TOWN BALL

TOWN BALL

The Glory Days of
Minnesota Amateur Baseball

ARMAND PETERSON

and

TOM TOMASHEK

UNIVERSITY OF MINNESOTA PRESS

MINNEAPOLIS

LONDON

Additional information is available on the book's companion Web site at
http://www.minnesotatownball.com.

Published by the University of Minnesota Press
111 Third Avenue South, Suite 290
Minneapolis, MN 55401–2520
http://www.upress.umn.edu

Library of Congress Cataloging-in-Publication Data

Peterson, Armand.
  Town ball : the glory days of Minnesota amateur baseball / Armand Peterson and Tom
Tomashek.
     p. cm.
  Includes bibliographical references and index.
  ISBN-13: 978-0-8166-4675-3 (hc/j : alk. paper)
  ISBN-10: 0-8166-4675-9 (hc/j : alk. paper)
  1. Baseball--Minnesota--History. I. Tomashek, Tom. II. Title.
  GV863.M6P48 2006
  796.35709776--dc22
                                              2006019433
Printed in Canada on acid-free paper

The University of Minnesota is an equal-opportunity educator and employer.

14 13 12 11 10 09 08 07 06   10 9 8 7 6 5 4 3 2 1

CONTENTS

about in the summer. We dreamed of one day playing for our town team, maybe even with Jiggs, a former minor-league pitcher, Western Minnesota League all-star and a player/manager in St. Peter, where during his college days at Gustavus Adolphus he lettered 12 times in four sports. He was also a consummate teacher and coach who could get his point across without raising his voice. And he had a tremendous dry sense of humor that made his explanations even more interesting. He could tease you without making you feel foolish, and he also had a self-effacing humor that made you realize that he was human.

But after more than two years of research, it became obvious that while Jiggs played an integral role in our lives, there were many other players providing thrills for youngsters and fans all over the state. Therefore we are dedicating this book to all the players, team officials, reporters, and loyal fans and supporters who made the postwar baseball scene so exciting.

We are grateful for those who shared their memories with us, and to the families of deceased players who have preserved the past in scrapbooks, photo albums, and tattered newspaper clippings. We have enjoyed our conversations more than we can express.

Our only regret is that time and space prevented us from mentioning the efforts of more towns and individuals who helped make this an extraordinary time in the state. Despite what we like to think of as a thorough search, we only scratched the surface. We apologize to those players and family and friends of players who went unmentioned.

We especially want to thank the city, county, and state historical society curators and newspaper editors who gave us access to their archives. We extend a profound and heartfelt thanks to New Ulm's Herb Schaper and St. Paul's Bob Schabert, two of the era's most enthusiastic and conscientious media contributors, who helped us track down players, photographs, and relevant facts that no one else seemed able to find. The baseball coverage by Ted Peterson, a *Minneapolis Star and Tribune* sportswriter, also proved to be a major source of information.

We are indebted to Brian Larson, a Minnesota Baseball Association statistician, and to the former players Bill Dudding and Don Gutzke, who gave us encouragement when we were just starting our quest and whose continuing support helped keep us going. Special thanks go to Pieter Martin, our editor at the University of Minnesota Press, for his patience and willingness to work with two enthusiastic and wordy first-time authors—who loved our subject so much that we couldn't stop writing.

May we also be so self-indulgent as to thank our families for their moral and physical support and their unyielding patience while we've spent countless hours in research or tethered to our computers. Laura and Linda, how can we thank you enough?

As for Jiggs, we thank him for that memorable September night in Chaska, the inspiration for this gratifying and nostalgic journey.

INTRODUCTION

OWATONNA RESIDENT HUGH HALL pulled into St. Cloud in mid-September 1959, found an apartment to rent within walking distance of Municipal Stadium, and then headed to the ballpark to watch the Minnesota State Amateur Baseball Tournament. Hall, a retired dairy herd inspector, had been traveling to every state tourney since 1942, from Detroit Lakes in the northwest to New Ulm and Faribault in the south. This baseball zealot's sentiments were written up by the *St. Cloud Daily Times* sportswriter Frank Farrington in his column, "The Fanning Mill."

"I like baseball. It's my hobby, my only hobby," Hall said. "I never keep score because I enjoy the crowds more than I do the games. I meet people at the tournament I've known for years. I see men in the stands now whom I watched play years ago. Now we watch their sons playing."

Fans like Hugh Hall were the standard-bearers for a large number of Minnesotans who shared the nation's love of baseball during the years immediately following World War II. They loved major-league baseball despite living several hundred miles from Chicago, the closest big-league city, and they rooted for the state's minor-league teams competing in the American Association and Northern League, but the backbone of Minnesota baseball was town team ball. The amateur game was up-front and personal. It offered townspeople the opportunity to embrace a team that included their family and friends, Main Street's professionals, tradesmen and merchants, high school teachers and their student-athletes, and farmers from the surrounding countryside.

By the beginning of the twentieth century, town team baseball was already a part of Minnesota's community fabric and continued to grow through World War I and the Great Depression. Participation plummeted during the four years of World War II, with membership in the Association of Minnesota Amateur Baseball Leagues slipping from an all-time high of 452 teams in 1940 to 162 in 1945. Once the war ended in the late summer of 1945 and the soldiers began marching home, a groundswell of interest in hometown baseball began to build. From 1945 through 1960, Minnesota experienced a magical era of amateur ball, setting records in town participation and attendance that have not been matched since.

With this book, we are celebrating the postwar era of town team baseball in Minnesota, a time we first shared as wide-eyed kids in the stands and later as young adults on the field. Through our research, we rediscovered the excitement the game inspired in Minnesota's communities, bringing together people of all ages, socioeconomic status, and gender. We learned how town team ball drove local businessmen to invest in their teams and communities, helping to build and improve ballparks, adding lights, and in some cases hiring outside players to make the team more competitive. Town team baseball was not just a popular entertainment but a vital civic institution whose fortunes rose and fell on the postwar boom economy and the changing landscape of popular culture. While ultimately unsustainable, town team baseball rode the wave of optimism that rippled across America after fifteen dark years of war and depression.

The first part of this book is a narrative overview of the era, beginning with town team baseball's postwar recovery, followed by its mercurial surge in interest, and finally ending with its gradual decline to a reduced but still respectable level of competition. With little competition for the entertainment dollar immediately following the war, town team ball became a summer staple for both hardcore baseball fans and entire families. Town participation made a giant leap from 1945 to 1950, when 799 teams began the season in three different divisions, with some communities fielding two and even three clubs. Once limited to Saturday or Sunday matinees, baseball schedules expanded through the installation of lights, and the fan base continued to grow. Crucial league games and marquee exhibitions drew crowds of two, three, and four thousand specta-

tors, with attendance sometimes surpassing the combined population of the towns.

The modern State Tournament was created in 1924 by Roy Dunlap and Lou McKenna of the *St. Paul Pioneer Press* and *Dispatch* newspapers. In 1925, participating leagues formed the AMABL (now called the Minnesota Baseball Association), which has governed competition and sponsored the State Tournament continuously since. In 1945 there were two classes of leagues in the state, and a third was added in 1948. Regional playoffs were held to determine State Tournament entrants in the two lower classes. League champions in Classes A and B were permitted to draft three players—in any combination of pitchers and catchers—from other teams in the league, while Class AA teams were permitted two. In the 1945–60 era, tournaments were generally held over a ten-day period, using two weekends. Attendance soared after the war, from 9,445 in 1945 to the record turnout of 35,318 in 1950. Attendance broke 30,000 three times during those years, and it exceeded 20,000 eleven times. By contrast, no State Tournament has broken 20,000 since 1959.

The second part of this book profiles Minnesota towns, big and small, that fielded teams during the era. The class structure was based on competition rules, not population. Quite simply, Class AA teams were permitted three outside players, defined generally by a 15-mile radius from the town, and Class A teams were permitted two. There were no restrictions on salaries. Class B towns were permitted no outside players, and could pay no salaries. The rules made for some unlikely competition. A comparatively small town like Litchfield (population 4,608) won a championship in Class AA, while hamlets such as Delavan (population 302) and Milroy (population 268) were able to hoist state championship trophies in Class A and B, respectively. Even small farming communities such as De Graff, Atwater, Fulda, Fairfax, and Iona chose to recruit talent to test their mettle in Class AA.

Minnesota discovered free agency long before it became a major component of the major-league salary structure. The Class AA level was dominated by the Southern Minnesota, Western Minnesota, and West Central leagues, all of which permitted rosters entirely made up of nonlocal talent. Many of these teams were stocked with college players from all over the country, but Austin's manager Emil Scheid developed his Southern Minnesota League power by luring professionals to Minnesota and forced others to follow suit. Later, Jim McNulty became the state's master recruiter. A product of the Dodgers' organization, McNulty guided Class AA championship teams in Fergus Falls and Fairmont, developing a dynasty in Fairmont using his "little black book" of professional prospects.

Class A or Class B teams, representing the vast majority of the state's membership, occasionally benefited from the professional ranks, but never on a wholesale scale. Some town officials took liberties with residency rules, and some had friendly school boards and businesses that offered jobs to help recruit top players. The vast majority of teams, however, relied on local talent. Most found, unfortunately, that they could not win a state championship with that philosophy, though there were exceptions, like Lester Prairie, Rollingstone, Milroy, and Cold Spring. Norwood and Brownton, although they won no state championships, became perennial powers using homegrown talent.

The third part of the book is devoted to the personalities, from the recruited ringers to the local heroes, who made town team ball not just entertainment but a cultural phenomenon. Major leaguers contributed an air of celebrity to the game, before or after their big-league careers. Minnesota natives such as Jerry Kindall, along with imports like future Yankee first baseman Bill "Moose" Skowron and Cleveland pitcher Herb Score, spent one or more seasons in Minnesota before working their way to the top. Dick Siebert, Howie Schultz, Rudy York, and Hy Vandenberg were among the former major leaguers to play town team baseball after their big-league careers ended. Towns attracted a wide collection of baseball nomads to the state, ranging from Negro League pitcher Gread "Lefty" McKinnis to minor-league standout Johnny Herr to rascals like Fat Johnny Burrows. Some of the notables associated with Minnesota baseball had either attained or would gain celebrity in other areas, including coaching greats Herb Brooks and Bud Grant and Gopher football legend Paul Giel. The most successful small towns were bolstered by large family trees, in some cases contributing four or more starters with the same surname. The Dolans of Milroy were recognized as the first family of Minnesota baseball after the tiny town won the Class B title in 1954, but they were just one of many family acts in the state.

The former Benson infielder Roy Berens echoed the sentiments of most who experienced the state's baseball glory days when he said, "We'll never see anything like that again. [Town team] wasn't the only summer activity in the state, but it was extremely important. We played the game hard while the fans provided major support, letting us know how much they appreciated us and the game."

Some observers have noted that the decline in town team baseball coincided with the arrival of the Minnesota Twins. However, peak participation occurred in 1950 and declined steadily afterward, long before the Twins had an impact. A wide range of societal changes—brought on by television, the new suburban lifestyle, the car culture, golf, summer vacations, lake cabins, air-conditioning, and much more—transformed our culture in the 1950s, and town team baseball was taken along for the ride.

Town team ball's glory days may never be duplicated, but it was a spectacular period that deserves to be chronicled for those too young to remember—or for those who want to remember. When one former town team standout was asked to recount his memories, he humbly responded, "I'm surprised that anyone remembers me." This book is our response. We remember not only his contributions but those of many others who were, and remain, our boys of summer. Our only regret can be summed up by paraphrasing an age-old lament: "So many stories, so little space."

Part I

THE TOWN TEAM BALL ERA

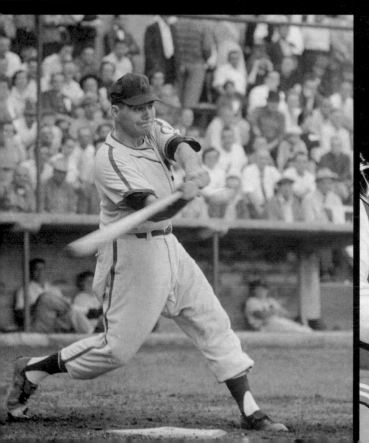

THE BOYS ARE BACK

1945–46

RED WING PITCHER HAL SWANSON PROBably wasn't thinking about the historic significance of the game as he threw the first pitch in the 1945 Minnesota Amateur Baseball Association State Tournament, held at Hayek Field in Albert Lea. If anything, Swanson was probably thinking about the weather. It was windy and wet, and the start of the game had been delayed almost two hours by rain. Fewer than two hundred fans huddled together in the stands. The game was played just eight days after Japan formally surrendered on the deck of the battleship USS *Missouri*.

Lingering fears about the Pacific war hung like a dark cloud over post–V-E Day celebrations earlier in the summer, but these were relieved on V-J Day. Finally, at last, the nation dared to look forward to peacetime. The country was poised at the beginning of an economic boom stimulated by wartime spending and consumer demand pent up by several years of rationing.

In Minnesota, Marsh Ryman, a University of Minnesota ticket manager, reported a big boost in season ticket applications for Gopher football, and weekend vacancies were hard to find in resort areas. South Dakota estimated it would have

an increase of close to 50 percent in nonresident pheasant-hunting licenses. The Minneapolis Park Board was planning expansions in all sports programs, and improvements at Parade Stadium. Towns and cities all over the state were looking forward to peacetime and their veterans coming home. In 1945 only 162 Minnesota teams made it through the season, compared to 452 who had

Excelsior's Roger McDonald gets a ride after throwing a no-hitter in the 1945 Class A championship game against Mayer. It was the first championship-game no-hitter in tournament history. *Star-Tribune* photograph; courtesy of the Minnesota Historical Society.

Excelsior, 1945 Class A State Champions. The team's pitching dominated opponents. Before McDonald's no-hit gem, Ed Poppitz and Vern Bruhn tossed three-hit shutouts to defeat Ashby 16–0 and De Graff 5–0. *Front row, left to right:* Vern Bruhn, Roger McDonald, Gordon Gelhaye, John Dellwo, Jesse Schwartz, Andy Green, Joe Hutton Jr., and Ed Poppitz. *Back row:* Bob Moore, manager Steve Eddy, Harold Voss, Lloyd Johnson, Al Litfin, James Hanson, Karl Sorenson, Dick Kartack, and Vance Crosby. *Star-Tribune* photograph; courtesy of the Minnesota Historical Society.

played in 1940. Strong baseball towns like Stark and Wells, who had each fielded two teams in 1940, did not have a single team in 1945. Fergus Falls and Moose Lake, who played in the State Tournament in 1940, were also forced to drop their teams during the war.

However, interest in baseball was picking up in 1945, especially at the end of the summer, when it was clear that the war and rationing were over. The *Minneapolis Tribune* reported crowds of 2,800 at two playoff games in early September and said that some teams had regularly been drawing crowds of 1,000 to 2,000 during the season. The Western Minnesota League was a hotbed. The three-game semifinal series between Springfield and New Ulm drew 3,960 fans, and the three-game finals between New Ulm and Sleepy Eye drew 7,280.

At the time, baseball truly was the national pastime. Almost all men had played it growing up. Athletes didn't train in their primary sport year-round as they do today. When summer came, football, basketball, and hockey stars played baseball. There was little competition for baseball on the nation's sports pages. The National Football

League was still a fledgling organization, taking a backseat to coverage of college football. The National Basketball Association hadn't been formed yet, and there was little interest in the National Hockey League outside Chicago, New York, Detroit, and Boston—the four American cities that had teams in the six-team league. At World Series time, radios in offices and stores were tuned to the games. Scoreboards posted in public areas throughout the country kept passersby up to date on progress of the games. Many, like the elaborate one in New York's Times Square, posted play-by-play results. Some grade and high schools transmitted radio broadcasts of the games over public address systems.

Down in Albert Lea, Swanson's pitch to Courtland leadoff hitter Mel Schiller on that rainy September day signaled the start of an unprecedented boom in town team baseball in Minnesota. Courtland defeated Red Wing 19–5 in the first game of what turned out to be a wonderful tournament. Excelsior won the Class A title on Sunday, September 16, beating Mayer 4–0 on a no-hitter by Roger McDonald, a Washington native attending St. Thomas College on a U.S. Navy V-12 program, an officer-training program that deferred students from the draft until they graduated. That was the third consecutive shutout by Excelsior pitchers. In the Class AA championship game, Albert Lea beat Minneapolis Honeywell 1–0 on a scratch single with two outs in the bottom of the ninth inning by pitcher Earl Steier. Hard-luck losing pitcher Jack Verby, a V-12 medical student at the University of Minnesota, was attempting to complete his second shutout in two days. On Saturday, he'd thrown a three-hitter to beat West St. Paul 3–0.

As good as the games were, though, the buzz at the tournament was about 1946. Organized baseball came back rapidly after the war. Major-league attendance had actually held up fairly well during the war. The nadir was reached in 1943, which, at 7.5 million, was 23 percent below 1941. Crowds increased to 10.8 million in 1945, finally topping 1941, but then rose another 71 percent to 18.5 million in 1946. The minor leagues, which declined to an estimated 6.0 million attendance in 1943, showed even more explosive gains. In 1946, the minors went from 86 to 314 teams, while attendance, at 32.0 million, went up 227 percent compared to 1945.

Minnesota's baseball resurgence in 1946 was as dramatic as in the minor leagues. Returning servicemen flooded the state, and almost 250 new teams started up. The renaissance was widespread. The Minneapolis Park Board leagues, which had 27 teams in 1940 and fell to 4 in 1945, came back with 16 teams in 1946. The situation was not quite as dramatic in St. Paul, which had 23 teams in 1940, 11 in 1945, but then rose to 16 in 1946.

Generally, teams in the southern half of the state got back into action in 1946. In most cases this involved reestablishing a team that had existed before the war, but new teams were also being formed. Many towns created second, or even third, teams to accommodate all the men who wanted to play. One of the state's baseball hotbeds was in the Stearns County area, which managed to maintain three leagues throughout the war. By 1946, two new leagues were formed as 13 new teams joined the 23 that had played in 1945.

In the traditionally strong New Ulm area, the powerful Western Minny League fell from six teams in 1940 to four teams in 1945, while the Brown County League went from nine teams to five. In 1946, the Western Minny and Brown County Leagues expanded to six teams, and the new six-team Tomahawk League was formed.

Teams in the northern part of the state were a little slower getting back into action. In 1946, the Red River Valley and Northern Minnesota Leagues, shut down during the war, restarted, and by 1948 four new northwestern leagues were created—Kittson County, Marshall County, Nor-Mah-Polk (nominally including Norman, Mahnomen, and Polk counties), and Lake of the Woods. In the Duluth and Iron Range area in the northeastern part of the state, only the Head O'Lakes League survived the war, but in the next couple of years there were six new leagues operating in the area—the Class A Arrowhead and the Mesabi and East, West, North, and South Itasca Class B Leagues.

These teams belonged to the Association of

The Pugg's Wigwam independent team from St. Cloud. Pugg Long *(back row, far right),* a businessman, sponsored and managed the team. *Front row, left to right:* Ruehle, Campbell, Fisher, Trebtoske, Stafford, Hall, and Gilliver. *Back row:* Hengel, Schnobrich, Nyberg, Weidner, Binsfield, Rader, Wickman, Albie Peckskamp, Pugg Long. *Bat boy (in front):* Buddy Binsfield. Photograph from the collection of the Stearns History Museum, St. Cloud, Minnesota.

Minnesota Amateur Baseball Leagues and therefore played in leagues whose playoff champions went on to regional and state championship tournaments. There were many others who did not play in organized leagues, for various reasons. Some were loosely organized groups who banded together to play a few games, while others had sponsors and uniforms and played an extensive schedule. The Pugg's Wigwam team of St. Cloud is one example of the latter. Sponsored by businessman Pugg Long, the team played—unsuccessfully—in the Lakewood League in 1946 and 1947. Long withdrew from the league but kept the team together to play an exhibition schedule. The team played over 20 games in 1948, frequently hiring outside pitchers for games against tough opponents.

However, independent teams were always scrambling to find opponents. Sundays were the best dates for attendance, but the organized leagues played their games on Sundays. Occasionally, if a league had an odd number of teams, a nearby independent could sched-

ule Sunday games with the bye team. In the immediate postwar years, the independents were able to play midweek twilight games (starting around 5:30 p.m.). But when teams whose home fields had lights began scheduling weekday league games, it became even more difficult to draw up a schedule.

Although many towns that had strong prewar baseball teams, like Buffalo, Delavan, Fulda, Hanska, Howard Lake, and Ulen, were not able to get started in time for the 1946 season, the AMABL registered 52 Class A and 7 Class AA leagues. Rules were basically the same as they had been before the war. Class A teams were permitted two outside players, while Class AA teams could have three. Although the Minneapolis, St. Paul, and St. Paul Suburban Leagues were automatically placed in Class AA out of a sense of fair play, population was not the determining factor for the rest of the state. Any league or town could choose to play Class AA if it wished. Thus the Southern Minnesota League elected to join Class AA in 1939. (However, if one team in a league had three outside players, the AMABL classified the whole league as Class AA.)

Residency had to be established before April 1. A "home player" was defined as one who resided within a 15-mile radius of the nearest city limit, but this could not extend into the city limits of another AMABL-affiliated team unless that team gave specific written consent. Rules gave teachers who were moving to new jobs the option of playing for their current or future town. A college player could play either for his hometown or for a team in the town where he was attending school, providing he maintained a residence there during the summer.

The rules said nothing about salaries. It had been common practice for teams to recruit pitchers and catchers. Top pitchers like Jack Verby (New Ulm), Claire Strommen (Springfield), and Arleigh Kraupa (Waseca) were reported to be receiving $50 per game, while others like Gene Cooney (Bloomington), Vern Bruhn (Shakopee), and Alex Romanchuck (Winsted) were receiving around $25 per game. Good-hitting catchers could draw up to $25 per game, and many position players got $5 to $10 per game. (Using the Minnesota Federal Reserve Consumer Price Index Calculator, $50 in 1947 would be equivalent to $438 in 2005.)

More common than salaries, however, was the practice of paying "shares." In this system, the players divided the money left at the end of the season after all expenses and taxes had been paid. Usually each player got one share, but some catchers were assigned 1.5 or 2 shares, and a player/manager might draw the same. Most pitchers were paid on a per-game basis in addition to a share. Jimmy Delmont, an Albert Lea columnist and also a member of Albert Lea's 1946 State Class AA champions, wrote that their pitchers were paid $50 per game, and that the season's player's share was $560 ($700 less $140 in taxes). That was a net of $13 per game. (They played 43 games.) That's probably the top marker for the state in 1946. Most teams that paid shares probably paid $50–$150 per share in the first couple of years after the war.

The average Class A team, though, had just two hired players—a pitcher and a catcher—and no shares split, although many teams were strictly amateur and paid no salaries or shares. There was a wide disparity from town to town and from league to league. Some Class A leagues limited the number of salaried players per team to two or three. (This was acceptable to the AMABL, since the rule was more restrictive than the state rule.) The Western Minnesota League was acknowledged to be the top Class A League, and it paid accordingly. The Minnesota Valley League was close, followed by the North Star, Wright County, Corn Belt, and North Central Leagues. Many leagues had only one or two teams that paid at all.

You might think that there would be a lot of complaining from the smaller towns or those that couldn't afford to pay for players, but little was heard as the 1946 season got under way. Perhaps this can be explained by the fact that paying for players was not a new phenomenon—just a continuation of a practice that had begun well before the war. If there were concerns, they were overwhelmed by the desire to enjoy peacetime baseball again. For now, just being at the games was enough for the overwhelming majority of fans.

There's not a lot of hard evidence about attendance that year. Contemporary news stories talked in general terms about "great" and "record" crowds, but exact numbers are hard to find. Minnesota baseball was mostly a Sunday game in those days. Except for Minneapolis and St. Paul, all leagues played a double round-robin schedule—that is, there would be 14 games in an eight-team league and 10 games in a six-team league, all scheduled on Sundays. Most teams played exhibition games during the week—twilight affairs mostly, because very few teams had lights. Serious teams—the ones which wanted to get to the State Tournament—played a lot of extra games. Albert Lea, for example, was 10–4 in league play, 4–0 in league playoffs, and 3–0 in the State Tournament, and 17–5 in exhibitions for an overall 34–9 record. Similarly, New Ulm was 10–0 in league play, 1–2 in playoffs, and 6–7 in exhibitions. For the year, New Ulm's 17 home games drew an average of 1,245 fans per game.

Young America catcher Harry Zellman tags out a Glencoe runner during the Region 12A playoff finals at Glencoe on Sunday, September 1, 1946. Glencoe brought in temporary bleachers to handle the crowd, estimated at 4,000. *Star-Tribune* photograph; courtesy of the Minnesota Historical Society.

Many teams played exhibitions after the regular season and State Tournament were over. New Ulm, in fact, after being upset by Gibbon in the first round of the playoffs, played one game with Albert Lea and two with Springfield as those teams prepared for the State Tournament. September and early October were also prime time for barnstorming teams like Babe Barna's All-Stars. Barna, a former major-league player, was a popular Minneapolis Millers slugger from 1944 to 1948 and assembled a team of current and former Millers and some old friends to extend their season and pick up a little extra money.

The Minneapolis Park National League played two games a week—on Saturdays and Sundays, for a total of 28 games. They played a split season, with the winners of each half meeting in a playoff to determine the league championship. The winner played a two-of-three series with the Park American League champion to determine the city's entry into the State Tournament. The Park American League played just one game a week during the regular season. St. Paul had a similar situation. The AAA League played twice a weekend—25 games total, five rounds through the six-team league—while the City League played once, for a total of 16 games. A two-of-three playoff was held between the two champions to determine the State Tournament entry. Both cities used their American Association parks—Lexington in St. Paul and Nicollet in Minneapolis—to make up for rainouts and to squeeze in playoff games before the State Tournament deadline.

Fan interest was high as league playoffs started all over the state in August. The Southeastern Minnesota League was bumped up to Class AA on the eve of the playoffs for excessive use of outside players. The specific violations are not known, but whatever they were, they could not have been that effective—league champion Zumbrota was beaten by Albert Lea 23–2 in the first round of the State Tournament.

The state playoffs were an unqualified success. In the Southern Minny, six playoff games drew 10,395 spectators. The largest crowd was 2,610 at the final game between Winona and Albert Lea. The *Minneapolis Tribune* estimated crowds of 2,000 at Park Board playoff games. The *St. Paul Pioneer Press* reported record crowds for games at Baker and Dunning Fields, and 3,000 at North St. Paul to see West St. Paul beat the Polars 5–4 on a long home run by former major-league player Bobby Reis. Crowds well in excess of 1,000 were reported all over the state. In Detroit Lakes, 1,900 watched the Lakers defeat Fergus Falls for the North Central Minnesota League championship. In Franklin, 2,600 saw Springfield beat Winthrop 6–1 for the Region 6A championship. The *Tribune* reported that 3,000 jammed into the Lester Prairie field to watch Glencoe defeat Belle Plaine in the first round of the Region 12A playoffs. Glencoe scrounged in neighboring towns for temporary bleachers to meet demand for seats for the final game of the regional playoffs. An estimated 4,000 saw Young America shut out Glencoe 10–0 to win a State Tournament berth.

One dark cloud hung over the State Tournament—the specter of paralytic poliomyelitis, often called "infantile paralysis." The polio virus was identified in 1908, and subsequent periodic outbreaks caused widespread fear, leading to the creation of the National Foundation for Infantile Paralysis in 1937, and the charity fundraising organization "March of Dimes." World War II had diverted public attention from polio, but large epidemics were reported immediately after the war ended. There was an average of 20,000 cases per year in the United States from 1945 to 1949. In 1946, Minnesota's polio cases soared to 2,882, with 226 deaths, compared to 233 cases in 1945.

Officials in Minnesota—not knowing how the virus was transmitted—reacted by closing many public places, especially in areas where new cases of polio had been reported. Around the state, many county fairs were canceled, and large public gatherings discouraged. The Capitol Theatre in St. Paul, for example, postponed the showing of the new Walt Disney movie *Pinocchio* from early August to late September. The State Fair Board played a waiting game. They'd had to cancel the 1945 fair because of postwar

The Minnesota restaurateur William Hanson washed coins in disinfectant twice daily during the national polio epidemic in 1946, when no precaution seemed too extreme. *Dispatch–Pioneer Press* photograph; courtesy of the Minnesota Historical Society.

transportation difficulties, and interest was high for 1946. Furthermore, the board feared it would cost them over $100,000 to terminate contracts they'd already signed. But in the end they couldn't take the chance that some polio cases might be traced to the fair, and on August 14 the board made the decision to cancel. Twin Cities schools shortly made the decision to postpone the start of classes until mid-September, in hopes that the epidemic would have run its course by then. Schools all over the state did the same. The Owatonna Health Board initially restricted State Tournament ticket sales to those age 16 or over but later lifted the ban.

Rain plagued the State Tournament, causing several delays and postponements. The opening games scheduled for the first two days, Friday and Saturday, August 30–31, were rained out, and only one game was played on the first Sunday. The AMABL pushed the championship games from September 8 to the fifteenth to help ease the schedule crunch and give surviving teams a chance to rest their pitchers. When it was over, the pretournament favorites were the winners—Albert Lea in Class AA (its third consecutive) and Springfield in Class A. Despite the rain, attendance hit 23,513, more than dou-

bling the previous all-time record of 10,993, set at New Ulm in 1941.

The "Mythical" Championship game was rained out once, too, and finally played on September 29, when Albert Lea beat Springfield 7–2 to capture its second consecutive Mythical Title. This game, matching the winners of Class AA and Class A, had been established in 1938 to determine an overall champion to send to the American Baseball Congress national amateur tournament in Battle Creek, Michigan. Minneapolis Heinies, the 1937 Class AA champions, had been invited to the ABC tournament that year, and when they couldn't go, St. Paul J. J. Kohn's, the state runners-up, went to Battle Creek and returned as national champions. J. J. Kohn's returned to the tournament in 1938 as defending champions.

Owatonna, the 1938 Class A Champion, upset the Class AA St. Paul Northern States Envelopes—chosen to represent the Twin Cities—

State officials gather in an Owatonna hotel to revise the 1946 tournament schedule after several rain delays. *Star-Tribune* photograph; courtesy of the Minnesota Historical Society.

area teams, although they had lost to St. Paul Park in the Class AA championship game—to win the first overall state championship. Unfortunately, the ABC and Minnesota State Tournaments overlapped, and it was decided to send Owatonna to the 1939 national tournament. Similarly, the 1939 and 1940 state champions were sent to the 1940 and 1941 tournaments, respectively.

The ABC tournament was canceled from 1942 to 1945 because of the war, but the AMABL continued to play the overall championship games. In a bit of embarrassment for the AA teams, the Class A champions won all the games from 1938 to 1944. Albert Lea finally broke the Class AA jinx when they beat Class A Excelsior 14–2 in the 1945 title game. In the past, that victory would have earned the Packers a berth in the 1946 ABC tournament. However, the AMABL decided to schedule the 1946 State Tournament a week earlier, permitting the overall champion to go to Battle Creek. As luck would have it, the rain delay made it impossible for Albert Lea to make the national tournament. By 1947, when Albert Lea won again, the ABC rules banning any form

of player compensation were being enforced and essentially prevented Minnesota Class A or AA teams from competing there.

Minnesota officials kept playing the game, and eventually people started calling it a "Mythical" Championship because the winner didn't go anywhere and didn't receive a trophy—it was strictly for bragging rights.

Newspapers reported a lot of talk behind the scenes at the State Tournament. Towns were plotting to make improvements in their teams for next season, and there were rumors about deals offered to some top players. One thing that wasn't a rumor was that dozens of towns were planning to install lights in 1947. Owatonna's impressive new lights were the envy of many towns. On a practical level, baseball officials saw how valuable lights were, as the four night games played during the tournament helped to make up for the equivalent of two full days of rained-out games. (New Ulm, in 1941 and 1944, was the only prior host town to have lights.) These officials were also salivating at the prospect of drawing big crowds at midweek night games in the future.

When it didn't rain, the 1946 State Tournament at Owatonna drew great crowds. In this Class A semifinal game, Springfield shortstop Art Marben scores on a passed ball while Detroit Lakes pitcher Harley Oyloe waits for the throw. The batter is Bassie Wagner. *Star-Tribune* photograph; courtesy of the Minnesota Historical Society.

LIGHTS ON THE PRAIRIE

1947

STATE MEMBERSHIP—THE AMABL HAD now been incorporated as the Minnesota Amateur Baseball Association (MABA)—grew another 26 percent in 1947. Most new teams were from towns that hadn't been able to get organized soon enough in 1946, but some towns also added second teams. Postwar prosperity made money available for recruiting top players and for building new fields or improving existing ones, and it seemed like everyone was talking about lights.

Over 150 towns did install lights in the next four years. It became a feeding frenzy—baseball fans and businessmen in one town would not sit idle while a nearby rival installed lights on its field. In early 1948 the *Minneapolis Tribune* columnist Joe Hendrickson wrote that "landmarks for a small town used to be a church steeple or a steel water tank, but now there is a new eye catcher as one motors down state highways—this might be called the age of the light tower."

In just a couple of years, whole leagues had lighted fields. In southwestern Minnesota the "First Night League" was formed in 1949—consisting of Iona, Marshall, Pipestone, Slayton, Wilmont, and Worthington—and claimed to be the first league to schedule all its games at night. Most leagues, though, maintained the tradition of Sunday-afternoon games and used lights only on weekdays.

Lights were not cheap—about $15,000 ($131,370 in 2005 dollars), depending on the amount of volunteer labor contributed for assembly and installation. Various means were used to raise the money, but in towns buying lights there were very few arguments about whether the money should be spent in the first place. Only a few opposed the spending. The methods chosen merely reflected a consensus on the best way to get the deal done, which varied from town to town.

A few examples show the diversity of funding approaches. Little Falls installed lights at its field at the Morrison County Fairgrounds in 1947. The total cost was $17,092. The team kicked in $1,935, and the $15,157 remaining was financed through the sale of shares—in amounts up to $100—to the public. Notes were issued for the shares and were to be paid back by withholding 20 percent of gate receipts for each game played under the lights.

13

seasons in the majors, and split 1946 between St. Paul of the Class AAA American Association and Chattanooga of the Class AA Southern Association. But signing of professional players was not limited to the state's Class AA leagues. Excelsior, of the Class A Minnesota Valley League, for example, signed Minnesota native Rollie Seltz, who had played with Allentown, Pennsylvania, in the Class B Interstate League in 1946.

Austin manager Emil Scheid broke new ground in 1947 when he signed pitcher Earl Mossor, a Tennessee native, and outfielder Ray Riley, a Cincinnati, Ohio, native, to play for Austin. Neither had any prior affiliation with Minnesota. Although relatively few out-of-state professionals came to Minnesota in 1947, their presence was watched with interest, and the pace of hiring them picked up in subsequent years.

College players were in demand all over the state, too. MABA rules permitted a college player to establish his residence—for eligibility purposes—either in his hometown or in his college town, provided that he actually lived there during the summer. On the other hand, the overall MABA hometown rule required residency to be established by April 1. Some teams took advantage of this rule and established April 1 residencies for their college players. "Establishing a residence" typically involved setting up a mailbox or mailing address but might have been as simple as just having the player say that he was living in the town by April 1. Thus, in 1947, Alex Romanchuck, who lived in St. Paul and attended St. Thomas College, and played with Winsted in 1946 as an outside player, was told to reply, if asked, that he was living in Winsted and drove to classes from there. A gentlemen's agreement prevailed—some teams might have grumbled about such arrangements, but if a player had been with a team all season, and

the team said he was a hometown player, very few protests were filed.

But, as in the past, the playgrounds of Minneapolis and St. Paul provided most of the "outside" players for the state's teams. Since most of the legends of Minnesota amateur baseball revolve around outstate teams, this may appear to be an incongruous remark, but the fact is that the Twin Cities population made up almost half of the state, and its boys had better opportunities to learn the game than rural youth. Both cities were full of neighborhood parks where pickup baseball games began at very early ages, and most parks were staffed by college-age athletes who helped set up and supervise games. Grade and elementary schools, especially in St. Paul, fielded competitive baseball teams, and settlement houses also sponsored youth teams. Both cities had well-organized midget baseball programs. The *St. Paul Pioneer Press* frequently printed stories of league and playoff games, including line scores and an occasional box score. Both cities had strong American Legion programs for older youth, as well as other junior leagues for 15- to 18-year-old boys. The St. Paul Park Board also sponsored the Capitol League, which was limited to players 18 to 19 years old.

In greater Minnesota, on the other hand, formal youth baseball programs were far more limited in scope. Only a few cities had midget programs until the early 1950s. While American Legion teams were sponsored throughout the state, many rural teams played only a few games a year. In the 22 State Legion Tournaments held between 1926 (the first one) and 1947, St. Paul teams won nine times and Minneapolis teams eight times. It should not be surprising to learn that so many good players came from Minneapolis and St. Paul. To start with, almost 40 percent of the eligible players lived there—38.6 percent, to be exact, according to the 1950 census. Add to that the fact that these city youth had far more opportunities to learn and play the game than their rural counterparts, and it would be safe to guess that 50 percent or more of the state's top baseball players came from the Twin Cities. This is not to denigrate the wonderful players who came from the rural areas. It's just a fact. If you were a baseball official in, say, Buffalo or Pierz or Belle Plaine, and looking for a pitcher, your first thought would probably have been, "I wonder who I can find in the Cities?"

The Minneapolis Park Board, under pressure by team sponsors, issued a ruling that made a player ineligible for Park Board competition if he played in league or exhibition games outside the city. During the summer several players were ruled ineligible for playing in exhibitions, but the league was shaken by a protest filed on the last day of the season. Honeywell had finished in last place in the first half of the 1947 Park National season but picked up some new players and rallied to lead the league going into the final weekend of the second half on August 9–10. They won on Saturday but lost 8–6 to Triangle Sales on Sunday to finish 7–3 and in a tie for first place with the Banana Distributors, who swept their weekend games. However, Honeywell manager Ralph Williams protested the eligibility of Triangles pitcher Lloyd Lundeen. The Park Board ruled in Honeywell's favor when they found that Lundeen had played six league games with Winsted of the North Star League and had pitched in an exhibition game against Belle Plaine of the S-C-S (Scott-Carver-Sibley counties) League. That gave Honeywell the second-half championship, and they went on to win a playoff with first-half champion Mitby-Sathers and a berth in the State Tournament.

The St. Paul AAA and Minneapolis Park National teams had to carry at least two pitchers each to handle their Saturday and Sunday schedules. That left the pitchers with one week between starts, and with the temptation to pocket $25 to $50 cash to pitch an exhibition game for an outstate team. There were many exhibition games played all over the state, and

The wholesale produce entrepreneur David Goldbloom sponsored the Minneapolis Banana Distributors, a perennial Park National contender. Goldbloom often brought stalks of bananas and distributed them to children. Photograph by Lefty Evans; courtesy of Don Evans.

Large crowds watched Minneapolis Park National League playoff game at Parade 4 in 1947. Second-half winner Honeywell beat first-half winner Mitby-Sathers 8–3 to sweep the best-of-three series. Here Sathers batter John Hruska and Honeywell catcher Arnie Johnson await a pitch from John Cowles. Photograph by Lefty Evans; courtesy of Don Evans.

a lot of teams looking for players for a single game. They needed pitchers for these games to rest their regular starter for a league game. They also hired other top players to strengthen their chances to defeat a regional foe or strong barnstorming team in an exhibition game.

Several informal networks matched teams and willing players-for-hire. First was the good-old-boy network—managers and players frequently had an old teammate who might be willing to play an exhibition game, or who knew someone who could. The members of the Northwest Umpires Association also facilitated the process. They umpired for 20 leagues in 1947, running in an area bounded by the Twin Cities, St. Cloud, Willmar, New Ulm, Mankato, Albert Lea, and Winona, and got to know many play-

ers and managers. The umpires fed games scores and highlights back to Bob Bullock, who published the weekly *Northwest Umpires Review*. The *Review* was a four-page newspaper; page 4 showed the standings in the 20 leagues officiated by the NW Umpires, while pages 2 and 3 gave highlights of games in those leagues. There were several versions of page 1 printed each week. The issue that was circulated in the West Central League area, for example, would contain more details about that league and usually printed the batting averages of the leading hitters in the league. Fans and players eagerly awaited each new issue. Fans caught up on other games in the league, and players checked to see if their names were printed in the highlights.

Managers looking for exhibition players often called Bullock for leads. He helped them when he could, by checking with other umpires in the association, most of whom lived in St. Paul

The May 11, 1947, issue of *Northwest Umpires Review*. Multiple issues were published each week; this one was for the Independent Central League. From the authors' personal collection.

NORTH WEST UMPIRES REVIEW

Vol. XIV—No. I   Sponsored and Edited by the Northwest Umpires Ass'n.   AP-N   May 11, 1947

St. Francis Assumes Independent Central League Lead

St. Francis stands alone at the top of the Independent Central League with two victories and is the only undefeated club in the league. Zimmerman has yet to win but were tremendously improved last Sunday.

Zimmerman goes to St. Francis today to try for their first win and hand St. Francis their first loss. Nowthen takes on Anoka at Anoka, Crown travels to Forest Lake, Rogers to Albertville, and Orrock to Soderville.

Cold, rainy weather has caused many clubs to go into action without much of a preliminary conditioning period. Early season weaknesses may disappear with warmer weather — if and when it comes.

Young America continued where they left off last season as they nosed out one of the Crow River Valley League favorites at Lester Prairie. Watertown, Waconia, and Victoria survived the first day's play.

Today Waconia plays at Lester Prairie, Plato at Victoria, Mayer at Watertown, and Young America at St. Bonifacius.

The Pomme De Terre League opens its season today with Hancock at Chokio, Hoffman at Cyrus, and Starbuck at Clontarf.

The Golden Valley League also lifts the lid with Echo at Morton, Olivia at Maynard, and Sacred Heart at Renville.

Kasson surprised Rochester at Rochester and other winners in the Southeastern Minnesota league were Claremont, Lake City, and Pine Island. The league seems to be very well balanced in strength and should have a great race.

One of the opening day winners will fall today in the Pine Island-Claremont tussle at Claremont, Rochester goes to Lake City, West Concord to Dodge Center and Kasson to Red Wing.

The St. Peter-Bloomington game today at St. Peter features the early season's play in the Minnesota Valley League. Both are unbeaten in two starts. Chaska, also unbeaten, crosses the river to Shakopee where the crafty Lefty Odenwald's crew lie in wait. This one should be a dinger.

Excelsior plays at Jordan and Hopkins tries for its first win at St. Louis Park. Shorty Dale's team will also be hot on the trail of a victory and a good game should result.

All of the winners tangle with each other in the West Central Minnesota League today. Montevideo plays at Benson and Bird Island meets Olivia at Olivia in a neighborhood scrap. Two of last week's losers will break the spell and jump into the win column.

Clara City is at Granite Falls and Lake Lillian at Willmar. This newly formed league bids fair to be one of the state's strongest even in its very first year.

In the Southern Minnesota League, Mankato sprung a surprise and knocked off Albert Lea's 1946 State Champions. Rochester, Waseca, Winona also dented the win column.

Today's feature is Waseca at Albert Lea. The Mankato-Rochester tilt should be no tea party. Owatonna travels to Austin and Winona to Faribault.

In the rough · tough Western Minnesota League, the ony two winners to face each other are Gibbon and Springfield at Springfield. Gibbon seems to enjoy the winning way they picked up in knocking New Ulm out of last year's playoff and started strong enough to beat Dick Lanahan last week.

St. James travels to Fairfax and can only win if more players than the pitcher do the hitting. New Ulm at Sleepy Eye should be worth going miles to see. If it is a warm day the season's largest crowd could result. Redwood Falls plays at home and may have its hands full to repeat last week's victory.

Waverly, Delano Elk River and Monticello were opening day winners

BIG 13

An eleven way tie for 13th position necessitates making the Big 13 the Big 23 for today's edition.

	AB	Hits	Pct.
Weertz, Brownton	5	5	1000
Mueller, Buffalo Lake	5	5	1000
G. Gussendorf, Cosmos	4	4	1000
Reis, Faribault	3	3	1000
Martin, Buffalo Lake	3	3	1000
Kelly, Waseca	2	2	1000
Barlau, Hydes Lake	2	2	1000
O'Brien, Belle Plaine	6	5	833
Dvorak, Lake City	5	4	800
Litfin, Winsted	5	4	800
O'Hara, Glencoe	5	4	800
Peterson, Forest Lake	5	4	800
Kelly, Hopkins	4	3	750
Molock Winona	4	3	750
Kennedy, Kasson	4	3	750
R. Steffenhagen, Lake City	4	3	750
Ditty, Delano	4	3	750
Lanahan, Sleepy Eye	4	3	750
Fritz, Dodge Center	4	3	750
Jenneke, Lester Prairie	4	3	750
Dollerschell, Litchfield	4	3	750
Cardinal, Benson	4	3	750
W. Stender, Hydes Lake	4	3	750

in the Wright County League. Waverly and Delano two of the winners, get together today at Delano and this early season feature should draw a great crowd with weather favorable. St. Michael plays at Maple Lake, Kimball at Elk River, and Annandale at Monticello.

West Lynn plays today at Stewart, Cosmos at Gibbon-Moeltke, and Buffalo Lake at Hector. Last week's winners in the 212 League were Hector, Buffalo Lake and Cosmos.

Of the three winners, Cosmos seems to face the lightest task today, and the Buffalo Lake-Hector game at Hector is an early season feature that should pack 'em in.

Two winners collide today in the S-C-S Tri-County League as Norwood plays at Chanhassen. This game should give some idea as to the real strength of the newcomer to the league. The third winner last Sunday was Belle Plaine which gives every evidence of great strength.

In addition to the game mentioned above, today's schedule is Hyde Lake at Cologne, Belle Plaine at Arlington and Green Isle at Hamburg.

The Minneapolis Suburban League swings into full action today with Robbinsdale at Columbia Heights, and Mape Plain at Osseo. Robbinsdale got the jump last week with a close win over Osseo while Maple Plain and Columbia Heights were idle.

Glencoe, Hutchinson Winsted, and Howard Lake got away to a winning start in the North Star League. Dassel blew a 9 to 1 lead to lose at Glencoe.

Today Brownton plays at Dassel, Litchfield at Winsted, Cokato at Hutchinson, and Howard Lake at Glencoe. The latter game involves two winners.

This Week's Puzzler

Chicago leads St. Louis at Chicago 4 to 1 as they go into the 9th. In the first half of the 9th, St. Louis scores 4 runs making the score 5 to 4 in favor of St. Louis. The first batter up for Chicago in the 9th hits a home run tying the ball game at 5 to 5, and with no outs, rain then halts all further play for the day.

Does the score revert to the 8th with Chicago winning, 4 to 1, or is the game a tie?

(Answer at bottom of Page)

HOME RUNS

Griffith	Mankato
Madson	Mankato
West	Albert Lea
Kranke	Owatonna
Cardinal	Benson
G. Petersen	Soderville
Klonowski	Anoka
Leathers	St. Francis
Hahn	Winsted
Wallner	Winsted
Rosenow	Litchfield
Grahn	Hutchinson
O'Brien (3)	Belle Plaine
Mowrey	Belle Plaine
Droege	Hamburg
Westphal	Belle Plaine
Reed	Austin

BATTING AVERAGES
INDEPENDENT CENTRAL

	A	H	Pct.
Peterson, Forest Lake	5	4	800
Volkman, Forest Lake	8	5	625
Kreger, Nowthen	5	3	600
Gagne, Rogers	5	3	600
J. Dehen, Albertville	10	5	500
Ledin, Crown	8	4	500
Hierlinger, Crown	8	4	500
Callender, St. Francis	8	4	500
E. Barthel, Albertville	6	3	500
Durant, Albertville	6	3	500
Chamberlin, St. Francis	6	3	500
Lundberg, Forest Lake	8	4	500
Hendrickson, Soderville	8	4	500
G. Peterson, Soderville	6	3	500
Klonowski, Anoka	4	2	500
Shaber, Rogers	7	3	444
L. Zachman, Albertville	7	3	428
Sorenson, Anoka	7	3	428
L. Stoeckel, Crown	7	3	428
Lyon, St. Francis	10	4	400
D. Eckmark, St. Francis	5	2	400
J. Jacobs, Anoka	5	2	400
Johnson, Forest Lake	5	2	400
Bakeberg, Forest Lake	5	2	400
E. Hanson, Orrock	5	2	400
Doty, Zimmerman	5	2	400
Bean, Zimmerman	8	3	375
Lamatsch, Zimmerman	8	3	375
L. Ebner, Nowthen	8	3	375
B. Mellis, Rogers	8	3	375
Eull, Albertville	8	3	375
Flynn, Anoka	8	3	375
Leathers, St. Francis	8	3	375
Grams, Crown	8	3	375
Julkowski, Soderville	8	3	375

WRIGHT COUNTY LEAGUE

	AB	H	Pct.
Ditty, Delano	4	3	750
Stendahl, Elk River	3	2	667
Meierhofer, Maple Lake	3	2	667
M. Dansberg, Delano	5	3	600
Starbuck, Delano	5	3	600
Don Boggs, Kimball	4	2	500
Main, Waverly	4	2	500
T. Litfin, Annandale	2	1	500
Mackie, Annandale	2	1	500
Rache, Maple Lake	2	1	500
Dixon, Delano	2	1	500
Mees, Delano	5	2	400
Cornelius, Elk River	3	1	xx?
Knaus, Kimball	3	1	333
Zeller, Waverly	3	1	333

Foreseen ...
By Harby Dicks

Brownton at Dassel — Dassel
Litchfield at Winsted — Winsted
Cokato at Hutchinson — Cokato
Howard Lake at Glencoe — Glencoe

Lester at Lester Prairie—Lester
Plato at Victoria — Plato
Mayer at Watertown — Watertown
Young America at St. Bonifacius — Young America

St. Michael at Maple Lake — Maple Lake
Waverly at Delano — Delano
Kimball at Elk River — Elk River
Annandale at Monticello — Annandale

Nowthen at Anoka — Anoka
Zimmerman at St. Francis — St. Francis
Crown at Forest Lake—Forest Lake
Rogers at Albertville — Albertville
Orrock at Soderville — Soderville

Waseca at Albert Lea — Waseca
Mankato at Rochester — Rochester
Owatonna at Austin — Owatonna
Winona at Faribault — Faribault

West Lynn at Stewart — Stewart
Cosmos at Moeltke — Cosmos
Buffalo Lake at Hector — Buffalo Lake

Norwood at Chanhassen — Norwood
Hydes Lake at Cologne — Cologne
Belle Plaine at Arlington — Belle Plaine

Green Isle at Hamburg — Hamburg

Kasson at Red Wing — Kasson
Rochester at Lake City — Lake City
West Concord at Dodge Center — Dodge Center
Pine Island at Claremont — Claremont

Lake Lillian at Willmar — Willmar
Bird Island at Olivia — Olivia
Clara City at Granite Falls — Granite Falls
Montevideo at Benson — Benson

St. James at Fairfax — Fairfax
Gibbon at Springfield — Springfield
Franklin at Redwood Falls — Franklin
New Ulm at Sleepy Eye — New Ulm

Maple Plain at Osseo — Osseo
Robbinsdale at Columbia Heights — Columbia Heights

Hancock at Chokio — Chokio
Hoffman at Cyrus — Cyrus
Starbuck at Clontarf — Starbuck

Echo at Morton — Echo
Olivia at Maynard — Maynard
Sacred Heart at Renville — Sacred Heart

Boardman at New Richmond — Boardman
St. Croix Falls at Osceola — Osceola
Clear Lake at Clayton — Clayton
Bayport at Deer Park — Bayport

Bloomington at St. Peter — St. Peter
Excelsior at Jordan — Excelsior
Chaska at Shakopee — Chaska
Hopkins at St. Louis Park—Hopkins

Answer to today's puzzler
The game is a tie — it is always a legal game if the team last at bat makes as many or more runs in any inning after the 4th inning as the team batting first has made when play is terminated.

or Minneapolis. When he couldn't, he posted the request at the Lowe and Campbell Athletic Goods store in downtown Minneapolis. Lowe and Campbell was an unofficial clearinghouse for the Twin Cities players market. Many managers called the store directly, and players looking for a game frequently stopped by or called the store to check for possible assignments.

Crowds for the 1947 playoffs exceeded those reported for 1946, topped by the 5,653 fans who watched Albert Lea defeat Waseca in the Southern Minny finals, in a game played on Wednesday, September 10, at Dartt's Park in Owatonna. It was a "home" game for Albert Lea, but the two teams (who didn't have lights at their home fields) agreed to play a night game on the neutral site to draw more fans. The State Tournament opened on Sunday, September 14, so there was no option to wait for the weekend to play the game.

Crowds at the 1947 State Tournament overwhelmed the seating capacity of Mankato's Tanley Field. On the final day, 7,715 fans—up to 20 deep inside the outfield fences on the playing field—pushed the total attendance to 28,336, almost 5,000 higher than at Owatonna in 1946. The presence of large crowds on the field caused problems in several games. In the second-round game in Class AA, Albert Lea had the bases loaded in the bottom of the eighth inning, with two outs, and trailing 2–1 to New Ulm, when Herb Terhaar hit a deep fly to left center field. New Ulm center fielder Stan Manderfeld picked his way through the crowd and caught the ball. The umpires signaled an out, and Albert Lea manager Shanty Dolan charged out of the dugout. He argued that the tournament ground rules stated that balls hit into the crowd would be called ground-rule doubles. Both dugouts joined in the argument, and the umpires cleared the field only after threat-

ening to call the police. After consultation with tournament officials, the umpires ruled that the ball—even though Manderfeld was clearly standing in the crowd when he caught it—had not yet reached the crowd and therefore did not qualify as a ground-rule double. Under this ruling, a batted ball would have to strike someone in the crowd to qualify as a ground-rule double.

Albert Lea scored two runs in the bottom of the ninth to win the game. The tying run scored—you guessed it—on a ground-rule double that bounced into the crowd. Albert Lea won four consecutive games to sweep the Class AA championship for the fourth straight year and then, one week later, beat Class A champion Chaska for its third straight Mythical State Championship.

The 1947 tournament was marked by the appearance of two black players: Gread "Lefty" McKinnis, from the Rochester Queens, and Charles Moore, from Backus. McKinnis was a native of Alabama and had pitched for the Birmingham Black Barons and the Chicago American Giants of the Negro American League. McKinnis was 3–1 as a starting pitcher in the tournament and was voted the Most Valuable Player. He beat Milroy 7–1 on Friday, shut out Glencoe 1–0 (winning the game with a home run) on Saturday, but then lost when he tried to pitch his third game in three days in the finals against Chaska on Sunday. Charles Moore was a college student from Georgia. He came to Minnesota to visit his mother, who was a domestic servant for a family who had a summer home on Pheasant Lake outside Hackensack. Moore played shortstop for Backus, who lost their first game to Aitkin 5–3 in Class A single-elimination play.

No blacks had played in the State Tournament since 1926 and 1927, when a mysterious man named Lefty Wilson pitched for Wanda. Wilson was an alias for Dave Brown, who had pitched eight years for the Chicago American Giants and New York Lincoln Giants in the Negro Major Leagues. In 1925 he apparently killed a man in a barroom brawl in New York City and escaped to the Midwest, where he pitched as Lefty Wilson for the Chicago-based Gilkerson Union Giants and other semipro teams. He led Wanda to victory in the B-W-R (Brown, Watonwan, and Redwood counties) Tri-County League playoff championships in 1926 and 1927, but lost 4–0 to St. Paul Armours in the 1926 State Tournament, and 6–0 to Minneapolis Franklin Creamery in 1927.

No black players made it back to the State Tournament until 1947, as the AMABL practiced a form of racism in the 1930s and into the war years. Although there were no specific state rules against black players, the association published a recommended constitution and bylaws for member leagues that carried a provision stating that "all colored players are barred."

Despite the apparent success of the 1947 tournament, there were some complaints about excessive recruiting by some of the teams in the tournament. Joe Hennessy, a *St. Paul Pioneer Press* sports columnist, observed that not all developments at the State Tournament were encouraging. "There is a new type of scout at state tournaments," he wrote, "in addition to major and minor leagues. Many scouts are from teams in Minnesota looking for talent in 1948." Hennessy also expressed concern about the rising salaries and other inducements being offered to amateur ballplayers.

AMATEURS GET THEIR OWN CLASS

1948

RUMBLING ABOUT RECRUITING CONtinued all winter and reached a crescendo in the spring of 1948, when teams started making player-signing announcements. The Southern Minny, which would have six towns with lights by the start of the season, went to a 28-game schedule, while the Western Minny, a six-team league in 1948, expanded its schedule to 20 games, and it became clear that the Class AA teams were going to step up their pay and recruiting. Albert Lea signed three former professional players, and Austin countered by signing Wandas Mossor, the older brother of their 1947 ace Earl Mossor, as well as Minnesota college stars Red Lindgren (Augsburg) and Dick Seltz (Hamline). Lindgren hit .348 in 1947 for St. Cloud of the professional Class C Northern League, and Seltz hit .306. The high-profile players Jiggs Westergard and Hal Younghans, both Minnesota natives, gave up their pro careers to sign with Southern Minny teams.

If signings like these had been confined to the Class AA leagues, the Minnesota Amateur Baseball Association would probably have been able to weather the storm of protests. However,

many Class A teams were also in the bidding wars. Things came to a head in the North Central League area when Detroit Lakes signed Bob Haas, the professional Northern League's leading pitcher in 1946 and 1947, and Bob Ball, his catcher at Fargo-Moorhead in 1947, and Fergus

Earl Mossor, one of the first out-of-state minor-league players to come to Minnesota, shows his grip to Albert Lea catcher Spike Gorham. Mossor, a postseason draftee from Austin, won two games for Albert Lea in the 1948 Class AA State Tournament, and Gorham was voted MVP. *Star-Tribune* photograph; courtesy of the Minnesota Historical Society.

Falls, who planned to sign four members of the 1948 Minnesota Gophers team, reportedly sent team president Bob Allison to the NCAA College World Series in Omaha to look for more players.

Vint McDonald, a *Clay County Press* sportswriter and manager of the Hawley Hawks of the Heart O'Lakes League, wrote an open letter to the MABA. He threatened that his league, as well as the Tourist League (with two eight-team divisions, including former North Central teams Erhard and Wendell) and the Red River League, would withdraw from the MABA unless the North Central was reclassified or seeded directly into the State Tournament. McDonald also claimed to have support from other leagues in the area. Farther south, towns were making similar arguments for moving the West Central League (Willmar, Clara City, Bird Island, Lake Lillian, Granite Falls, Benson, Olivia, and Montevideo) up to Class AA.

The MABA could sit idle no longer. On April 19, 1948, it created a new class that was to be reserved for strictly amateur teams. Class B teams would not be permitted any outside or salaried players. The North Central and West Central Leagues were left in Class A, but the MABA said they must strictly adhere to the rules. Except for the Heart O'Lakes—strangely, since they were among the most vocal in protesting—and the North Central, the other leagues in that area immediately reclassified themselves to Class B.

The number of teams in the state shot up to 665, an increase of nearly 30 percent from 1947. The new class was an immediate hit—339 teams, from 47 leagues, chose to play Class B. Half of the Class B leagues were new ones, while the other half were former Class A leagues who chose to move down. Many Class AA and A teams—perhaps feeling there wouldn't be any more complaining about outside players—stepped up their recruiting. Not much was heard from towns in Class AA—who had made the choice to compete in the state's "big leagues"—but a lot of Class A towns were still unhappy, and the MABA was forced to act again. On Friday, August 20, right in the middle of playoffs, the MABA bumped the North Central and Bi-State Leagues into Class AA. The association cited Fergus Falls and Detroit Lakes as violators in the North Central, and the Rochester Queens and Winona Merchants in the Bi-State. They were all charged with having more than two outside players.

Fergus Falls was the most egregious of the violators. They had four players from the University of Minnesota baseball team—one whose home was in Fargo and three from Minneapolis—who probably could have been made "hometown" players under the relaxed rules interpretations of the time. However, two college players from Baylor, pitcher Fred Copeland and shortstop Hal Harris, weren't even signed until early May and didn't play their first games until June 24 and July 9, respectively. (MABA rules required a player to become a full-time resident by April 1.) Second baseman Jim McNulty, who had been playing for a Brooklyn Dodgers farm team in Abilene, Texas, played his first game on July 4. When asked how Fergus Falls thought they could get away with bringing in these players so late in the season, Harley Oyloe, who was one of five local residents on the team in 1948, said they really didn't think about it. "We weren't hiding anything," he said. "Everyone was doing it."

Why would players give up their minor-league careers and come to Minnesota to play "amateur" baseball? The explanation comes down

A *Life* magazine cover story featured the Brooklyn Dodgers' new training facility in Vero Beach, Florida, and the 550 players trying out for positions on the team's 25 minor-league farm teams. Copyright Time Inc.; courtesy of *Life* magazine.

LIFE

DODGER ROOKIES

APRIL 5, 1948 **15** CENTS

to numbers and dollars. Minor-league baseball grew rapidly after the war. In 1948 there were 438 minor-league teams, compared to only 86 in 1945. They didn't carry very large rosters, but at 16 players per team, the minor leagues would have had 7,008 players—all competing for 400 roster spots on the 16 major-league teams in operation at the time.

Life magazine's April 5, 1948, cover story on the Brooklyn Dodgers' spring training camp in Vero Beach, Florida, although not written to do so, showed what an uphill struggle it was for a prospective player to make the major leagues. Built on an abandoned wartime naval air station, "Dodgertown" hosted 550 players invited to try out for the 25 farm teams operated by the Dodgers in 1948. Ken Staples, a St. Paul native, recalled his first day at the training camp, when one of the instructors told catchers to report to a distant practice field. When he got finally got there, Staples observed that "the line of catchers looked a block long!" Another St. Paul native, Bob Bartholomew, was an outfielder in the Dodger farm system. He hit .348 for Class C Abilene, Texas, in 1948 and was "rewarded" by being assigned to Class C again in 1949. "There were 30 guys just like me in the system," Bartholomew said, "just waiting for Duke Snider [the Dodger center fielder] to break a leg or die."

Professional baseball didn't pay that well in the late 1940s. The Reserve Clause was still in effect, which bound a player to a team once he signed a contract. A player could not break or play out his contract and sign with another team—but the team could release a player with just 10 days' notice. Free agency was far off in the future. Before 1946 there was no required minimum salary for the major-league teams. Late in the season, the owners—reacting to the threat posed by the upstart Mexican League, which had used large

cash bonuses and higher salaries to talk 18 active major-league players into bolting to the new league—enacted a $5,000 minimum salary requirement ($50,080 in 2005 dollars). At the time it was enacted, 50 major-league players were making below $5,000, and only 15 were making more than $20,000. In 1946 the St. Louis Cardinals' Stan Musial, who hit .365 and won the National League's Most Valuable Player Award, was paid only $13,500 ($135,210 in 2005 dollars).

Minor-league pay was abysmal. Bartholomew was paid $225 per month in 1949 at Idaho Falls in the Class C Pioneer League. This was only a six-month job, from April through September. Teams did not pay salaries until the league schedules began, and before the Mexican League scare, they did not pay any training-camp expenses except for transportation to camp. Thus Bartholomew made only $1,350 per year playing baseball at a time when the national average annual salary was $3,600. Minor-league players like him needed to find decent jobs in the off-season, especially if they had families. Luckily, jobs were plentiful in the postwar economic boom. Many minor-league players spent their winters in auto assembly plants and textile mills.

Bartholomew quit after the 1949 season and returned to St. Paul. During the winter, Bob Balance, a teammate at Idaho Falls who had been hired as player/manager for the Waseca Braves in the Southern Minny, talked Bartholomew into signing with Waseca for $25 per game, plus a full-time job with E. F. Johnson Radio. At first glance, that may not sound like much. However, the Southern Minny played a 35-game schedule in 1950, and with exhibitions and playoffs, Bartholomew would have earned at least $1,000—and it was now bonus money on top of the earnings from his regular job. Many players, once they settled down in Minnesota, used their baseball earnings to make a down payment on a house or to make other large purchases such as an automobile. (A full-sized Detroit car sold for about $1,750 in 1950.) Bartholomew made that baseball money playing three games a week, compared to almost every day with Idaho Falls the year before.

Road trips were much easier, too. At Waseca, he slept in his own bed after every game. Winona, at 103 miles, was the longest trip for Waseca. The other six towns in the league were an average of 35 miles away. By contrast, the team closest to Idaho Falls in the Pioneer League was 53 miles away, while Billings, Great Falls, and Boise were 384, 359, and 288 miles away, respectively. The team traveled on crowded, non-air-conditioned buses and sometimes stayed four to a room in fleabag hotels. Although making the decision to play baseball in Minnesota meant the end of the dream of playing in the major leagues, it was not the end of the world. Indeed, Minnesota baseball was so pleasant and financially rewarding that some of the former pros probably wondered if they were dreaming.

The Bartholomew case is representative of many pro players who came to Minnesota. Other players signed different contracts or found different jobs, but their experiences were similar. Some came and stayed, while others just came for the summers. Ray Riley and Earl Mossor, who came to Austin in 1947, are examples of both cases. Riley found a good job at Hormel, married a local woman, and settled down in Austin. Mossor, on the other hand, pitched three summers in Minnesota but left in 1950 to restart his professional baseball career. Mossor played 10 more years in professional baseball, including three

seasons with the St. Paul Saints of the American Association, and three games with the Brooklyn Dodgers in 1951. Bartholomew was a native Minnesotan who, like many others, used his baseball skills to find a job and eventually learn a trade and settle down. There were only a few former pro players in the state in 1948, but they came in increasing numbers the next few years.

The arrival of out-of-state professionals was the last phase in the recruiting wars that had accelerated rapidly since 1945. At first teams looking for more or better players searched around the state for talent, especially in the Twin Cities area. It became difficult for St. Paul and Minne-

John Cowles, one of many Twin Cities stars to be recruited by out-state teams, played Minneapolis Park Board ball for free in 1947. In 1948 he received $50 per game pitching for Buffalo in the Class A Wright County League. Photograph by Lefty Evans; courtesy of Don Evans.

apolis teams to retain their players. Team sponsors paid park boards for league entry fees, which also covered umpires, purchased uniforms, and some equipment. However, they couldn't raise any money by ticket sales, since the park boards owned the fields and did not charge admission. Several city pitchers were thought to have been paid a little under the table, but it couldn't have been much, judging by the mass exodus of players to outstate teams.

Early in the 1947 season, for example, Edison High School star pitcher Johnny Garbett, pitching for Triangle Sales in the Park National League, beat Honeywell's John Cowles (North High School, 1940), 3–2. One year later they had two more pitching duels—but they had both moved to the Class A Wright County League. Garbett was being paid $75 a game by Maple Lake, while Cowles was paid $50 per game by Buffalo. Pay was higher for pitchers, but it wasn't limited to them. John Leighton, a Honeywell teammate of Cowles, moved to Bird Island of the West Central League in 1948, where he played shortstop for $25 a game and got a job working at a local car dealer. Many other players interviewed said that leagues surrounding the Twin Cities commonly paid at least $10 to $15 per game for good infielders and outfielders.

State college players were in the next phase, as teams were able to offer well-paying summer jobs to attract them. The colleges were swamped with returning veterans taking advantage of the GI Bill, so there were a lot of men to choose from. School boards frequently helped by hiring teachers and coaches who were also baseball players. A typical story was told by Wayne Dietz, a Sanborn native and Minnesota High School Baseball Coaches Hall of Fame coach. Dietz, who had played at St. Olaf College as well as with town teams in Northfield and Sleepy Eye, figured he had a pretty good chance of landing a job when the Hector School

Board president asked him, before his job interview started, "Do you play baseball?"

Teams started looking for out-of-state college players in 1948. Fergus Falls was the first to send a scout to the College World Series, but other teams quickly followed. Gopher coach Dick Siebert used his connections to find players for Litchfield when he managed there from 1951 to 1954, and some teams, like Morris, formed informal alliances with colleges. In the early 1950s the West Central team usually had several players from Michigan State University. Similarly, Springfield tapped into the University of Wisconsin. Once a college player spent a summer in Minnesota, he became part of a referral network that brought many more. For example, in 1951, when Litchfield needed an infielder who could also do some catching, Ray Gebhardt, an All–Big Ten player at Ohio State University in 1949, suggested to manager Siebert that he call Gebhardt's former Buckeye teammate, Bob Montebello.

College players were paid by their summer employers to protect their eligibility, but the NCAA didn't do much policing until the late 1950s. Some individuals have suggested that baseball teams might have subsidized employers at times but kept the transactions off the books. No records have been found to substantiate this, but it probably happened. Most college players were paid about $300 per month, but a few got considerably more. University of Alabama pitcher Al Worthington (who later played for the Minnesota Twins) was paid $500 per month at Fulda in 1950, and Ohio State University All-American pitcher Paul Ebert received $400 per month at Marshall in 1954. College players typically worked as coaches for summer recreation programs or as lifeguards, or did park and field maintenance, although many worked in grocery stores or on city construction and maintenance

The "baseball train"—an eastbound Chicago and North Western "Minnesota 400"—crosses the Mississippi River at Winona on August 23, 1947. Photograph by Ken Zurn; from the collection of Chicago and North Western Historical Society.

crews. Whatever the job, baseball was their priority, and players were given generous time off to practice and travel to games. The players roomed with local citizens and generally paid a nominal rent out of their salaries.

The first former professionals who played in Minnesota were those who had some connections to the state. Men like Hy Vandenberg (Springfield), Tony Jaros (Faribault), Howie Schultz (Willmar), Rollie Seltz (Excelsior), and Jiggs Westergard (Mankato) were Minnesota natives who returned to their homes when they quit or retired from pro baseball and started playing in the state's amateur leagues. Others like Bobby Reis (West St. Paul) and Bob Haas (Detroit Lakes) were not from Minnesota but played here at the end of their pro careers.

The second wave of professionals extended to players from all over the country. Wags in south-

ern Minnesota christened the Chicago and North Western 400 train the "baseball train" because it carried prospective baseball players to and from Minnesota. It was joked that some towns always had one player coming and one player leaving on the 400. Hecklers were often unmerciful with hired players who were having a bad night, yelling at them to come to the grandstand to pick up their tickets for the 400.

It didn't take teams long to figure out that former pros were the way to go—if they could afford them. Each team who won the Class AA State Tournament from 1948 to 1953 had a pitching staff dominated by former pros. In 1954 and 1955, when the state was down to two Class AA leagues and the Western Minny and Southern Minny decided the State Championship in the "Little World Series," Fairmont won both years with pitchers from the Class A, AA, and AAA minor leagues. The advantage the former pros had over Minnesota players was experience. Minor-league pitchers pitched every fourth game in those days, and against tough competition, especially when they rose to Class B and above. Minor leaguers at other positions played about 140 to 150 games a year, plus six to eight weeks of spring training. A typical Minnesota town team player wouldn't get that much experience in four seasons.

In July 1948 Max Lanier's All-Stars barnstorming team made a big splash in the state. The All-Stars were a group of major-league players—and a few minor leaguers, as well—who had been lured into the independent Mexican League in 1946 by the multimillionaire Jorge Pasqual, who owned the *entire league* and was offering huge bonuses and annual salaries. Within two years, almost all of the defectors came back to the states, but they were banned from professional baseball.

Lanier organized the barnstorming team in 1948, complete with its own streamlined bus. The team played about 70 games that summer, including six in Minnesota from July 8 to July 23. Three games were rained out in Minnesota, and one in Detroit Lakes was canceled when several Lakers players decided not to play, fearing they would be suspended from professional baseball. Lanier's All-Stars demanded a $1,000 to $1,500 guarantee and generally had no trouble booking games, as towns were anxious to see real major-league players in person. Advance publicity was a bit overboard—the booking agent claimed that the team, if permitted to play in the major leagues, could challenge for a pennant.

The All-Stars had three fairly close games in the state, beating Austin 5–1, Fergus Falls 9–7 and Springfield 3–1. They beat Buffalo 9–1 and routed a collection of all-stars from the Gopher League 22–0 in Slayton, and some Shakopee-area all-stars 10–2 in Shakopee.

Barnstorming teams of all stripes roamed across Minnesota in the late 1940s, ranging from pickup teams of former University of Minnesota athletes to the bearded House of David team to some tough Negro Major League teams like the Kansas City Monarchs. Until 1948, most leagues in Minnesota played a Sundays-only schedule, and few teams had lights. Midweek twilight exhibition games were one way for teams to pick up a little extra money. After the war, people were starved for entertainment, and it was easy to fill the stands for almost any game. The extra games also gave players more practice and permitted teams to try out prospective players. Many towns also scheduled day-game exhibitions on the Memorial Day (then called Decoration Day), July 4, and Labor Day holidays.

Many of the exhibition teams were collections of athletes brought together for just a few games. For players on these teams, the games were an opportunity to pick up a little extra spending money. Teams with names like the St. Paul All-Stars, Minneapolis All-Stars, and Mill City All-Stars were thrown together to play exhibition games. Their rosters varied depending on who was available, and being a resident of St. Paul, for example, wasn't essential to playing on the St. Paul All-Stars, especially when they were

Max Lanier's All-Stars team offered Minnesota fans a chance to see real major-league players in action. In the days before television, most fans had never seen a major leaguer except in newspaper wire photographs or an occasional movie theater newsreel. Poster courtesy of Don Cook.

★ MAX LANIER'S ★

ALL

STARS

HARRY FELDMAN
Pitched 800 Ball for N. Y.
Giants—'42

MAX LANIER

MAX LANIER
Pitched in 3 World Series
Selected on 2 All Star Teams

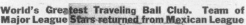

**World's Greatest Traveling Ball Club. Team of
Major League Stars returned from Mexican League**

MYRON HAYWORTH
Catcher for the World
Champion Browns—'43

JAMES STEINER
Former Boston Red Sox
Catcher

15
Former
Major League
Players

GEO. HAUSMANN
Former Star Infielder
for N. Y. Giants

LOU KLEIN
Former Second Base
Championship Cardinals—'43

FRED MARTIN
Former St. Louis Cardinal
Pitching Sensation

15
Former
Major League
Players

vs

Springfield Tigers

MONDAY JULY 19, 1948, - 8:15 p. m.

RIVER SIDE BALL PARK

ADMISSION: Adults, $1.00, Plus Tax   Children, 50c, Plus Tax

The Greatest Attraction of the Year!

In 1948, Winsted, with a population of 941, attracted baseball crowds more than twice the town's size. Courtesy of *Herald-Journal*, Winsted, Minnesota.

looking for a player to fill a spot in the lineup. A team calling itself the Golden Gophers traded on the immense popularity of the University of Minnesota football team and drew pretty well wherever they played.

As more teams got lighted fields, the appetite for exhibition games grew, and the state began to see more professional barnstorming teams. The bearded House of David team dated back to the 1920s and was always a popular drawing card. The Negro League teams liked to travel in the upper Midwest. Although they certainly encountered racial prejudice in Minnesota, they found fewer problems with eating and sleeping accommodations than in the South or East.

Teams like the Kansas City Monarchs, Birmingham Black Barons, San Francisco Cubs, Cuban All-Stars, Indianapolis Clowns, Chicago Barons, and the Brooklyn Colored Clowns made regular appearances in the state. Some of these teams played the game straight up, while others clowned in the mold of the Harlem Globetrotters. A typical stunt was one performed by Odell Livingston of the Colored House of David team, and one that would be featured in the pregame advertising. Livingston always caught one inning while sitting in a rocking chair. The Clowns entertained fans with batting exhibitions and sleight-of-hand infield drills before games.

Generally, barnstorming teams played for a share of the gate, negotiated in advance. From time to time, though, a little wagering was done on the day of the game. They might agree, for example, to a 60–40 or 75–25 split, with the winner taking the larger share. In anticipation of this, many local teams "drafted" ringers to pitch or play against the touring team.

By early August 1948, teams were once again battling for positions in the State Tournament. Most towns claimed crowds were better than in 1947. The *Marshall Messenger* reported that Milroy beat Wanda 4–3 in a Redwood County League playoff game before 2,300 fans in Milroy, attendance that was five times the combined population of the two towns! The State Tournament promised to be a good one. The Class AA field was up to seven teams. Albert Lea had finished in fourth place in the Southern Minny but won the playoffs and was back to seek its fifth consecutive championship. Twin Cities writers Ted Peterson (*Minneapolis Tribune*) and Bob Schabert (*St. Paul Pioneer Press*) felt that either Fergus Falls or Springfield would dethrone the Packers. Twin Cities fans were optimistic that their teams would do well. The St. Paul Union Printers, returning from 1947, and the Banana Distributors managed to hang on to more top players than most Twin Cities teams, and each

had won exhibition games against tough outstate rivals during the season.

The Union Printers had won the 1946 National Printers Championship, played in Boston's Fenway Park. They had also done well in the 1947—held in Lexington Park—and 1948 National Championships. The *Pioneer Press* and small printing job shops around the city supported the team by hiring good baseball players as apprentice printers. They also kicked in to pay entry and operating costs for the team, and each provided a uniform, with the shop's name on the back of the jersey.

Shakopee, the host, had eliminated Chaska, the 1947 Class A champion, in the Minnesota Valley League playoffs and then won Region 1A

Union Printers, 1947. The team won the 1946 National Printers Championship in Boston's Fenway Park and went to the State Class AA Tournament in 1947 and 1948. *Front row, from left:* Roy Heuer, Klink Hoium, Paul Guertin, Bob Fernlund, Bill Schliek, Paul Berberich, Charles Smith. *Back row:* Harold Yahnka, Bob Kueppers, Len Brix, manager Bud Ryan, Bob Matz, Jerry Tuckner, Lou Schultz, Bob Stoltz, Jack Nentwig, John Anderson. Courtesy of Jack Nentwig.

State Tournament game at Shakopee's Riverside Park, Sunday, September 12, 1948. The overflow crowd was permitted to sit on the playing surface, right up to the foul lines, and along the warning track in fair territory. *Dispatch–Pioneer Press* photograph; courtesy of the Minnesota Historical Society.

to qualify for the tournament. Peterson and Schabert favored Shakopee to win the state Class A Title. No one knew what to expect in the new Class B, but the presence of nearby Lester Prairie and the Springfield Cubs was expected to draw big crowds.

Shakopee had done a great job on their $20,000 upgrade to Riverside Park, which included new lights, a new infield, new fences, and increased seating capacity. Players from the Minneapolis Millers, who visited the State Tournament on Tuesday, September 14, declared the playing field better than any in the American Association, with the possible exception of Indianapolis or Columbus—and certainly better than either Nicollet or Lexington Park, homes for the Millers and Saints. The *Pioneer Press* sportswriter Joe Hennessy described the Lexington infield as "a rough dirt pile with

almost no grass." And furthermore, "the outfield is burned out."

The Twin Cities teams got off to a good start in the Class AA bracket, beating some tough pitching opponents. The Union Printers beat the Rochester Queens and Lefty McKinnis 3–2, and the Bananas topped Hy Vandenberg and the Springfield Tigers 6–1. The Bananas beat the Printers in a wild 14–13 game, but went on to lose two games to Albert Lea, 5–2 and 11–0, but did finish in second place in the tournament.

Thanks to the solid pitching of Earl and Wandas Mossor, postseason draftees from Austin,

Albert Lea won Class AA again. Winsted won Class A, in a bracket featuring excellent play and close games, and the St. Cloud Moose won the inaugural Class B title. Attendance, at 34,280, set a record for the third consecutive year. Shakopee paid off half of the new facility's debt with profits earned at the tournament. Unlike 1946 or 1947, there weren't many complaints behind the scenes at the tournament. The creation of Class B solved a lot of problems, and it looked as if more teams would join the MABA in 1949.

Not many people paid attention when KSTP became the upper Midwest's first television station in April 1948. There were only an estimated 2,500 television sets in the Twin Cities area at the time. Stanley Hubbard, KSTP president, and Rosy Ryan, Minneapolis Millers general manager, announced that all Millers home games would be televised, except for Sundays and holidays. KSTP sports director Jack Horner was at the microphone for the Millers home opener with the Louisville Colonels on Tuesday, April 27.

The first televised World Series game—between the New York Yankees and Brooklyn Dodgers—had been broadcast by NBC from Yankee Stadium on September 30, 1947, to four eastern cities: New York, Philadelphia, Washington, and Schenectady. Together, the four cities had only 150,000 television sets. However, fans flocked to the 3,000-plus bars in New York City equipped with sets. For the 1948 World Series, RCA and Gillette spent $25,000 to install 100 television sets on the Boston Common. An estimated 15,000 fans showed up each day to watch the hometown Boston Braves play the Cleveland Indians.

Annual production of television sets went from 179,000 in 1947 to 975,000 in 1948. Industry officials attributed much of the increased demand to the popularity of televised sporting events and predicted that replaying highlights of games during evening news shows would cause a boom in attendance for almost all sports. Frank Shaughnessy, president of the professional International League, seemed to be the lone dissenter. He feared that television would destroy baseball's minor leagues, especially those in the range of major-league broadcasts.

The 1948 State Tournament featured some great matchups. Here Belle Plaine catcher Gene O'Brien reaches home plate after a home run against Milroy in a first-round Class A game. In this game, three O'Brien brothers from Belle Plaine faced four Dolan brothers from Milroy. *Star-Tribune* photograph; courtesy of the Minnesota Historical Society.

SWINGING FOR THE FENCES

1949

TELEVISION WAS BUT A DISTANT RUMBLING in Minnesota as the 1949 baseball season began. Membership in the Minnesota Amateur Baseball Association grew by 38 to 703 teams. The West Central League opted to play in Class AA, which silenced critics in that area who had complained about the excessive use of outside players by the league. The two leagues bumped to Class AA in August 1948 went in different directions—the North Central League decided to stay in Class AA, while the Bi-State returned to Class A. If there was a significant trend to be found, it was that more teams decided to move down to the strictly amateur Class B. The number of Class A leagues went from 35 in 1948 to 22 in 1949, and the number of teams from 263 to 170. Class B enrollment went from 339 to 469.

For most towns, the home team's baseball games were the highlight of the weekly social calendar. Each town seemed to have one or two places where townspeople gathered to talk over the last game and speculate about the next one. Barbershops were usually on this list. Many businessmen had regular appointments—weekly or biweekly haircuts were the norm in the 1940s and 1950s—and others frequently stopped in just for the conversation, which was usually about baseball. At Ike's Barber Shop in Springfield, for example, barber Fats Johnson, a member of the baseball team board of directors, got a lot of free advice on how to run the team. Similarly, farmers—when they had time between planting and harvesting—would meet for morning coffee at local cafés to discuss the weather, of course, and dispense their baseball wisdom.

Fan interest wasn't limited to men, either. The *Minneapolis Tribune* wrote about an athletic banquet at Winthrop High School, attended by approximately 200 fathers and mothers. "We can't hold our bridge and women's club sessions when there is an athletic event," one Winthrop mother told the reporter. Baseball games were must-see events. In small towns, where cars were permitted to park along the foul lines, people would often park their cars at the field early Sunday morning and then walk to church, returning in time to watch the game. During the game, the car horns would be honking for key hits and good defensive plays. In New Ulm, for big games where

Town team ball was up close and personal in parks like Hamburg, where early-bird fans parked their cars along the foul line fences. Courtesy of Lois Droege.

attendance was expected to be high, some fans paid children 25¢—the child's ticket price—to enter the park as soon as the gates were opened and reserve seats in desirable locations. When the adults showed up, the children would move to other unoccupied, but less desirable, seats.

Locals would stop players on the sidewalk to talk about baseball and mingled with them at cafés and taverns, and appreciative fans frequently bought them lunches and drinks. Saturday nights were big, when farmers came into town to shop and catch up on local gossip—and talk about Sunday's game. Harold Witte, who started playing for Hector in 1948 while still in high school, said, "You really felt important on main street when you played on the town baseball team." Minneapolis native Johnny Garbett agreed. "It was unreal," he said. "I couldn't believe it when I first came to Maple Lake in 1948 [as a 19-year-old pitcher]. People were so nice. They treated me like I was family." He was paid $75 per

game and had a job at a gas station. "I pumped gas for a few hours a day," he said, "but mostly I just sat around and talked about baseball."

Local businesses donated gift certificates and merchandise for players making key plays. Season openers were big events—prizes might be given for first hit, first walk, first extra-base hit, first home run, first double play, and so on. Some gifts continued throughout the season—a case of beer, for example, for each home run, or, in some places, a case of Wheaties for each home run. Many gifts were awarded on the spur of the moment, in appreciation for a good play. Many players went home with chickens, sacks of potatoes, and other groceries or gift certificates.

On occasion, for a home run or a big hit that turned the tide against a bitter rival, a player

Fergus Falls players Dick Fisher *(left)* and Jim McNulty pick up the cases of Wheaties they'd won for hitting home runs, while Harry Hill can only cradle his bat and dream of hitting one himself. Courtesy of Harley Oyloe.

might get an unusual curtain call—to walk beside the dugout and collect one-, five-, and at times ten-dollar bills rolled up and stuffed into the fence by overjoyed fans. After the game, the winning pitcher or game hero was sometimes surprised to find a paper bill in his hand after a congratulatory handshake from a fan who had won a big bet on the game.

Betting on games was pervasive. Most of it was casual—maybe a few dollars between friends from different towns, but some men were betting up to $100 or more per game. Reed Lovsness, a Cottonwood native, said he was surprised at the amount of open betting he saw when he started pitching at Milroy in 1953. "Some guys were walking around waving $10 and $20 bills, looking for a bet," he said. "Talk about pressure on a pitcher!" The larger bets were not out in the open, however. Usually, some local businessman or wealthy farmer was the bookie. Willing bettors knew who they were, and how to contact them. Some sat in their cars during the game, while others had a favorite spot in the stands

where they could be found. Popular bars also served as clearinghouses for bets on games.

The games were raucous affairs. Roger Edgar, later a member of Waseca's 1957 Class A State Champions, recalled going to Springfield games with his father in the late 1940s. "Game days were exciting," he said. Signs would be placed out on streets advertising the game. These would not merely give the game time and opponent. "See Hy Vandenberg battle Leo Leininger and the New Ulm Brewers," they might read. People in town had been talking about the game all day, and anticipation was high as the first fans entered the field. At first, while the players warmed up and played catch, the only sound was the good-natured banter between the players, and the zip from the seams of the thrown balls and the smack of balls hitting gloves. By the time batting practice started, more fans were beginning to arrive, polka music began to be played over the public address system, and smoke from the concession stands' grills drifted over the stands. By the end of batting practice, it was hard to hear the crack of the bat over the other competing noises. While the teams took infield practice and the pitchers warmed up, the voices of hecklers would rise above the din, starting to work on their favorite targets—the opposing pitcher, manager, or some other player they thought they could rattle.

The jeering got louder as the game got under way. Each town seemed to have at least one heckler whose voice could be distinctly heard on the field. Some were funny; others just nasty. Milroy's Spike Dolan recalled a game against Marshall, when he got doubled off first on a line drive to the second baseman. As Spike started to walk off the field, the second baseman yelled, "How do you like that, you [unprintable]?" Dolan turned around and ran back onto the field. "What did you call me?" he shouted. "I wasn't talking to you,

Umpires had a tough job. Here one of the men in blue gets some "helpful" advice, while fans in the stands are prepared to contribute theirs. *Dispatch–Pioneer Press* photograph; courtesy of the Minnesota Historical Society.

Dolan," came the reply. "It was that loudmouth SOB behind first base!" He was referring to Milroy's "designated heckler," Ferp Phillippe.

But everyone joined in, and chatter from the dugouts could be unmerciful. You wouldn't hear "Hum battah, hum battah" or "let's go boys." More likely it would be "stick it in his ear" or "who was that I saw with your wife last night?" Play on the field was rough, and brawls were not uncommon. Fans occasionally ran onto the field to take part, as they did in Watertown during a July 1949 game with Winsted, the defending Class A State Champions, who were tied with Maple Lake for first place in the North Star League. On that day, however, Winsted was get-

ting beat by seventh-place Watertown, 3–1, and not taking it well. The game was frequently interrupted by arguments and shoving contests. The *Carver County News* of Watertown observed that "a Winsted strikeout wasn't official until the victim had complained for at least a minute and a half." Of course, Winsted supporters argued that they were the victims of poor umpiring. In the eighth inning someone threw a beer bottle onto the field, just missing Winsted first baseman Cobby Saatzer. The umpires immediately warned the Watertown bench that any further incidents like that would result in a forfeit. That temporarily quieted the crowd, but when Saatzer caught a pop-up on the next play to end the inning, he wheeled around and threw the ball into the screen in front of the first baseline bleachers. Fans jumped onto the field, and players from both dugouts joined in the melee. Police had to be called to break up the riot.

Police occasionally had to escort umpires to their cars after games to protect them from fans angry at real or perceived bad calls. Fans had long memories, and an umpire unfortunate to have drawn their ire over a prior game's controversial call would be taunted from the time he walked onto the field. Although some of those fans probably thought they could intimidate an umpire and cause him to make favorable calls, most were just yelling because it was part of the game. Not many came to the games just to sit and watch. Many were like Dorothy French, whose husband Hugh played on the Zumbrota team of the late 1940s. "I didn't know much about baseball," she admitted, "but when Hugh's sister Rae, who was an avid baseball fan, stood up and shouted, I did too, even though I didn't always know what I was shouting for." When fans yelled, "Did you forget your glasses?" at an umpire, it wasn't necessarily a personal insult. It was just part of the game. Fans came to cheer and yell, and when the home team wasn't doing anything to cheer about, they yelled insults at the umpires or other team.

Some umpires probably did deserve criticism. Older ballplayers, particularly those who played in the forties, frequently mentioned that many umpires were incompetent and inconsistent. The surge in teams from 162 in 1945 to 799 in 1950 was a major factor; the demand for umpires simply outstripped the supply. For a few

postwar seasons, some leagues used hometown, volunteer umpires. While this might have been adequate for low-key recreational leagues, it was a recipe for trouble in towns starting to spend money to assemble competitive teams.

The Northwest Umpires Association, formed in 1917, was the oldest in the state. Most of its members lived in the Twin Cities, and they covered 21 of the state's 58 leagues in 1946. As the demand for umpires grew, other umpires organizations were formed. D. W. "Doc" Henry of Marshall formed the Southwest Umpires Association in 1947, and it soon became affiliated with leagues in that region and also stretched into the west central area. The Minnesota-Wisconsin Umpires Association started in the southeastern part of the state and by 1953 was handling all three of the remaining Class AA leagues. The Northwest, Southwest, Minnesota-Wisconsin, Lake Region, Inter-State, and Central Minnesota Umpires Associations formed the League of Minnesota Umpires Association in 1953 to discuss common issues and to standardize the training and certification of umpires. The increasing professionalism of umpires greatly reduced the complaints about their performance. Unfortunately, leagues frequently undermined umpires' authority by reversing decisions made in the aftermath of brawls and arguments. Players who bumped or struck umpires often got off with light penalties.

Town team games were major attractions for children, even those who weren't interested in baseball. It was a place to congregate. Many towns, like Rollingstone, had a park or picnic area next to the baseball field. On Sundays, families met at the park, and while most of the adults watched the game, children were left on their own to play with friends or wander over to the game. A gang of boys would usually assemble to chase foul balls. They were paid a nickel or dime to return the balls to team officials. Others made money by helping the concession stands. In towns that permitted beer sales—many were in dry counties or prohibited sales on Sundays—children could make a dime or quarter per case for returning empty bottles. Rules on sales of beer were fairly relaxed, and some groups of men used a young boy to carry beer from the concession stands to their seats. In return, they saved their empties for him to return, and gave him a small tip. At 50¢ each or three beers for a dollar, the empty cases filled up quickly on hot summer afternoons. Some teams used children to walk through the stands carrying popcorn and paid them a penny for each 10¢ bag or box of popcorn they sold.

After the game, players and their families and other local fans would often stay near the field or adjoining park area to socialize and talk about the game. Where permitted, teams might donate a couple cases of beer and soft drinks. In some towns, players would retreat to a machine shed or Legion hall or someone's garage to have a few drinks—sometimes with players from the opposing team. Many rural players and fans can recall rushing home after Sunday afternoon games to finish chores so they could return to town for a picnic or cookout.

Each town developed its own postgame tradition. In Belle Plaine, for example, players usually gathered at manager Gene O'Brien's garage, where they talked over the just-completed game. Soon the talk drifted to tales of games and seasons long gone. It wasn't unusual for this to go on for hours, with participants coming and going. Similarly, players in Ivanhoe gathered at Wayland's Barbershop, where they would drink a few beers and discuss the game while they waited to use the shop's single shower. Sometimes the discussions didn't break up until sunrise. In Nor-

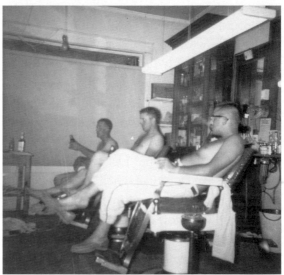

(**TOP**) Some of the mellowest moments for Norwood players came after games when they relaxed with fans and rehashed the plays. Courtesy of Lois Willemsen.

(**ABOVE**) Ivanhoe players Chuck Frisby, Jim Muchlinski, and George Briffett wait patiently to use the single shower in Wayland's barbershop. Postgame discussions could drag on until the early-morning hours. Courtesy of Jim Muchlinski.

wood, players and families and some fans would linger at the field for a while and then go out to the picnic area at nearby Eagle Lake. Local businessmen or other supporters occasionally provided steaks or hot dogs and hamburgers.

In 1949 fans attended games in even greater numbers than in 1948, which had also been a record year. Most teams did not regularly report exact numbers, but newspapers wrote of "record crowds," "the biggest crowd in history," and "another overflow crowd" without giving the details. Teams reporting specific attendance figures showed some impressive numbers. Austin drew an average of 2,227 per game for 17 regular-season Southern Minnesota League games, and a total of 37,859, including exhibition and playoff games. The three-game semifinal playoff series with Albert Lea drew 2,888 per game, while the three-game finals with Rochester averaged 3,543.

New Ulm drew 36,345 fans for 20 home games—13 league games, 4 exhibition, and 3 playoff. The 1,817 per-game average was an increase of 428 per game from 1948. Baseball-mad Fergus Falls drew 38,400 fans to 29 home games. Of these, there were 10 league and 3 playoff games. The other 16 were exhibitions, ranging from games with the Minneapolis Banana Distributors, St. Paul Harding Boosters, and the Northern League's Fargo-Moorhead Twins to barnstorming teams like the Brooklyn Colored Clowns and an ad hoc group calling themselves the Minneapolis All-Stars. Attendance topped 1,000 for most of the exhibition games. The largest regular-season crowd was 2,300 for a game against archrival Detroit Lakes, and the largest playoff crowd was 3,031, also against the Detroit Lakers.

Fans also flocked to games as the West Central League began operation as a Class AA league. Montevideo, which had folded during the 1948 season, and Granite Falls opted not to move up in class. Atwater (population 880) and De Graff (population 270) joined in their place. Amazingly, the league—with holdover

Lake Lillian at 358—had three teams with populations less than 1,000. Clara City (1,106) and Bird Island (1,333) were not much larger. That didn't seem to be a deterrent. Towns held various fund-raisers and solicited contributions to help finance their teams. Love of baseball wasn't the only factor. Most supporters donated out of a sense of civic pride—they were proud to be in the "big leagues." Some old regional rivalries transferred to the playing field. Everyone loved to beat Willmar (population 9,410), which had more than double the population of Benson (3,398), the next-largest city in the league. De Graff and nearby Benson also became bitter enemies on the field. De Graff drew over 1,500 fans for games with Benson and Willmar.

New lighting systems, combined with continued fan support, led teams to increase their schedules, especially in the Class AA and A leagues. Installation of lights in Waseca and Faribault—the only two teams without lights in 1948—early in the season permitted the Southern Minny to go from a 28-game to a three-games-per-week, 35-game schedule. The six-team Western Minny went from 20 games to 25, while the North Central went from a 10-game schedule in 1948, when it was a six-team league, to 20 games in 1949, when it was a five-team league.

Many Class A leagues followed suit. The North Star League, home of Winsted, the 1948 State Champion, went from 14 to 28 games. The Minnesota River League went from 14 to 21, and the Minnesota Valley League went from 10 games to 20. This was a struggle for the league, where Shakopee was the only team with lights. They played once a week through June and then started playing midweek twilight games in July. The new six-team First Night League, which billed itself as the first league to schedule all night games, including Sundays, played a 20-game schedule.

Most leagues had only one or two teams with lights and stayed with double-round-robin 10- or 14-game schedules. Twilight games were poorly attended in rural areas of the state, where field-work and daily chores made it difficult for farmers to come to the games. The Minnesota Valley League, with teams from Bloomington, Chaska, Excelsior, Hopkins, St. Louis Park, and Shakopee, was a unique case. Chaska and Shakopee were the only teams who attracted significant numbers of farmers.

Class A or B towns with lights, especially those with the ambition to qualify for the State Tournament, scheduled extra exhibition games to get their teams better prepared. The Little Falls Red Sox, the 1949 Class B State Champions, for example, played 7 exhibition games in addition to its 14-game Great Central League schedule. Many towns rented nearby lighted fields to play midweek exhibitions or to make up rained-out league games. Norwood was more fortunate

than most—its Crow River League rival Young America's lights were barely a mile from Norwood's home field.

Economically, the extra games made sense. First of all, fans kept buying tickets. In Class AA and A, this paid for the extra expense of hiring at least one additional pitcher. Curiously enough, this also made it easier for teams to expand from a two-games-a-week schedule to three games. With only two games per week, there wasn't enough work for two pitchers, unless the team scheduled exhibition games. Three games weekly appeared to be the ideal mix. Two starters could alternate games, so one pitched Sunday-Thursday-Tuesday-Sunday, and the other pitched Tuesday-Sunday-Thursday-Tuesday.

Night game at Winona's Gabrych Park. Towns raced to install lights in the late 1940s and frequently drew huge crowds to midweek games. The Southern Minny expanded its schedule to 28 games in 1948 and to 35 games in 1949, when it started playing three games a week on Sunday, Tuesday, and Thursday. Courtesy of Winona County Historical Society Archives.

The extra revenue from more ticket sales permitted teams to recruit and sign more professional and college players. Teams also began to sign players out of the Negro Major Leagues and from black touring teams.

The Negro Major Leagues declined rapidly after 1946, when the Brooklyn Dodgers signed Jackie Robinson to play with their Montreal farm team in the Class AAA International League. Within a few years, most young black players were signing with major-league organizations, and black fans turned their attention away from the Negro Major Leagues. The Negro National League ceased operating after the 1948 season, and though the Negro American League continued to operate through 1960, it was not considered "major" in status anymore. All-time home-run king Hank Aaron started the 1952 season with the Indianapolis Clowns, but his contract was sold to the Boston Braves, and he spent the remainder of the season with Eau Claire in the Class C Northern League. Aaron was the last player from the Negro American League to make the major leagues. Many veteran black players, too old by now to be sought by the white major leagues, were able to sign onto formerly all-white "amateur" and semipro teams. The leagues in Western Canada attracted the most, but quite a few players found their way into Minnesota.

The Rochester boxing and entertainment promoter Ben Sternberg was the pioneer in bringing black players to Minnesota. He met Abe Saperstein, owner of the Harlem Globetrottters, while arranging playing dates for the basketball team, and formed a long-distance friendship with the Chicago native. Saperstein was a booking agent for most of the Negro American League baseball teams, as well, and promoted the Negro Leagues' famous East-West All-Star Game. Saperstein was one of several white businessmen who were influential in black baseball. He was a silent partner in the Ethiopian Clowns, the baseball equivalent of the Harlem Globetrotters, and the Birmingham Black Barons of the Negro American League. He also owned the Chicago American Giants of the Negro American League.

Sternberg had signed Gread McKinnis, the MVP of the 1947 State Tournament, on a recommendation by Saperstein. McKinnis also pitched for Sternberg's Rochester Queens in 1948. At the time, Rochester had two separate baseball organizations. The Queen City American Legion Post sponsored the Queens, who played in the Bi-State League. The Rochester Baseball Association fielded

Team birthday party for Rochester Royals manager Ben Sternberg at Bruno's Café, August 1949. *From left:* Mel Carter, Sam Jones, John Creevey, Gene Carroll, Spike Powell, Bob Petersdorf, chef Angelo Perini, Bruno Lisi, Ida Perini, Stan Partenheimer, Sam Hill, Artie Osman Jr., Bud Wolfe, and Sternberg. Courtesy of Phil Dixon.

three additional teams—the Aces in the Class AA Southern Minny, the Blue Sox in the Class A Wabasha County League, and the Red Sox in the Class A Southeastern Minnesota League. The Aces had a disastrous year, finishing 2–26, and the other three teams often had trouble finding fields. The two organizations decided to merge for 1949 and appointed Sternberg to run the Southern Minny team, now named the Royals.

Under Sternberg, the Royals finished in second place, with a 21–14 record. He recruited an almost completely new team, carrying over only Stan Partenheimer from the Queens and Bud Wolfe from the Aces. Abe Saperstein furnished him with three key players: Marlin "Mel" Carter, Sam Hill, and Sam "Red" Jones. Carter and Hill played on Saperstein's 1948 Chicago American

Giants. The 37-year-old Carter's career in the Negro Leagues stretched back to the early 1930s, and the 20-year-old Hill had been an East-West All-Star Game outfielder in 1948.

The 23-year-old Jones had pitched for the Homestead Grays in 1946 and the Cleveland Buckeyes in 1947 and 1948. Jones pitched a no-

---

Hall of Fame pitcher Hilton Smith *(front row, second from right)* was lured to Fulda by team manager Dick Reusse in 1949. Smith's great years were behind him by then; he pitched a few games, but Earl Ashby *(front row, far left),* a journeyman catcher in the Negro American League, pitched the key playoff games. *Front row, from left:* Ashby, Bill Busch, Louie Miller, Lefty Hanson, Smith, Red McCarthy, batboy Tom Gits. *Back row:* Toussaint, Dick Reusse, Doug Gits, Ken Bothwell, Alvin Elting, Delly Koopman, unknown, Stan Cosgriff, Vick Gits, John Tuseth. Courtesy of the Ken Bothwell family.

hitter during the season against Owatonna, winning 12–3 on 12 strikeouts and 6 walks, despite 5 errors by his teammates. He lost the first game of the playoff finals to Austin 4–3 on a three-run home run by Dick Seltz. Then, in the second game—six days later because of two rainouts—Jones threw a no-hitter, striking out 15 and walking 7. Austin took a two-games-to-one lead the next night, and Rochester decided to use Jones in the fourth game of the series with only one day's rest. The Royals were handicapped because their second starter, lefty Stan Partenheimer, had to leave for Ohio and his high school teaching job. Jones was knocked out in the seventh inning, and Austin clinched the championship, 6–1.

On August 31, the Chicago American Giants and Cleveland Buckeyes played a regular-season American Negro League game at Winona's Gabrych Park. Ted "Double Duty" Radcliffe, who pitched for the Rochester Aces early in 1948, caught for the Giants and hit the game-winning home run in the bottom of the 11th inning. Lefty McKinnis pitched the first three innings for the Giants, striking out 6 and giving up 2 runs. Red Jones and Ben Sternberg were among the 400 spectators who braved cold temperatures and threatening skies to attend the well-advertised game. The *Winona Republican-Herald* speculated that Sternberg might have been scouting for next season. They may have been right. Sternberg brought McKinnis back to Rochester in 1950. He also signed Gene Smith, a Chicago American Giants pitcher who didn't play in the game at Gabrych Park. Jones signed a minor-league contract with the Cleveland Indians and eventually pitched 12 season in the major leagues.

In 1949 the Fulda businessman and baseball booster Dick Reusse and his friend George Rauenhorst drove to Kansas City on a recruiting trip. They signed Hilton Smith, the great Kansas City Monarchs pitcher. A longtime teammate of Satchel Paige, Smith was voted into the Cooperstown Hall of Fame in 2002. He remains the only man who played in Minnesota in the 1945–60 era to receive that honor. Reusse felt that Smith would help boost interest in baseball and ensure that the city would approve a bond issue to install lights for the 1950 season. He advertised widely and booked exhibition games with all comers. The team went 7–1 in the five-team Centennial League but also won 14 of 21 exhibition games. Reusse's gambit was successful—Fulda made the Class A State Tournament in 1949, and the city, by a vote of 234–78, approved a bond issue to spend over $14,000 to light the city baseball field.

Many other teams also recruited black players in 1949. Although few had connections like Sternberg or the audacity of Reusse, many had played against barnstorming black teams and knew promoters who worked with them. Because of the deterioration of the Negro major leagues, some black players were willing to sign contracts to play in rural towns with no black population.

Minnesota teams, except for Sternberg's Rochester Royals, seemed to pick off the more veteran black players, or the very young. Hilton Smith was 37 in 1949, and his arm had lost its zing. He was effective at times, using his guile, but Cuban-born Earl Ashby, the second black player on the Fulda Giants, pitched the key playoff games at the end of the season, while Smith played right field. Slayton signed 42-year-old Leroy Matlock, a star pitcher in the Negro major leagues in the 1930s. Delano signed Ernie "Schoolboy" Johnson, an 18-year-old who had played with the Colored House of David touring team in a game in Delano in 1948. Johnson left Delano to play with the Kansas City Monarchs after a few early games. He returned to play a few more games in July but did not finish the season in Delano. Other Minnesota towns had similar experiences. Many black players, like their white professional counterparts, were, quite simply, baseball vagabonds, drifting from job to job in search of better pay. Very few of those signed in 1949 played out the season or returned in 1950.

Jud Roseland managed the Banana Distributors, Mitby-Sathers, and DeVac's to Minneapolis Park Board championships in six of nine years between 1946 and 1954. The Bananas lost to Albert Lea in the 1946 and 1948 Class AA championship games. Photograph by Lefty Evans; courtesy of Don Evans.

The MABA awarded the State Tournament to Detroit Lakes, by far the northernmost city to be the host—and 207 miles from Shakopee, the 1948 site. Detroit Lakes had installed lights in 1948 and improved the grandstand and bleacher seating in 1949 to accommodate up to 5,000 fans at Washington Park. The baseball-mad town spent an estimated $50,000 on the park over a two-year period. State officials were gearing up for an anticipated fourth consecutive year of record-breaking attendance.

For the first time since 1943, Class AA would have a new champion. Five-time defending champion Albert Lea finished in fourth place in the Southern Minny and then lost to Austin in the first round of the playoffs. Austin dominated the regular season, finishing with a 28–7 record, eight games ahead of second-place Faribault. Austin manager Emil Scheid felt confident enough to stand pat with his roster for the State Tournament and selected no postseason draftees. Austin was the clear favorite to win the Class AA championship. A pre-playoff favorite would have been Springfield, who ran away with the Western Minny pennant with a 22–3 record. However, third-place New Ulm, just 14–11 on the season, upset Springfield in the finals of the league playoffs.

Fergus Falls and the Minneapolis Banana Distributors were the only 1948 tournament teams to repeat. The Distributors, despite their second-place finish in 1948, were not given much of a chance. Manager Jud Roseland, who took over the team in 1946, did a masterful job of assembling a competitive team composed mainly of former high school players from the South and Roosevelt areas, but he couldn't financially compete with out-state teams for pitchers. Marley Denzer, a 40-year-old veteran, was his ace. The youthful St. Paul Harding

Player	Team	AB	H	BA
Dick Kaess*	Albert Lea	146	58	.397
Tony Jaros	Faribault	135	53	.393
Ed Puchleitner*	Waseca	113	44	.389
Red Gleason	Owatonna	121	46	.380
Mel Carter	Rochester	137	52	.380
Larry Rosenthal*	Winona	132	50	.379
Dick Seltz*	Austin	127	48	.378
Spike Gorham	Albert Lea	138	52	.377
Ole Lucken*	Faribault	122	44	.361
Chet Wieczorek	Rochester	114	40	.351
Marty Lee*	Winona	123	43	.350

Top hitters of the 1949 Southern Minnesota League. Asterisks denote St. Paul natives.

Boosters were the surprise winners in the St. Paul AAA League but were not given much of a chance, as the appeal of pay-for-play continued to drain the city of its top players. For example, 6 of the top 11 hitters in the Southern Minny were St. Paul natives.

Fergus Falls eliminated Detroit Lakes three straight in the finals of the North Central League playoffs, breaking the hearts of Lakers fans who had hoped they would be able to root for the home team in the State Tournament. Fergus Falls, 41–7 overall on the season, was given an outside chance to win, especially since it was expected that its fans would flock to the games. They were only about 50 miles from Detroit Lakes, compared to 300 miles for Austin's fans.

Defending champion Winsted returned in Class A and was a prohibitive favorite. Milroy, the only other returnee, won a tough region and was given an outside chance, as was Fulda, who had beaten First Night champion Worthington in the regionals. Class B seemed to be anyone's guess. Taconite, a first-round loser in 1948, was the only returning team. Little Falls, Perham, and Elk River, based on their tough schedules, were early favorites.

The tournament got off to a great start, with a first-day record crowd of 4,456, but rain canceled one day's games and forced several other postponements. An Austin–Fergus Falls game helped draw a record 4,735 fans to a weekday session. Austin won 8–3 behind the pitching of Earl Mossor. The Packers swept through the tournament with five consecutive victories. They beat Fergus Falls a second time in the finals, 13–3. A 30-mile-per-hour wind from home plate to center field turned the game into a home run derby. The Packers hit seven home runs, including two each by pitcher Bob Kuhlman and outfielder Mel Harpuder. The losing Red Sox hit three solo shots.

Excelsior, with its all–Hamline University infield—manager Rollie Seltz at second, Don Eliason at first, Joe Hutton Jr. at short, and Dick Mingo at third—marched through the Class A field. Excelsior dethroned Winsted with a 17–1 shellacking in the semi-finals, and then veteran Gene Cooney outpitched Winnebago's 20-year-old fastballer Mike Schultz in the finals, 7–2. For Schultz, who had just signed a minor-league contract with the New York Yankees, it was his third game in six days. He shut out Milroy 2–0 in their tournament opener and threw four innings in relief two days later, picking up a win in a 3–1 victory over Blooming Prairie.

Similarly, Little Falls blasted into the Class B semifinals with identical 14–1 wins over Rosemount and Comfrey. They squeaked out a 4–3 victory over Elk River in the semifinals and then outslugged La Crescent 23–10 in the championship game. Minnesota Gopher basketball star Whitey Skoog, a postseason draftee from Brainerd, started the games against Rosemount and Comfrey—played on the same day because of rescheduling forced by rain delays—and also started and pitched six innings in the Elk River game.

Total attendance of 28,564 fell 5,716 short of the record set at Shakopee in 1948, but edged out Mankato's 1947 figures for second place on the list. That was quite an accomplishment, considering the weather and the northern location. Railroads were a big help in providing transportation. Special coaches brought Elk River and Little Falls fans to the tournament for their Class B semifinal game, for example.

Other Class AA teams in the state took notice of the composition of Emil Scheid's Austin Packers. All three of his pitchers—Earl Mossor, Bob Kuhlman, and Sam House—were recruited from professional baseball. Seven out of eight of the position players starting in the championship game were also former professionals. First baseman Red Lindgren and shortstop Dick Seltz were Minnesota natives, but each had played in the professional Northern League and were recruited to Austin to play baseball. Lindgren found a job with Hormel, and Seltz was hired to teach and coach at Austin High School. Only two players, second baseman Bob Beckel and infielder Warren Austinson, were Minnesota natives with no professional experience.

Fergus Falls, on the other hand, was a college-oriented team. The starting lineup in the final game against Austin had seven current or former college players:

Bob Beckel and Warren Austinson were the only two players without professional experience on the 1949 Class AA state champion Austin Packers. *Back row, from left:* Bud Thompson, Billy Campeau, Bob Kuhlman, Bob Beckel, Red Lindgren, Dick Seltz, Don Turck, Earl Mossor. *Front row:* Mel Harpuder, Warren Austinson, Ray Riley, Sam House, John Miller, Jack LaVelle, Emil Scheid, batboy Terry Strong. Courtesy of Larry Scheid.

Position	Name	College/University
SS	Don McNally	Lafayette, Pennsylvania
RF	Duane Baglien	University of Minnesota
3B	Harry Hill	Lafayette, Pennsylvania
LF	Jerry Smith	University of Minnesota
C	Lyle Westrum	none
1B	John Norlander	Hamline University
CF	John DeWitt	Texas A&M
2B	Jim McNulty	none
P	Fred Kroog	Lafayette, Pennsylvania

Manager Jim McNulty, a Brooklyn Dodger farmhand, was the only former pro in the lineup. Westrum, from Clearbrook, Minnesota, was the brother of the New York Giants catcher Wes Westrum. Lyle played briefly in 1947 for Hickory of the professional Class D North Carolina State League and spent 1948 with Park Rapids in the North Central League. Westrum signed a minor-league contract with the New York Yankees after the State Tournament. (In 1950 his .333 batting average at Joplin, Missouri, in the Class C Western Association was second on the team. A young switch-hitting shortstop named Mickey Mantle led the team with .383, plus 26 home runs and 136 RBIs.) Norlander played pro basketball with the NBA's Washington Capitols. The team's second pitcher was Fred Copeland, from Baylor University. Number three pitcher Harley Oyloe and reserve Stan Banholtz were Fergus Falls residents, and relief pitcher and spot starter Lefty Sycks was from Backus. (Oyloe had pitched for Grand Forks in the Northern League in 1941 and was appearing in his seventh state tournament.)

McNulty made no secret of his intention to bring in more professionals in 1950, and other Class AA teams, looking at Austin's success, felt they would have to do the same. Some of the state's top Class A teams also started to look for former professionals. As MABA officials met in the fall to make plans for the next season, it couldn't have looked brighter. More towns were planning to install lights and expand their schedules and it also looked as if more towns would be forming new teams.

A SEASON
TO REMEMBER

1950

RECRUITING OF PROFESSIONAL PLAYERS did step up all over the state in 1950, particularly in the Southern Minny League. The other Class AA leagues were still relying on college players but were looking for a few key pros for special needs. For example, the Willmar Rails built their nucleus around local standouts like Howie Peterson and Art Grangaard, and outside players like Joe Hutton Jr. Then they added two pros to bolster the team. Gene Kelly, a 1945 University of Minnesota graduate and a veteran of five seasons in the minor leagues, was hired to run the city's recreation department and pitch for the Rails. Howie Schultz, a St. Paul native and former Brooklyn Dodgers first baseman, was added to give the lineup a home run threat.

The First Night League elected to move up to Class AA. New members Fulda and Sibley, Iowa, joined carryovers Iona, Marshall, Pipestone, Slayton, Wilmont, and Worthington to make it an eight-team league. Class AA ball, on the other hand, turned out to be too expensive for several of the West Central's small 1949 teams. Bird Island, Lake Lillian, and Clara City withdrew and joined the Class A Western Central League, while Olivia

moved over to the Western Minny, but there was no shortage of replacement candidates. Alexandria, Glenwood, Litchfield, and Morris joined the league to keep its membership at eight.

Litchfield didn't even make the decision to field a team until December 1949. The city had been without a team since 1947, when its North Star League entry had won only two games. The arrival of Dr. Jack Verby—formerly an ace pitcher and now one of the state's most feared hitters—at a local clinic, however, reignited baseball interest in the town. On December 22, 1949, the Litchfield Baseball Corporation was formed in a large meeting at the community center. Gopher coach Dick Siebert had been invited to speak before the meeting. He told them that he "was surprised to find out that Litchfield did not have a lighted baseball park," and went on to say that he believed that "every town over 500 population in Minnesota had some sort of ball team and most of them had lighted fields." Siebert started the fund-raising by donating $25. Doc Verby followed by donating his services as a player.

In short order, the group got permission from the school board to make improvements to the

57

Final-day action in the 1950 State Tournament featured four exciting games. Here a Le Center runner scores in the team's 4–3 victory over Winsted in the Class A championship game. *Star-Tribune* photograph; courtesy of the Minnesota Historical Society.

field at the high school, and launched a public campaign to raise funds for lights (required to be accepted in the Class AA West Central League), hired a manager, and began to recruit players. The *Litchfield Independent Review* sportswriter Lee Meade reported that baseball enthusiasm had taken over the city. "It's impossible to walk down the streets," he wrote, "without running into two or more people discussing the future baseball plans in Litchfield and this area."

The Litchfield association broadened its scope by traveling to surrounding communities not only to look for donations but also to solicit fans for the area's new "big league" team. Foundations for the new lights were poured in early April, and the installation was completed—with a temporary main power line—in time for the first night game on May 21. A standing-room-only crowd of over 1,500 watched Litchfield down Willmar 10–9.

Although no one knew it at the time, 1950 would be the high-water mark for Minnesota baseball. The total number of teams in the state increased to 799, up 72 from 1949. Thanks to

Litchfield baseball boosters met with representatives of surrounding towns in December 1949 to solicit support for a new Class AA team. Casey Dowling, Dassel teacher and future Litchfield catcher, is standing at right; slugging Dr. Jack Verby is left and center, wearing an overcoat with a fur collar and lapels. Courtesy of Casey Dowling.

the addition of the First Night League and an increase in the number of teams in the Twin Cities, the number of Class AA teams rose to 81. The downturn in Class A teams continued as the roster dropped from 22 leagues to 18, with a reduction of 33 teams, while Class B ranks rose from 469 to 581.

Outside the Twin Cities, there were 76 towns that had two or more teams. Clear Lake (which could draw players from the nearby St. Cloud area), Pierz, Sleepy Eye, and Winona fielded three each. Twenty-four towns or unincorporated villages with populations under 1,000 fielded two teams, including Buckman (population 173), Effie (202), St. Stephen (234), and Courtland (251). Leavenworth, an unincorporated village in Brown County between Sleepy Eye and Springfield, actually had four teams! Their number one team played in the Brown County League and had gone to the State Tournament in 1949 and won the league title again in 1950. The Leaven-

worth Juniors and North Leavenworth played in the Junior Pasture League. Mulligan, a township just two miles south of Leavenworth, also had a team in the Junior Pasture League. Mulligan township and North Leavenworth had their own fields, while the two Leavenworth teams shared a field on the west side of town.

There was no reason to think that the Minnesota Amateur Baseball Association would not continue to grow. Two factors help explain the rapid postwar growth and optimism for the future. First, the growth was only natural. The state was down to 162 teams in 1945, but it had been at 452 in 1940, and it was reasonable to assume that participation would eventually return to the prewar level. Returning servicemen and civilians exhausted by the war yearned to return to the life that existed before Pearl Harbor—a life that included Sunday-afternoon baseball games.

The second factor was the economy. At first there were fears that the dramatic decrease in defense spending would lead to an economic slowdown. However, the economy actually picked up speed in the euphoric days following the end of the war and kept on expanding. A demand for consumer goods, pent up for 15 years by the Depression and the war, created an unprecedented boom in all sectors of the economy. In 1946 and 1947 there was a 12- to 18-month waiting list for some automobiles, but production ramped up dramatically. U.S. car sales went from 2,148,600 in 1946 to 6,665,800 in 1950. The story was similar for toasters, refrigerators, Pyrex baking dishes, dress shoes, farm machinery, tricycles, outboard motors, and card tables.

Returning servicemen found jobs plentiful,

and their families started raising the baby boomer generation. In the Twin Cities, home construction skyrocketed in Richfield, Roseville, and other inner-ring suburbs. Small rural towns that had been suffering since the start of the Depression suddenly came alive again. It wasn't unusual for a town under 1,000 to have three or four gas stations, two car dealers, two or three farm implement dealers, two grocery stores, two clothing stores, two or three general stores, a furniture store, plumbing and heating shop, two or more electricians, several restaurants, two grain elevators, at least one doctor and dentist, one newspaper, a bank, and a K-12 school. Towns as small as 300 had their own K-12 schools and were contemplating new construction or additions to existing buildings to accommodate the surge in enrollment coming from the baby boomers. Outside the towns, large farm families were still the rule. In a typical section there might be at least three or four families, each with four to six children.

The GI Bill helped fuel a sense of optimism for the future. It enabled a whole generation of men to go to college. Many were like H. D. "Dee" Elverum, who pitched for Honeywell, Maple Lake, and Annandale and later became an executive at Honeywell. "I wouldn't have gone to college without the GI Bill," he said. "Before the war I wasn't even thinking about going to college." Besides tuition and books, the GI Bill provided a stipend for living expenses—$50 a month for single men and $75 for married men. The program transformed our society. In 1950 twice as many men graduated from college as in 1940. The GI Bill also fueled the housing boom, as veterans were able to secure low-interest-rate loans with no down payment.

Money was readily available for civic projects. There was no problem raising money to pave a gravel road leading to main street, build a fire station, fund a school addition, build a tennis court—or to build a new grandstand or install lights at the local baseball field. Similarly, it was relatively easy to raise money to support a baseball team. It seems insane for De Graff (population 270) and Lake Lillian (358) to challenge Willmar (9,410) or for Iona (355) to challenge Marshall (5,923), but that's exactly what they did. Farmers, merchants, and fans donated money and provided full-time and seasonal jobs to help the home team hire the players needed to field a good team. Class B teams didn't require as much money, but it could cost about $2,000 to $3,000 a season to pay for uniforms, equipment, bats and balls, umpires, field maintenance, and travel expenses. Class A teams could spend from $5,000 to $10,000 per season, while the top Class AA clubs were spending $15,000 to $20,000 in players' salaries alone.

Thanks to the economy, money wasn't a problem in 1950, and new teams continued to be formed at the same time that towns spent more money on their existing clubs. Attendance reports continued to be strong. Five teams in the Southern Minny averaged more than 2,000 per game, led by Austin at 2,691 and Faribault at 2,346. To put this in perspective, the American Association teams averaged 1,991 fans per game in 1950. Kansas City, at 3,168, was the only team to beat Austin's average attendance. St. Paul and Minneapolis averaged 1,633 and 1,561, respectively. Other leagues were not as detailed in their reporting, but some teams did report downswings in attendance. Fergus Falls, notably, saw its total attendance drop 10,920—from an average of 1,324 per game in 1949 to 886—as local fans were starting to lose interest in lopsided exhibition games and league games with the weaker teams. A first-round playoff game against the last-place Moorhead Chix drew only 200 fans. However, the league playoff finals games with Detroit Lakes all drew over 2,000. Attendance at Chaska and Shakopee was

The nine-day 1950 State Tournament was played in St. Cloud's Municipal Stadium, home to the professional Class C Northern League Rox. Photograph from the collection of the Stearns History Museum, St. Cloud, Minnesota.

also down. They had bolted from the Minnesota Valley League—home of defending champion Excelsior—to the Minnesota River in the hope of improving attendance. Winsted, despite making the State Tournament for the third consecutive year, also reported lower attendance.

Barnstorming teams continued to crisscross the state. Hall of Fame pitcher Satchel Paige excited Minnesota fans with several appearances. Paige was the marquee player for the barnstorming Negro League teams. He'd made the cover of several national magazines in the 1940s, and capacity crowds turned out whenever he was scheduled to appear. On occasion, rumors spread that Paige would be coming to town with one of the barnstorming teams, even though the pregame publicity said nothing about him. Paige

made the major leagues in 1948—at the age of 41, although his exact birth date was often in dispute—when he was signed by the Cleveland Indians. The Indians released him in February 1950, and he went on a personal barnstorming tour in the summer, promoted by J. L. Wilkinson, the white businessman who had owned the Kansas City Monarchs for almost 30 years.

Paige was paid $400 to pitch four innings for the Moorhead Red Sox against Fergus Falls in a game played in Barnett Field in Fargo on June 4. On June 7 he pitched three innings for the Class

B Austin Queens in an exhibition game with the Southern Minny Austin Packers. The Packers tagged him for three hits and two runs in three innings. The *Austin Daily Herald* reported that those were the first runs scored off Paige in 20 innings of barnstorming. For Paige, it was a fairly leisurely tour. He traveled between games in a black Cadillac convertible and took time to go fishing whenever he could.

St. Cloud was selected to host the 1950 State Tournament at Municipal Stadium, home of the professional Northern League St. Cloud Rox. Before the tournament, the MABA made a ruling to help make the Minneapolis and St. Paul Class AA teams more competitive. They were permitted to draft two city residents who played on out-state teams who did not qualify for the State Tournament. The Minneapolis champs, Mitby-Sathers,

picked up Springfield ace and former big leaguer Hy Vandenberg and Dale Engstrand, a former University of Minnesota pitcher who had played for St. James in the Western Minny. The St. Paul Nickel Joints decided to stand pat.

Twin Cities newspapers eagerly awaited the eight-team Class AA tournament, which promised to be much more wide open than in prior years. Defending champion Austin was back with an offensive juggernaut—compiling a .323 team batting average—but their pitching was suspect. They lost ace Earl Mossor to the pros and struggled to a 21–14 regular season record, tied for first place with Waseca. Fergus Falls, the 1949 runner-up, improved its lineup with three former professional players: pitcher John Kelly, who was 21–1 coming into the tournament, catcher Joe Colasinski, and shortstop Hal Younghans, a former Dodgers farmhand who had also played for Waseca in the Southern Minny. Pitcher Gail Mayo, the ace of Albert Lea's 1947 championship team, was 21–0 on the year and made Cannon Falls a dark horse. The Bananas had finished in second place in 1948 and fourth in 1949, and Minneapolis boosters hoped that the Mitby-Sathers might be able to make a run with Vandenberg and Engstrand.

Minnesota River League champion Le Center defeated defending Class A champion Excelsior in the Region 1 playoffs and was a co-favorite with North Star champ Winsted, who won the State Championship in 1948 and lost to Excelsior in the semifinals in 1949. Defending champion Little Falls returned in Class B and was the prohibitive favorite. Most of the other Class B teams were unknown quantities.

Austin's Red Lindgren stretches to force out a runner in a 5–1 victory over previously unbeaten Fergus Falls on Sunday, September 17, 1950. The game was Austin's fourth in two days. The win forced one more game for the Class AA championship, but the weary Packers lost 3–0. *Star-Tribune* photograph; courtesy of the Minnesota Historical Society.

Class AA Team	1950 Population	League
Austin	23,100	Southern Minny
Cannon Falls	1,831	St. Paul Suburban
Fairfax	1,143	Western Minny
Fergus Falls*	12,917	North Central
Litchfield	4,608	West Central
Marshall	5,923	First Night
Mpls Mitby-Sathers	521,718	Park National
St. Paul Nickel Joint	311,349	AAA

Class A Team	1950 Population	League
Cold Spring	1,488	Great Soo
Granite Falls	2,511	Western Central
Harmony	1,022	Fillmore County
Le Center*	1,314	Minnesota River
Milroy	268	Redwood County
Red Wing	10,645	Goodhue Wabasha
Winsted	941	North Star

Class B Team	1950 Population	League
Ashby	443	Tourist
Bloomington	9,902	Sun Valley
Cass Lake	1,936	Lake Region North
Duluth Teve's	104,511	Head O'Lakes
Fertile	890	Nor-Mah-Polk
Foley	1,089	Lakewood
Keewatin	1,807	West Mesaba
Lester Prairie*	663	Crow River Valley
Little Falls	6,717	Great Central
Olivia	2,012	Super Eight
Pine City	1,937	Eastern Minnesota
Santiago	556	Independent Central
Stewartville	1,193	South Border
Ulen	525	Heart O'Lakes
Warroad	1,276	Lake of the Woods
Woodstock	277	Gopher

Populations of 1950 State Tournament entrants. Asterisks denote champions.

Only three were returning from 1949: Cass Lake, Ulen, and Warroad.

There was an overlap in population for the 8 Class AA, 7 Class A, and 16 Class B teams entered in the tournament, demonstrating the democratic nature of Minnesota baseball in 1950. It showed that many teams chose the class of ball they played based on factors other than the size of the town. For example, four Class A and nine Class B towns were larger than Class AA Fairfax. Milroy, the smallest team in the tournament, was in Class A.

The tournament drew 35,280 fans, beating the record set at Shakopee in 1948 by 1,038. Crowds were enthusiastic all week and were treated to exciting games in all divisions. The *Minneapolis Star* said that it was easily the best tournament in the 27-year history of the event. "No other tournament," the *Star* reported, "ever produced a better trio of championship games."

Lester Prairie won Class B with four impressive complete-game pitching performances. Doug Dibb tossed a three-hit 8–1 victory over Ulen in the first round, and then shut out Duluth Teve's 2–0 on four hits in the championship game. Lester Prairie scored two runs in the bottom of the eighth off Duluth's George Koskovich to break up a tense pitching duel. Teve's had rallied for three runs in the seventh and five in the eighth to overcome an 8–1 deficit to upset defending champion Little Falls 9–8 in the semifinals. Lester Prairie postseason draftees Ed Hoese (Mayer) and Bert McCarthy (Green Isle) had thrown four-hitters to beat Bloomington 8–0 and Foley 6–2 in the quarter- and semifinals.

Le Center, who had beaten defending State Champion Excelsior in regional play, came into the tournament as a co-favorite in Class A with Winsted, the 1948 State Champion. Neither team disappointed its followers. Winsted beat Har-

mony 14–4 in a seven-inning shortened game in the first round and then beat a tough Milroy squad 5–1 in the semifinals. Le Center squeaked by Granite Falls 4–3 in 11 innings in the opening round. Le Center lefty Jim Dalton pitched 4⅔ innings in relief of starter JeRoy Carlson, a postseason draftee from Belle Plaine, to earn the victory. Le Center beat Cold Spring 12–2 in the semifinals to set up the championship matchup with Winsted.

Le Center left 13 runners on base and Winsted 11 in a tense game. Winsted scored three in the top of the sixth inning to grab a 3–2 lead, but Le Center tied the game with a run in the bottom of the sixth. Carlson relieved Dalton in the seventh for Le Center and blanked Winsted the rest of the way to earn the victory. Catcher Gene

---

Fans jammed through the turnstiles to watch some great pitching duels in the 1950 State Tournament. Photograph from the collection of the Stearns History Museum, St. Cloud, Minnesota.

O'Brien, like Carlson a postseason draftee from Belle Plaine, doubled in the bottom of the seventh, moved to third on a ground ball, and scored the winning run on a sacrifice fly by Bob Moravec.

The Class AA tournament was a classic. The defending champion Austin Packers got off to a good start. Roman Bartkowski threw a no-hitter to blank St. Paul Nickel Joint 16–0 on opening day, Saturday, September 9, but they were upset by Litchfield 3–2 on Sunday. In that game, Litchfield scratched out three runs in the top of the first inning, and Johnny Garbett, a postseason draftee from Morris, made the runs stand up with a gritty pitching performance. That loss put Austin in a tough position. The way the eight-team double-elimination tournament schedule was laid out, the Packers would now have to win two games on the final Saturday and three games on Sunday to win the championship. That would put a strain on the Austin pitching staff.

But it wasn't that much easier for the Fergus Falls Red Sox. They didn't play their second game until Friday night, when Fred Kroog beat Marshall 7–4. On Saturday Austin advanced in the losers' bracket by beating Marshall 3–1 and Fairfax 5–0. In the nightcap, behind pitcher Mel Henson, a draftee from Detroit Lakes, Fergus Falls beat Litchfield 3–1, making them the sole undefeated team.

That set up one of the most exciting final days in State Tournament history. In the first game, starting at 1 p.m., Austin's Roman Bartkowski pitched his second shutout of the tournament to eliminate Litchfield 3–0, and to set up a showdown between Austin and Fergus Falls in the finals for the second consecutive year.

Both teams watched Le Center beat Winsted 4–3 for the Class A Championship and then laced up for the 6:30 p.m. game. Bill Davis, a veteran left-hander who hadn't joined the Packers

The 1950 State Tournament attendance at St. Cloud was a record 35,318. Photograph from the collection of the Stearns History Museum, St. Cloud, Minnesota.

until late July, made his first appearance in the tournament. The Red Sox starter, John Kelly, was well rested, too. He hadn't pitched since Tuesday night. The game was a classic pitchers' duel through eight innings, but Austin broke the game open with four runs in the top of the ninth to win 5–1 and force one more game for the championship. Purdue slugger Bill Skowron, who had signed a $30,000 bonus contract with the New York Yankees on the eve of the tournament, hit a two-run home run in the rally.

The large group of Fergus Falls fans—the *Fergus Falls Daily Journal* estimated there were about 1,000—who had caravanned together to

The 1950 State Tournament and Minnesota Amateur Baseball Association officials presided over the most successful event in the State Tournament's 27-year history. *From left:* Ernest W. Johnson, MABA secretary; George Fabel, MABA director; William Burkard, St. Cloud tournament chairman; Karl Raymond, MABA director; Joe Cory, MABA second vice president; Al Zieper, MABA first vice president; Tom Mallery, MABA president; John Dey, aide to Minnesota governor Youngdahl; James Quigley, master of ceremonies. Photograph from the collection of the Stearns History Museum, St. Cloud, Minnesota.

St. Cloud were clearly worried. They recalled two devastating losses to Austin in the 1949 tournament and feared that the ninth inning outburst by the Packers was an omen of things to come in the final game. Managers Scheid and McNulty were also worried, as both teams had used up their top pitchers to get to the final game. Austin had used four starters in two days—Marquardt and Kuhlman had pitched complete games on Saturday, while Bartkowski and Davis did the same on Sunday. Scheid actually collapsed in the dugout at the end of the game and had to be carried into the dressing room. He recovered with a little rest and decided to go with spot starter Sam House, who was 4–2 for the year but hadn't started a game since late June. Although House was primarily a position player at Austin in 1950, he won a game in the 1949 State Tournament and as recently as 1947 had pitched at Little Rock, Arkansas, in the professional Class AA Southern Association.

McNulty had used his three top starters—Kroog on Friday night, postseason draftee Mel Henson (from Detroit Lakes) on Saturday, and Kelly on Sunday. He was leaning toward starting Kroog on only a day's rest, but catcher Joe Colasinski lobbied hard for their rested third starter Harley Oyloe, who was 10–2 for the year. Colasinski figured that Oyloe would offer a perfect contrast to the fire-balling Kelly, whom Austin had just faced. "Harley's breaking stuff will drive them nuts after facing Kelly," he said.

Colasinski was right. Oyloe's curveball and assortment of slow balls kept Austin off balance all night. He had pinpoint control, too, and forced 13 ground-ball outs. The Red Sox infield made several sparkling plays, and left fielder John DeWitt threw out two Austin runners trying to take extra bases. House was nearly as effective. Third baseman Eddie Piacentini, who was voted the tournament's MVP, doubled in a run in the fifth inning, and the Red Sox scored unearned runs in the sixth and eighth innings to win 3–0.

The three championship teams went home to be honored by parades and other civic celebrations, and MABA and tournament officials could be excused if they patted themselves on the back for a job well done. Faribault had been chosen as the site for the 1951 State Tournament, and officials were looking forward to another record-breaking year.

CRACKS IN THE FOUNDATION

1951–52

THE 1951 SEASON WAS NO RECORD. In fact, team participation took a nose-dive. The ranks of the Class AA leagues dropped to nine just before the start of the season when the North Central League dropped to Class A. More Class A teams continued to drop down to Class B, as well. There were now 17 Class A leagues and 113 teams, compared to 18 and 137, respectively, in 1950.

More ominously, the ranks of the Class B teams fell from 581 to 451. The Korean War draft was a major factor, making it difficult for some small towns to find players. Many towns folded their teams completely or dropped sponsorship of a second team. Interest in town baseball teams was also beginning to decline, partly because of competing interests, and partly because of over-exposure. Fans were also tiring of the constant fund-raising required to support the local teams.

The North Central League's difficulties illustrate the financial pressures teams and leagues were facing all over the state. Fergus Falls' attendance in 1950 was down almost 11,000 compared to 1949, and the team had to solicit donations and ask local merchants to sign notes

for the team to pay off over $6,000 ($48,500 in 2005 dollars) in debt. Fergus Falls officials were convinced that they needed a strong six-team league, playing three games a week—like the Southern Minny, Western Minny, West Central, and First Night Leagues—to survive financially in Class AA baseball. The attendance drop in 1950 showed them that a constant diet of exhibition games no longer satisfied hometown fans.

But other teams in the North Central League, except for Breckenridge/Wahpeton and Detroit Lakes, were fed up with Class AA baseball. The three teams tried to join the West Central, but the league already had eight teams and was skeptical about the extra travel that would have been required by adding three new northern teams. Fergus Falls boosters didn't feel their fans would support Class A ball after having a top Class AA team for three years, but went along with Detroit Lakes and Breckenridge/Wahpeton and moved the North Central down to Class A. Crookston and Fargo-Moorhead joined to make it a five-team league.

In 1950 the two closest Class A leagues had been the Great Soo and Stearns County, both

(**ABOVE**) Winona topped the Southern Minny in 1952 with an average attendance of 2,191 and was the only team besides Mankato to show an increase over 1950. Here a record crowd of 3,537 watches a playoff game against Albert Lea. Officials estimated an additional 500 people watched from areas outside the fences. Courtesy of Winona County History Society Archives.

(**RIGHT**) The 1952 financial report for the Rochester Royals shows how complex the business of "amateur" ball had become. Note that donations were essential to keeping the team afloat. From Clint Dahlberg scrapbook.

clustered just west of St. Cloud. In fact, except for those two leagues, and now the North Central, everybody else in Minnesota north of St. Cloud played Class B baseball. Teams like Little Falls (the 1949 state Class B champions), New York Mills, Wadena, Brainerd, Park Rapids, and Bemidji seemed logical choices for Class A teams but were not ready to make the jump. These towns were also a little nervous about competing with Fergus Falls and Detroit Lakes. Bemidji had seen enough after its one year in the league in 1949. Brainerd, which had fielded two Class B teams in 1950, decided to form an independent team in 1951. They hoped to boost attendance by hiring college players and young professional prospects and playing a tough exhibition schedule.

The West Central and First Night Class AA leagues were also showing some financial strain. Most of the teams had been forced to solicit donations to pay operating expenses in 1950, and the increase in recruiting over the winter made

1952 Financial Report

ROCHESTER BASEBALL ASSOCIATION, INC.

Statement of Income & Disbursements

	1950	1951	1952
Income:			
Income from previous year ......$	75.19	$ 0	$ 622.90
Income from admissions	30,163.50	28,688.72	20,003.16
Miscellaneous income	17.00	382.40	1,382.92
Donations received	5,980.00	6,145.00	9,476.88
Stock sold	890.00	270.00	380.00
Net concession rental	1,948.44	2,072.07	1,183.20
Adm. tax collected but not paid..	1,698.07	0	0
	$40,772.20	$37,558.19	$33,049.06
Disbursements:			
Team manager salary ....$	3,000.00	$ 3,000.00	$ 3,000.00
Business manager salary	800.00	800.00	300.00
Social Security expenses	387.88	249.53	269.16
Cub team promotion	828.50	0	0
Electric and water	846.44	528.16	644.19
Laundry and cleaning	135.09	111.15	176.93
Ushers, sellers, takers, parkers ..	1,299.58	980.90	893.47
Field expense	1,113.38	1,029.44	1,530.07
Grandstand promotion	268.56	0	0
Stationery and office Sup. & Ptg.	311.17	452.47	243.37
Secretary expense	15.22	0	0
Advertising	388.75	391.00	484.03
Insurance	854.32	1,052.27	712.89
Directors expense	182.30	0	127.13
Equipment expense	1,681.71	1,654.03	1,317.10
Team travel expense	789.71	727.75	883.95
Miscellaneous expense	43.50	223.88	227.87
Business manager telephone	134.03	209.00	261.01
Team manager telephone	422.64	0	78.95
Light and grandstand payments .	4,000.00	4,000.00	2,567.00
Police expense	270.00	84.00	80.00
Umpire expense	1,286.00	1,185.00	1,195.00
Ball shaggers	152.00	134.00	170.92
Players salaries	21,598.29	16,328.76	17,633.21
Players travel and Misc. Exp....	932.43	861.95	687.92
New batting cage	0	272.30	0
Previous years' bills paid	0	2,801.55	0
	$41,741.50	$37,077.14	$33,484.17
Starting bank balance ....$	1,031.15	$ 61.85	$ 542.90
Plus year's income	40,772.20	37,558.19	33,049.06
Less year's disbursements	41,741.50	37,077.14	33,434.17
Ending bank balance	61.85	542.90	107.79

it certain that fund-raising would be required again in 1951. So far, though, local merchants and fans seemed willing to continue to support their hometown teams. Atwater, with a population of 880, the second-smallest town in the league, withdrew, but Olivia, which had bolted the league for the Western Minny in 1950, came back to keep the league roster at eight.

Several teams had severe financial troubles in the First Night League in 1950, but the league decided to continue in Class AA. Wilmont dropped out before the season started but was replaced by Lamberton. Worthington, the largest city in the league, tried to make a go of it by using local players but soon realized they would not be competitive and began to hire college and pro players. The dugout was like a merry-go-round, with new players constantly coming in for tryouts. Through the first 22 league games, they used 44 different players. Then they got caught using two players under assumed names—they were brought in after the July 15 signing deadline—and forfeited three games in the protest. Team officials realized these three losses doomed them to miss the playoffs and, on July 31, folded the team. The team's finances were already deep in red ink, they said, and without gate receipts from the playoffs, it would get much worse. Glenwood also tried a limited-budget approach in the West Central League. In July, mired in last place with a 3–22 record and still losing money, Glenwood threw in the towel.

Class AA baseball was definitely getting expensive. Pennant-winning Owatonna topped the Southern Minny with a $24,587 payroll ($184,710 in 2005 dollars). New Ulm spent $18,928 in the Western Minny. Litchfield and Willmar topped

Hamburg raised enough money in its annual Shafskopf (Sheepshead) tournament to meet its Crow River Valley season budget. Courtesy of Lois Droege.

the West Central League. Litchfield spent $17,387 in player salaries, and Willmar was estimated to be at about the same level. Marshall was estimated to be at $15,000 to $18,000 in the First Night League. Other teams ran in the $10,000 to $15,000 range. No team could break even without outside fund-raisers and donations. New Ulm, for example, took in $24,032 on receipts from ticket sales of 39,521. (They averaged 1,520 per game for 26 home games: 4 exhibition, 18 regular season, and 4 playoff.) Total disbursements were $34,815. The difference was made up by contributions and button sales of $4,200, concession profits of $5,860 and $850 in advertising revenue. Owatonna, averaging 1,400 fans per game, needed $8,000 in donations to break even. Marshall raised $10,000 in contributions to meet its budget.

Some teams raised extra money by selling rights to reserved seats—foreshadowing the "seat licenses" used to help finance many of today's big-league stadiums. Austin, for example, sold

1,500 seats—for regular season games only—at $5 each. This guaranteed the holder a specific seat in the grandstand but still required the purchase of a regular admission ticket for each game. Most towns that tried this, however, managed to sell only 50 to 100 reserved seats.

A deficit did not necessarily mean that a team was close to folding, though. The majority of towns still took pride in their teams, and many fund-raising projects were eagerly awaited social functions. Wrestling matches, donkey baseball games, raffles, card games, and holiday picnics were popular ways to raise money. Some Class A and B teams raised almost enough money in one function to support the team for a whole season. Delavan (population 302) served 1,200 to 1,500 at its annual Spring Smorgasbord at the local high school. All of the food was donated and prepared by local residents, and players served as busboys. Entertainment accompanied the meal, and a separate bingo room was also set up. Hamburg was famous for its Schafskopf Tournament, held on the first Sunday in Lent. Schafskopf, or "Sheepshead" in English, was a card game popular in the German communities in the Crow River Valley League area. The tournament consisted of 80 hands of card

playing. The first shift started at 2 p.m., and the second round shortly after they finished. Many players stayed to play poker after the Schafskopf players were finished. Typically, the Hamburg community hall was packed with 400 to 500 players at each session. Entry fees were not much—75¢—and about $120 in prizes were awarded. Most of the money the team raised was from beer sales.

Dick Siebert, who was the player/manager at Litchfield, defended "amateur" baseball's expenses in an interview with the *Minneapolis Tribune's* Joe Hendrickson. He said that "the civic glee and advertising which accompanies a state tournament triumph is good for any city." Even in other cities, the players brought to town assume important roles in the community. "In fact," he said, "the state baseball program has been a big boost for community athletic development, including paying for facilities. The kids flock out to compete in programs directed by their heroes, the stars of the town baseball team." Siebert argued that expenses

Hutchinson Hornets players Jiggs Westergard *(left)* and Gene Olsen conduct sliding lessons in a peewee clinic. They were among many players who guided community summer youth baseball programs. Courtesy of Chuck Westergard.

players permitted. The latter would redefine an "outside" player as one who does not maintain a year-round residence in the town.

At a meeting in New Ulm in November 1951, the delegates came to an agreement on a reserve clause to limit the bidding wars for players. A salaried player under contract in 1951, for example, would not be permitted to sign with another team if he was offered a new contract by January 31, 1952. The leagues also agreed to adopt a common constitution and rules and to establish a voluntary Board of Control to oversee competition. The leagues also requested to pull out of the Mythical State Championship Game. The game was a money loser for the Class AA champs, and the games had not been real contests for the past several years.

Meanwhile the Twin Cities and St. Paul Suburban League teams were fed up with Class AA. They knew they couldn't compete financially with out-state teams to attract the high-caliber college and former pro players who were flocking to the state. An incident recalled by Jerry Schaber, a St. Paul Harding and Hamline University athlete, illustrated the problem. In the 1951 State Tournament, Litchfield, which was paying Schaber $35 per game, was in the midst of clobbering St. Paul Nickel Joint 23–0 in a seven-inning no-hitter by Stetson University pitcher Dick Donnelly. During a time-out, Schaber was standing on second base, talking to Don Klark, second baseman for the Nickels. Klark shook his head and confided to his old friend, "I just don't understand it, Jerry."

Schaber, who played for the St. Paul Harding Boosters team in the 1949 State Tournament, said that he did understand. "We're all professionals," he replied. "You guys don't have a chance anymore."

St. Paul's AAA League champs had been routed in the first round of the last three State Tournaments. The Harding Boosters lost 19–0

In a strategy meeting in New Ulm, Minnesota, on November 5, 1951, Class AA officials make plans for the 1952 season. Seated, from left, are L. R. (Lefty) Ringhofer, Owatonna; Phil von Fischer, Springfield; Ernie Herriges, New Ulm; Victor Sondag, New Ulm; and H. V. Swanson, Mankato. Courtesy of Herb Schaper Historical Baseball Collection/*New Ulm Daily Journal.*

to Fergus Falls in 1949, getting only one hit. The Nickel Joint was no-hit by Austin, 16–0, in 1950, and by Litchfield, 23–0, in 1951. Cannon Falls, the St. Paul Suburban League Champion from 1949 to 1951, beat the Harding Boosters and Benson in 1949 but lost two straight in 1950 and won only one game in 1951, 6–2 over the Minneapolis champs, Mitby-Sathers. Neither Cannon Falls nor the rest of the league felt they could afford to compete with teams in the Southern Minny, Western Minny, and West Central, and they strongly wanted out of Class AA.

The MBA decided to approve the move of the St. Paul Municipal and St. Paul Suburban Leagues to Class A. That left Minneapolis in a tough position. With the ability to draft pitchers from outside the city leagues for the State Tournament, they felt their teams could remain competitive in Class AA. There was also the stigma of the largest city in the state not being able to compete. However, Mitby-Sathers's only win since the pitching-draft rule was instituted was a 7–2 victory over St. Paul Nickel

Joint in 1950, and then they lost to Cannon Falls and Nickel Joint in 1951—two foes who would be in Class A in 1952. In the end a compromise was made. The Minneapolis Park National League would remain in Class AA, while the Park American would move down to Class A. That wasn't a good bargain for the Park American—they were placed in Region 1A, with the powerful Minnesota River and Minnesota Valley Leagues.

Class A had a net gain of 13 teams in the 1952 season, owing to the addition of 27 teams from the metropolitan leagues dropping down from Class AA. A troubling sign was that attendance was down consistently all over the state. Southern Minny teams averaged 1,611 per game, compared to 1,925 in the peak year of 1950—a 16 percent reduction. New Ulm was down to 1,145—a 37 percent reduction from the 1,817 figure reached in its peak year of 1949. Most towns didn't publish attendance data, but their newspapers did write with concern about the decline.

Declining revenue from ticket sales caused some teams to suffer competitively. At Winsted, for example, where the Warriors were winning their fifth consecutive pennant, the team was forced in midseason to release their number two pitcher, Vern Wroge, to save money. This forced them to use starter Alex Romanchuck three times in a week during the Wright Star league playoffs, and the team lost to Maple Lake. In a bit of poetic justice, Wroge was picked up by Glencoe and drafted by Brownton after they won the Twin Trails League playoffs. Wroge shut out Maple Lake 2–0 in the Region 2A championship game.

The State Tournament at Austin's Marcusen Park promised to have at least two new champions. Defending Class AA champion Litchfield lost to Willmar in the finals of the West Central League playoffs, while defending Class A

Albert Lea catcher Del Marquardt raps out a hit in a 1952 Southern Minny playoff game against Winona at Hayek Park. The Winona catcher is Norm Snyder. The five-game championship series, won by Albert Lea, drew 11,789 fans. Courtesy of Winona County History Society Archives.

TWO STRIKES ON CLASS AA

1953–54

THE 1953 SEASON TURNED OUT TO BE a watershed, marked by a continued march of teams down from Class AA and Class A. Minneapolis, after watching the Mitby-Sathers get shut out 9–0 and 12–0 in the 1952 State Tournament, petitioned to move the Park National League down to Class A. The roster of Class AA leagues was now down to three: the Southern Minny, Western Minny, and West Central. Out-state, 23 more teams moved from Class A to Class B. The Wright Star League, home to 1948 Class A champion Winsted and 1951 champion Watertown, and once considered one of the strongest Class A leagues in the state, moved down to Class B. The venerable Stearns County League, long a fixture in Class A, also moved to Class B, while the powerful Western Central League, which sent Granite Falls to the 1950 Class A State Tournament, and Bird Island in 1951 and 1952, did the same. Elsewhere, the Great Soo and Southwestern Leagues also dropped from Class A.

The folding and reshuffling of leagues caused many teams to scramble to find a new league to enter. Other teams moved around, trying to find a

level of competition they could afford and handle. Olivia, for example, a charter member of the West Central League, moved to the Western Minny in 1950, then back to the West Central in 1951, and in 1952 moved to the Class B Super 12 League, a

New Ulm's civic leaders worked hard to promote State Tournaments. In November 1952, New Ulm mayor Roman Schnobrich applies a little "schmooze" by polishing the shoes of Minnesota Baseball Association president A. L. (Tom) Mallery, while *(left to right)* Walt Schleuder, Ernest Herriges, Willard Kunz, and Roy Gebhard look on. Courtesy of Herb Schaper Historical Baseball Collection/*New Ulm Daily Journal.*

move made out of economic necessity. But the local fans didn't respond well to Class B baseball, and the baseball club decided to move to the Class A Twin Trails League in 1953, in the hopes that a better brand of ball would bring the fans back. Many other teams made similar journeys.

In 1953, fund-raising fatigue was also becoming more evident. Merchants and fans who five years ago might have walked up to a player or team official on Main Street to talk about the team or offer to buy lunch might now avoid eye contact and duck inside a store. They were worried they might be hit up for another donation. Teams were in a tough spot. Most needed to hire outside players to be competitive, but ticket revenues were not covering the costs as they had two or three years earlier. The alternatives were to do more fund-raising or cut back on salaries. Winsted's experience in 1952 was a cautionary tale for anyone thinking about making surgical cuts in a roster.

A postcard sent out by the Lake Lillian Athletic Association. Many towns were forced to try similar strategies to raise money to keep their teams in operation. Courtesy of the Kandiyohi County Historical Society.

BASEBALL MASS MEETING

TONIGHT, THURSDAY, JUNE 11, 1953
LAKE THEATRE AT 8:00 P. M.

THIS MEETING IS BEING CALLED BY THE BOARD OF DIRECTORS OF THE LAKE LILLIAN ATHLETIC ASS'N FOR THE PURPOSE OF GAINING FINANCIAL SUPPORT FOR YOUR TEAM. FUTURE BASEBALL IN LAKE LILLIAN WILL DEPEND ON YOUR ATTENDANCE. IF AID IS NOT FORTHCOMING. BASEBALL WILL HAVE TO BE DROPPED IMMEDIATELY. HELP US CONTINUE THIS GREAT AMERICAN PASTIME IN YOUR COMMUNITY.

Some teams tried to compete by using inexpensive or unpaid local players, but none of these efforts seemed to work unless the team dropped down a class. For example, Wells decided to field a team of young local players in the 1952 Class A Faribault County League. Unfortunately the team was not competitive, and local fans rewarded the team by staying away in droves. Attendance was so bad that the team played their last few home games on the road, hoping to share some of the gate receipts. Before the 1953 season, Wells tried to convince the league to restrict teams to local players or drop down to Class B. The other five teams in the league felt they couldn't field good teams without hiring outside players and were concerned that fans wouldn't support an inferior grade of baseball. (Wells's 1952 experience was all the proof they needed.) Consequently the league voted to remain in Class A and booted Wells out of the league.

The need to cut costs led some teams to go to extraordinary means to fill their rosters. Redwood Falls was a case in point. The Redbirds had a good year financially in 1950, when they won the Western Minny pennant but lost in the playoffs. They fell to sixth place in 1951 and bounced back to third in 1952 but had to raise $5,000 in nonticket revenue each year to balance the books. For 1953 the board of directors decided to contract with Lou Hillie, a former major-league scout serving in the air force in Waco, Texas. John Hoepner, chairman of the Redbird player-acquisition committee, had met Hillie on a previous scouting trip in Texas. Hillie offered to supply Redwood with a package deal, consisting of a manager and six or seven top youngsters, all attending college on baseball scholarships and all considered major-league prospects. Redwood Falls had six college players on its 1952 team, and the board had been impressed with their hustle and spirit. After much debate, the board approved the Hillie deal. They would save money compared to the 1952 salary structure but also hoped that the blue-chip players from Texas would produce a winning team and help boost attendance.

Unfortunately the team broke out of the starting gate with eight consecutive losses. The Texas youngsters were probably talented prospects, but Hillie had seriously underestimated the brand of baseball in the Western Minny. The Redwood board fired manager Ed Knipper, a Waco High School coach, and three players voluntarily returned to Texas with him. After the board scram-

New Ulm used a jeep at the 1953 State Tournament to transport pitchers from the bullpens beyond the left-field fence to the mound, long before such conveyances were used in major-league games. Courtesy of Herb Schaper Historical Baseball Collection/*New Ulm Daily Journal.*

bled to find replacements, they released Hillie's three other Texans. The Redbirds finished in the cellar with a 9–25 record and were the butt of jokes in newspapers in other towns in the league.

Almost all Class AA teams reported losing money in 1953. In the West Central, Morris and Benson–De Graff folded in midseason. (Heated rivals Benson and De Graff had merged before the 1952 season, a decision that baffled most residents of the two towns. They hated each other. In earlier seasons, the games between the two were easily the best-attended ones of the year.) In the Western Minny, Winthrop and St. James folded.

The State Tournament was held in New Ulm and drew 31,031 fans—trailing only the 1950 and 1948 tournaments—and gave hope to many that interest in baseball hadn't fallen off as much as the 1951 and 1952 tournaments had suggested. The location helped some, to be sure. Sixteen of the 27 teams entered were within a 100-mile drive of New Ulm. The presence of only three Class AA teams probably hurt attendance. The MBA had tried to have the three Class AA leagues send two entries each, but all turned down the opportunity.

Austin returned as the Southern Minny champion after a year's absence and once again found itself in the losers' bracket, as in 1950 and 1951. Austin lost to Litchfield 3–2 but then beat Fairmont twice, 4–2 and 8–4, before beating Litchfield 8–1 for the Class AA championship. In the Class A field, attention was focused on teams from three former Class AA leagues. Defending champion Cannon Falls was back from the St. Paul Suburban League, while Kohl's was back from the St. Paul AAA League. Park National champion DeVac's would be the first Class A entrant from Minneapolis. When it was all over, though, tiny Delavan (population 302) was the new champion. Delavan High School coach Rich

NNew Ulm attracted 31,031 fans for State Tournament play in 1953, approximately 13,000 more than had turned out a year earlier in Austin. Courtesy of Herb Schaper Baseball Collection/*New Ulm Daily Journal.*

Weigel was voted the tournament MVP. He shut out Jordan 1–0 on a four-hitter in the first round, then threw another four-hitter to beat Minneapolis DeVac's 5–2 in the semifinal game, and saved the 5–3 win over Little Falls in the championship game with 2⅓ innings of scoreless relief pitching. The 3,263 fans who watched the final set the record for a State Tournament Class A game.

Class B was also a Cinderella affair. Rollingstone (population 315) defeated Holdingford (458) 7–1 for the championship. They had overcome much larger towns in the semifinals to get there—Rollingstone beat Ada (population 2,121) 6–2, and Holdingford beat Pine City (1,937) 6–3.

The 1953 season marked the continued decline in the number and quality of barnstorming teams touring the state. Particularly noticeable was the reduction in black touring teams, who had been so popular in the late forties. Although some of the decrease can be attributed to the general decline of the Negro Leagues, most of it was due to exhibition fatigue by Minnesota fans. By the early fifties, many towns were playing two and three regularly scheduled league games a week and found it difficult to sell tickets to exhibition games.

Black teams had been a novelty item for many out-state fans, who were drawn to the games by curiosity—many had never seen a black person—

Austin's Red Lindgren *(right)* hit his first home run of the season to spark the Packers to an 8–1 victory over Litchfield in the 1953 Class AA championship game. Courtesy of Herb Schaper Historical Baseball Collection/*New Ulm Daily Journal.*

and by the mystique that had grown up around the Negro Leagues. Fed by the press coverage given to Satchel Paige even before Jackie Robinson broke the color barrier, and the success of the first black players to make the major leagues—men like Larry Doby, Roy Campanella, Don Newcombe, Willie Mays, and Monte Irvin, in addition to Robinson—fans were anxious to see in person other black players who might have been denied a chance to play major-league baseball.

By 1953, however, the novelty had worn off. Some black teams still toured the Midwest and made occasional appearances in Minnesota, but not to the excitement that greeted them in earlier years. In 1951 and 1952, a black touring team was based in Minnesota. The Duluth Travelers played exhibitions throughout northern Wisconsin and Minnesota, with occasional stops in the Dakotas. The players were not Duluth residents, in fact, and played very few games at "home"—and those hardly attracted much notice. Very few game results were ever reported in the *Duluth News-Tribune*. The Travelers won three of

five games against the independent Brainerd Braves in 1951, including two against future major-league star Herb Score.

Exhibition games against ad hoc celebrity teams, such as a collection of former University of Minnesota athletes, were also becoming less popular. Most "barnstorming" in the state consisted of individual Minnesota teams arranging their own exhibitions. Games on the three big summer holiday weekends—Memorial Day, July 4, and Labor Day—were popular dates. Soderville and Minneapolis DeVac's are examples of teams who arranged for holiday games in places like Brainerd, Little Falls, and International Falls. Families often accompanied the players to the resort destinations.

But teams still did play exhibition games. One of the more creative ideas was the "Fatted Calf Circuit," originated by Little Falls in 1952. The circuit purchased a five-week-old calf at the beginning of the season, with the calf going to the champion at the end of the season. Little Falls, Pierz, and the Brainerd Braves were league members in 1953, playing a 10-game schedule. It was an unlikely alliance—Little Falls played in the Class A Big Dipper League, Pierz was in the Class B Great Soo, and the Braves were independents. Since the games were outside the jurisdiction of the MBA, the teams used outside players and ringers with impunity. Little Falls, for example, hired Brooklyn Dodgers farmhand Arnie Banals to pitch some Fatted Calf games while he was doing National Guard duty at nearby Camp Ripley. Bud Grant pitched two games for Pierz.

Russ Meyer's All-Stars, a collection of major-league players, made one appearance in Minnesota in 1953, in a game in Rochester on Sunday, October 11. (Postseason barnstorming by major-league players had been a common practice dating back to the 1920s, but Minnesota was not a popular destination because of the uncertainties of October weather in the state.) Meyer, a Brooklyn Dodgers pitcher, put together a team including Carl Erskine and Rube Walker of the Dodgers, Clyde McCullough and Warren Hacker of the Cubs, Rip Repulski (a Minnesota native) and Pete Castiglione of the Cardinals, Ted Kluszewski and Roy McMillan of the Reds, and John Wyrostek and Ken Silvestri of the Phillies.

The game, which took place just five days after the Dodgers lost to the Yankees in the World Series, had originally been scheduled for Austin. Rochester promoter Ben Sternberg had been offered the game by a Dubuque attorney who was booking the games for the All-Stars, but Sternberg worked with Austin manager Emil Scheid to promote the game, probably figuring that Austin had more players left in town than Rochester to field a team. The Austin board, however, balked at the $1,200 guarantee demanded by the All-Stars. (They had lost $300 in a similar game played against Hal Lanier's All-Stars in 1948.) Scheid and Sternberg were not deterred. They moved the game to Rochester.

A crowd of 2,100 saw the Packers win an entertaining 11–10 game. Two members of Austin's 1950 state runner-up team, Bill Skowron and Harry Elliott, returned to lead the Packers. (Skowron hit .318 for Kansas City in the Class AAA American Association in 1953, and Elliott hit .328 in the Class AA Texas League before being called up for 24 games with the St. Louis Cardinals.) Nine home runs were hit in the game, two by Skowron and one by Elliott.

As MBA officials met in the fall to plan for 1954, they might have been excused if they looked forward to the new year with optimism. New Ulm had run a great State Tournament. The city conducted parades, hosted scenic tours—

trips to local breweries were popular—and generally made all the teams and their fans feel welcome. The MBA scheduled the 1954 State Tournament for St. Cloud, the site of the record-breaking 1950 tournament, and hoped that 1951 and 1952 were just temporary bumps in the road. The decline of the draft after the Korean War also gave them optimism.

But a lot had changed in four years. Foremost was the fact that there would be no Class AA teams in St. Cloud for the 1954 State Tournament. The West Central League dropped down to Class A after the 1953 season, leaving the Southern Minny and Western Minny as the only remaining Class AA leagues. In an effort to increase the number of the popular Class AA games at the State Tournament, the MBA tried again to have the leagues send two teams each. The leagues refused again, as they had in 1953, citing the fact that Class AA teams competing at St. Cloud would lose money—their share of gate receipts would not cover salaries, let alone traveling and per diem expenses. After some negotiations, the MBA permitted the two leagues to conduct a best-of-seven "Little World Series" to determine the Class AA champion, with games played at the home sites of the competing teams. The leagues agreed to pay the MBA 4 percent of net receipts.

There was some excitement for the series as the two leagues' playoffs got under way. Austin had restored the Southern Minny to dominance by winning the 1953 State Championship, after the North Central and West Central had "stolen" their crown from 1950 to 1952. The Western Minny, curiously enough, had never won a Class AA championship, but its followers felt that the addition of Marshall in 1953 and Litchfield and Willmar in 1954 had strengthened the league. Besides, they argued, a double-elimination tournament using draft choices wasn't a fair way to determine the real champion. A best-of-seven series with no draft choices would settle the argument for sure.

By this time, the Southern Minny rosters were stocked mostly with former professional players. Fifty percent of Western Minny players were former professionals, 30 percent were college students, and 20 percent state or local residents. Marshall and Litchfield were the only teams with more college players than pros. Fairmont, on the other hand, had no college players. The only non-pros on the roster were Bruce Frank, a Fairfax native and longtime player in the state's Class AA leagues, and Red Malcolm, a Fairmont native and former Little All American

Cuban-born Preston "Pedro" Gomez bounced around in the minor leagues before playing for Mankato and Springfield from 1952 to 1954. He eventually became a major-league manager. Courtesy of Herb Schaper Historical Baseball Collection/*New Ulm Daily Journal.*

fullback at Gustavus Adolphus College, playing his fourth year in the league.

Many players arrived from out of state for trials and were dispatched quickly when their play wasn't up to the competition. Turnover on some teams was high, and with so many players coming and going from so many places, there were bound to be some culture clashes. Cuban-born Preston "Pedro" Gomez, who had played eight games with the Washington Senators in 1944, but had kicked around in various minor and semipro leagues since, stepped off the Chicago and North Western Minnesota 400 in Springfield in 1954 and asked for a cab. Surprised to find that the town had neither a cab nor a hotel, he almost got back on the train.

Gomez eventually warmed to the town—he had played with Mankato in the Southern Minny in 1952 and 1953, so he was no stranger to Minnesota. He even stayed in Springfield during the winter but left in the spring for greener pastures. He was a coach with the 1965 Los Angeles Dodgers and took time to visit old friends in Springfield during the World Series. He managed three major-league teams between 1969 and 1980.

Fairmont won the Western Minny pennant and playoffs, while Rochester, who tied for second during the year with Faribault, won the Southern Minny playoffs. The *Rochester Post-Bulletin* confidently predicted a Royals victory, maybe in five games. When Rochester won games one and three, it looked like it might be an easy victory. However, Fairmont swept the next three to win the championship. The series drew only an average of 1,608 fans, topped by 2,917 at the opener in Rochester and 2,100 at the final game in Fairmont. A low of 513 suffered through the sixth game on a frigid September 22 Wednesday night. By contrast, Rochester drew an average of 1,806 during the regular season and 1,735 in four play-

teams dropped down to Class B—each in a different league.

The Southern Minny, on the other hand, decided to play Class AA baseball again in 1957. There was some discussion about dropping down to Class A, but teams felt that their local fans would not support a lower brand of baseball after so many years of Class AA operations. Mason City, Iowa, entered the league in place of Waseca-Owatonna, which had withdrawn from the league in July 1956 in a protest over a league ruling.

The withdrawal had been triggered by an incident in a game at Owatonna on July 3. In the top of the third inning, Faribault Lakers first baseman Howie Schultz hit an apparent home run. However, after Schultz completed his circuit around the bases and entered the dugout, home plate umpire Joe Bedor called Schultz out, stating that he had failed to touch home plate. The Faribault bench immediately jumped onto the field to protest. Lakers manager Pete Deem got into a shouting and shoving match with Bedor. Deem threw a punch, and Bedor was knocked unconscious. Now the rhubarb turned into a riot, and police were summoned to separate the players and umpires.

Bedor soon regained consciousness and, after conferring with the second umpire, declared the game a forfeit win for the W-O Twins. Southern Minny League secretary L. R. (Lefty) Ringhofer was at the game and verified that the umpire had the authority to make that decision. The next morning, though, league president L. J. Plotnick (from Faribault) and vice president Walter Bruzek (from Rochester) met with Ringhofer and reversed the umpire's decision. They ruled that the game must be replayed from the point of the interruption of the game. Deem was temporarily suspended pending an official ruling by the Southern Minny Board of Directors.

Umpire Joe Bedor filed assault charges against Deem, and officials of the Northwest-Minnesota-Wisconsin Umpires Association threatened to not furnish any more umpires to the league unless Deem was suspended for 16 months, starting immediately.

League directors met on July 16 to review the case. They imposed a six-game suspension on Deem, as well as a $100 fine, but upheld the decision to replay the game from the point of the interruption. They stated that they didn't think there were grounds to forfeit the game, and that the Faribault team and fans should not be penalized for one man's actions.

Waseca and Owatonna officials were livid. Replaying the game would cost them an extra $125, with no new revenue. It felt like they were being punished, instead of Faribault. Furthermore, they were angered at the way the league meeting on July 16 was conducted. Neither team president Wayne White nor any other W-O supporters who witnessed the incident were allowed to testify. White had run onto the field during the melee to try to protect the umpires.

Team officials voted unanimously to withdraw from the league. White informed the league that the Twins last game would be at Austin on July 17—the last day of Deem's six-game suspension—unless the July 3 game was termed a forfeit and Deem was given a tougher penalty. League president Plotnik replied that the league's six directors other than Faribault and Waseca-Owatonna had voted 6–0 at the meeting and would not revisit the decision. There was a suspicion among some of the other teams in the league that the Twins had been planning to fold the team all along and were just using the Deem incident as the excuse.

Meanwhile Twins manager Emil Scheid was working behind the scenes to try to save the franchise. Following the game on July 17, which the Twins lost 12–8, he invited the team members to his home in Austin to discuss his proposal. (The players had been paid by the Twins following the game and given their releases.) Scheid offered to take over the franchise, financially and on the field, for the remainder of the season. The Waseca-Owatonna Baseball Association had earlier agreed to turn the franchise over to Scheid if the league board of directors approved.

League officials met on July 18 and approved Scheid's plan. The team would finish the season as the "Travelers," playing all of their games on the road, but with a twist—home games originally scheduled for Owatonna or Waseca would be played at the visiting team's field. The Travelers would take the field as the "home" team and pocket the gate receipts less umpires costs and a rental fee. The team played a little better as the Travelers. They went 6–8 and finished at 17–25, tied for sixth place with Winona.

In the off-season, Owatonna and Waseca were asked if they were interested in rejoining the league, but there was little appetite in either city. Both were still soured by the Deem incident and tired of the constant fund-raising required to support a Southern Minny team. Waseca mayor I. W. Tobin expressed their sentiments when he said, "The farther away we can stay from any league or towns connected with the Southern Minny, the better off we'll be."

Reactions to the Deem incident outside the league were unfavorable. This was a significant departure in public sentiment, which in the past had brushed off stories about umpire-player altercations as part of the game. Local newspapers generally defended their players, claiming that umpires were incompetent or had incited the players. The general tone of outside news stories about the incidents was one of amusement.

That is, until the Deem incident. The *Minneapolis Star* columnist Charles Johnson berated the Southern Minny for not standing behind the umpires. He said that Waseca-Owatonna's withdrawal from the league "could be the beginning of the end of a circuit that always has rated so highly in baseball circles." Although some Southern Minny newspapers defended the league's action, most players realized that their confrontations with umpires had to be toned down.

CLASS A LOSES CLOUT

1957–58

THE NUMBER OF TEAMS IN THE STATE continued to slowly decline in 1957, leveling off at 541, down 59 since 1955. Class A, which had been declining steadily since 1948, the year Class B was created, held steady, but only because of a protest. The historic Class A First Night League, the first to claim that all its teams had lights, folded after the 1956 season. League members Pipestone, Worthington, and Lismore joined the existing Class B Jackson-Nobles League, while Milroy and Wood Lake formed the new Great Western Class B League with Cottonwood, Marshall, Redwood Falls, and Granite Falls.

The MBA had problems with the Great Western almost immediately and in late June moved the league up to Class A. The problem involved the eligibility of several players in the league who were nonresidents of the towns they played for but, the league claimed, were within the legal 15-mile boundaries. Some Redwood County League teams had complained that Great Western teams were poaching players from their territories. They suggested that the players must be getting paid or they would not be traveling to play

on teams farther away from their homes. Great Western officials met with the MBA but could not get them to budge on the issue of reclassification. When the league threatened to withdraw from the MBA, they got a return threat. "It's easier to drop out than to get back in," MBA president Al Zieper told them.

Ultimately the league decided to stay in Class A but to abide by Class B rules. All teams agreed not to pay salaries or to pick up any outside players. Most felt the MBA was still smarting over Milroy's successful fight to stay in Class B in 1954. Some cynics also pointed out that the state had 11 leagues and six regions in Class A at the start of the year, and moving the Great Western to Class A simply made it an even two leagues per region for the playoffs.

The fact that more leagues were electing to play in Class B did not mean that the competition would be any less fierce. Some Class B leagues, to be sure, were mostly recreational. However, others, like the Arrowhead League, were as competitive as any in the state. The Arrowhead, consisting of Iron Range towns running from Grand Rapids to Ely (plus International Falls), was formed in

1948 as a Class A league but dropped to Class B in 1950. Ely and Hibbing, league champs in 1950 and 1951, lost in the regional tournaments to Duluth Teve's, but the Arrowhead playoff winners won their way into the State Tournament the next nine years. Marble went three times, while Hibbing and Grand Rapids each went twice, and Virginia and International Falls once.

Competition was fierce and cutthroat. Jobs were plentiful, and towns used them to attract college players for the summer and to induce older players to move to the community. The outsiders—established as "hometown" players—supplemented local talent pools that included athletes like John Mayasich, whom some called the greatest American hockey player ever, and Gino Cappelletti, a future University of Minnesota and Boston Patriots football star.

College players like Dave Lesar and Bob Streetar, 1955 graduates at Grand Rapids High School, found good summer mining jobs in Marble. They worked full shifts but were able to adjust their schedules for games and road trips. There was no direct pay for baseball, but a lot of fringe benefits. Marble played or practiced almost every day, and Lesar and Streetar were given gas to travel from their homes and were supplied with gloves and spikes. Fans frequently passed money through the fence for good hits or defensive plays during the games, and many special prizes, such as $100 for the first home run of the game, were also offered. "Players argued for the leadoff position," Streetar joked.

Marble manager Bob "Windy" Anderson was perhaps the most zealous recruiter. He scoured the Iron Range for players, and his teams were strong contenders throughout the decade, but he was a lightning rod for criticism by his opponents. In 1952, while leading the league with a 13–4 record, Marble was forced to forfeit seven games for the use of two players who were signed with and also playing for a team in the neighboring Mesaba Itasca League. This dropped Marble to last place in the six-team league. However, they rallied with three straight wins to finish 9–11 and in a tie for fourth place to force a playoff for the last playoff position.

Just before the tie-breaking game could be played, Hibbing protested two more Marble players. The league found that their contracts had not been submitted to the league before the signing deadline. Anderson vehemently argued that he had turned them in and accused "someone" of tampering with them. After a long shouting and cursing match, league president Swede Pergol of Chisholm resigned, but the rest of the league board stood its ground and forfeited Marble's last three games, eliminating them from the playoffs. Pergol told the *Hibbing Tribune* that his resignation was "due to Windy Anderson and the Marble organization. I refuse to take cursing from anybody. I have taken as much as I possibly can." Anderson threatened to file a court injunction to stop the playoffs, but nothing came of it.

Marble probably should have won another title in 1954, when their 22–6 record ran away with the league pennant, but they lost to archrival Hibbing two games to one in the playoff finals. This was not an unusual outcome for the league—pennant winners often struggled in the playoffs. Nothing could be taken for granted. Competition was strong, and teams played hard-nosed baseball. Brush-back pitches and hard slides were expected, but frequently resulted in scuffles and fistfights. Some suggested that this hard play had to do with the hockey heritage in the Iron Range. Whatever the case, each year's playoff winners knew that they had been in a battle.

Barnstorming teams were becoming rare commodities by 1957, but one team that had

The All American Girls Baseball team played exhibitions against Minnesota men's teams from 1955 through 1958. They traveled in one station wagon (shown here) and a four-door passenger car. *Left to right:* manager Bill Allington, Joanne Weaver, Dottie Schroeder, Katie Horstman, Joan Eisenberger, Gertie Dunn, Ruth Richard, Dolores Lee, Jean Smith, Jean Geissinger, Maxine Kline. Courtesy of the Northern Indiana Center for History.

been coming to the state since 1955 was raising eyebrows—a team calling itself the Original All-American Girls Baseball Team. Thanks to the 1992 Penny Marshall movie *A League of Their Own,* most modern baseball fans are aware of the All American Girls Professional Baseball League, formed by Chicago Cubs owner Phillip Wrigley in 1943. They are probably not aware that the AAGPBL grew steadily through 1948 and finally ceased operations after the 1954 season.

In 1955, manager Bill Allington—whose Rockford Peaches had won the league playoffs four times—formed an all-star team and worked with agent Matt Pascale of Omaha, Nebraska, to set up a barnstorming schedule. The team traveled over 20,000 miles a year in a Studebaker station wagon and one sedan for the next four years, playing about 80 games a year. Ten to 12 players and Allington stuffed themselves into the

Heinrichs, now a postseason draftee from Fulda, finally got his State Championship. He'd been Pipestone's manager when they finished in third place in Class A in 1956 and lost in the semifinal round in Class B in 1957.

The MBA made a special presentation during the awards ceremony to the *Star-Tribune* writer Ted Peterson and the *Dispatch-Pioneer Press* writer Bob Schabert. They had been covering town team baseball since the war and also drew up the schedules and did other administrative work for the State Tournaments. Schabert also provided historical material for the State Tournament programs and was the tournament's unofficial record keeper. Peterson's *Sunday Tribune* town team articles were eagerly awaited by fans throughout the state.

Western Minnesota Press Writers Association, August 1954. *Front row, from left:* vice president Wes James, Marshall; president Herb Schaper, New Ulm; secretary-treasurer Loren Wolfe, Willmar. *Back row:* Al Anderson, Redwood Falls; Joe Martinson, Willmar; Jack Krebs, Fairmont; Pat Maloney, Springfield. Courtesy of Herb Schaper Historical Baseball Collection/*New Ulm Daily Journal.*

Local writers and newscasters in this era were strong boosters of their town baseball teams, and most successful teams got extensive—often on the front page—coverage during the season. (For less successful teams, the chicken-or-egg argument might apply: was the coverage extensive because the team was good, or did the team become good because of the interest created by favorable news coverage?) Even during the winter, many papers carried stories about the coming season, speculating on who was coming back from last year and who might be signed for the new season, and reporting rumors heard about the plans of rival towns.

Town team baseball was a fixture on local radio stations. The opening-round game between Class AA Litchfield and Fairmont in the 1953 State Tournament was carried live on six stations: Alexandria, Willmar, Marshall, Mankato, Montevideo, and New Ulm. Other stations popped in to cover games of interest in their areas, as well. The popular announcer Chuck Williams from Winona KWNO flew into New Ulm on game days to cover the Rollingstone Merchants for his local audience.

There had been a time when baseball officials were concerned that live radio broadcasts of games were cutting down on attendance. The Western Minny once tried to enforce a rule prohibiting radio broadcasts by visiting teams. Teams in the league were fairly close together, and Springfield, for example, was worried that fans from New Ulm might not follow their team to Springfield if the game were broadcast. Eventually restrictions like this fell to the wayside as officials realized that television and other leisure pursuits were more to blame for losses in attendance than radio broadcasts. In fact, many were now coming around to the belief that the radio broadcasts actually helped attendance by stimulating interest in the game.

Newspapers played a prominent role in local affairs, from promoting business to developing cultural amenities, and saw no conflict of interest when writers promoted the baseball team or served on a team governing board. Writers and newscasters felt that successful baseball teams contributed to civic pride, and were unashamed cheerleaders for the local teams. The Western Minny and Southern Minny had formal Press Associations, but writers in many leagues got together informally to discuss issues of mutual interest.

After the tournament, Austin beat Pipestone 5–1 in the Mythical State Championship game and then beat Prescott, Wisconsin's Class A champion 17–2 in the first "Interstate Series." Pipestone followed with a 2–1 win over Bangor, Wisconsin's Class B champion.

New Ulm drew 26,094 fans, the most since 1953, when the tournament was also held at New Ulm, but no one in the MBA saw this as a good omen. New Ulm always drew well for the State Tournament, and there were already signs that more teams were going to fold in 1959.

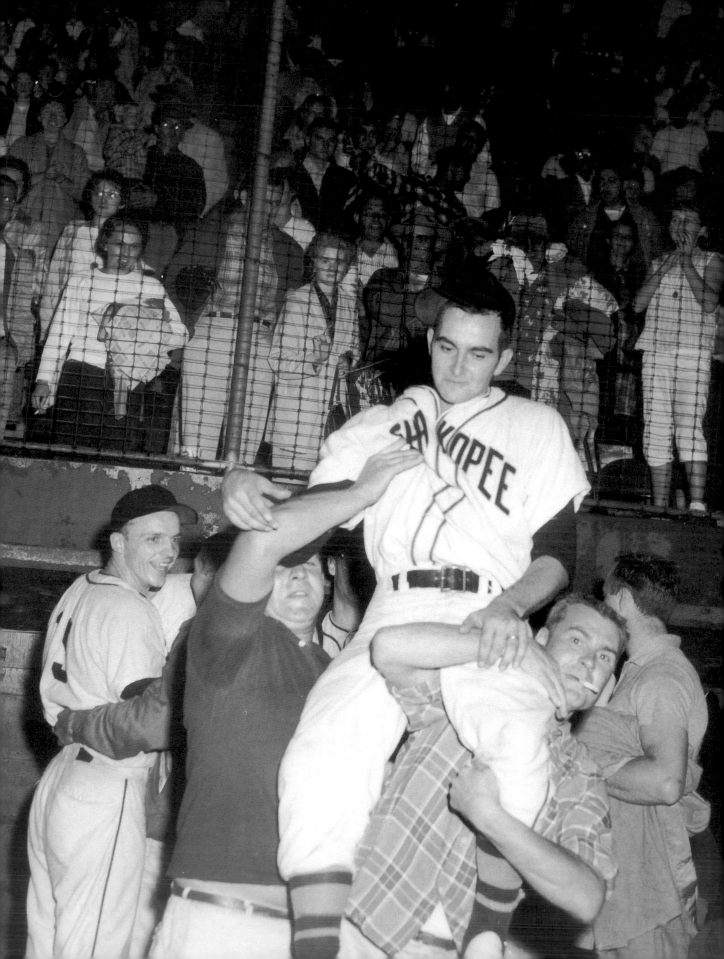

FINAL INNINGS

1959–60

THE CLASS A LEAGUES WERE RESHUFFLED once again before the 1959 season when the West Central League folded. It had been a fixture in the state since 1947, but three of the five members of the league in 1958—Alexandria, Fergus Falls, and Moorhead—were no longer interested in paying the costs of Class A baseball. Little Falls and Breckenridge tried to find other teams to join with them but found no takers. Times had certainly changed in 10 years. In 1949, seven of the eight teams—three of them from towns with populations under 1,000—in the West Central league that gladly jumped into Class AA baseball were smaller than Breckenridge-Wahpeton, the smallest team in the league in 1958.

This development left the Little Falls Red Sox stranded. They'd been runners-up in the State Class A tournament in 1953, 1954, 1956, and 1958, and third place in 1955. Class A baseball now was confined to a small triangular section of the state bounded roughly by a line from the Twin Cities down Highway 169 to the Iowa border, east to the Wisconsin border, and then back to the Twin Cities. Ultimately, Little Falls

dropped its Class A team but continued to support two Class B teams—the Indians in the O-T-W League, and the Cowboys in the Victory. (After they moved up to Class A in 1952, Little Falls had also fielded two Class B teams in 1952, 1954, and 1956–58.) The Indians made the Class B State Tournament in 1959 for the second consecutive year. Shortstop Jerry Wilczek was the only Red Sox player who moved to the Indians.

There were now only three Class A leagues in the state outside the metropolitan area—the Century, Minnesota River, and the Southern Minny. Backroom negotiations over the winter in the old Southern Minny towns had been extremely complicated, and heated. Rochester's experiment in the professional Three-I League fell apart in 1958 due to lack of support, and the team had finished the season in Winona. In 1959, Rochester baseball boosters still didn't want much to do with the Southern Minny and decided to support the Redcaps, who had played in the Class B Downstate League in 1958. They entered the Redcaps in the Class A Century League. Winona briefly looked at securing a franchise in the professional Class C North-

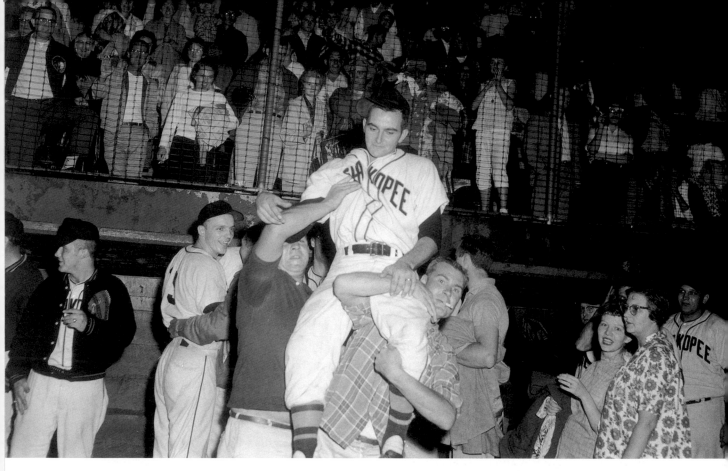

son draftee from Chaska and a former Dodgers farmhand, set a new state record by striking out 21 in a 1–0 victory over Belgrade.

Springfield and Shakopee met in the championship game. For Springfield, it was their third consecutive Class B State Tournament since the Class AA Western Minny folded. The team was built around a new crop of local youngsters, led by catcher/manager Norm Wilson, who abandoned his pro career in 1953 to move to Springfield. Shakopee had a similar story. They last played Class A baseball in the Minnesota Valley League in 1954, and the current team represented a new generation of local players. They lost to runner-up Norwood in the 1957 State Tournament but did not make it back in 1958.

The championship game was one of the most dramatic in State Tournament history. Springfield carried a 2–0 lead into the bottom of the ninth inning, and pitcher Jerry Friedman, a postseason draftee from Milroy, appeared to be cruising.

Shakopee's Fred Kerber is given a victory ride after the 3–2 victory over Springfield in the Class B championship game. Kerber's two-run home run with two outs in the bottom of the ninth tied the score, and the winning run scored two batters later. Photograph from the collection of the Stearns History Museum, St. Cloud, Minnesota.

But with two outs and a runner on first, Friedman hung a one-ball, two-strike curveball, and Shakopee's Fred Kerber hit it over the left-field fence to tie the score. Howie Heller, the next hitter, walked, stole second, and scored the winning run on an error. Fulton Weckman, a 17-year-old postseason draftee from Jordan, was voted the tournament MVP. Although he didn't get the win in the championship game—he was removed for a pinch hitter in the bottom of the eighth—he had pitched complete-game victories over Lake Henry and Virginia earlier in the tournament.

One of the highlights of the season had been the return of the famous Satchel Paige to play several exhibition games in the upper Midwest. About 1,100 fans showed up in Fairmont to see Paige pitch two innings for the Cuban Stars barnstorming team. The 53-year-old Paige—his exact age was always in question—gave up two runs, including a solo home run by Milt Nielsen, in the Martins' 3–1 victory. Fairmont manager Jim McNulty observed that Paige wasn't at his best, but that the umpire "wasn't giving him his favorite knee-high strike." Ten years earlier, Paige's appearance would probably have attracted twice as many fans. He returned to the state with the Cubans in 1960 and played a game in Bagley. The day of barnstorming teams was almost done. Except for a few celebrities like Paige, the traveling teams had lost their drawing power.

The 1960 season put an exclamation point on the trend moving baseball power toward the Twin Cities metropolitan area. The Bloomington Athletics finally won the State Class A Championship, after having been a pretournament favorite every year since 1956. Manager Herb Isakson—the same man whose residency was protested in 1958—led a team of minor-league and state Class AA veterans to the title with two victories over previously undefeated St. Paul Como Recreation. It was the first time two Twin Cities teams had met in a state championship game since 1939.

Subsequent years would see a further separation between the state's metropolitan and out-state teams. By 1962 Class A would be reduced to four leagues—Minneapolis, St. Paul, St. Paul Suburban, and Southern Minny. These were the same four leagues that formed the state's Class AA leagues in 1945, the beginning of the era. By 1966, only the Class A championship game was played at Belle Plaine, the site of the Class B tournament. The other rounds of the Class A Tournament were held at St. Paul's Dunning Field.

Perhaps it was fate that Bloomington won the championship. Although fans at the State Tournament did not know it for sure, Bloomington's Metropolitan Stadium would become the home of the American League Minnesota Twins in 1961.

Membership in the MBA stayed fairly constant in 1960. The Minnesota River League, which was organized in 1948 and produced three Class A state champions—Le Center in 1950, St. Peter in 1955, and Waseca in 1957, and three state runners-up—folded after the 1959 season. (Most of its original members were gone by 1958, actually.) The Great Western League moved—voluntarily, this time—up from Class B and kept the state Class A roster at six leagues. In the Southern Minny, Rochester, Mason City, and Winona dropped out. Rochester's experiment with two Class A teams had been a disaster. In 1959 the Yankees won the Southern Minny pennant, only to lose in the playoffs, while the Red Caps won only three games in the Century League. Neither team drew much fan support. In 1960 Rochester entered a four-team municipal league in the MBA Class B. Its champion, Kahler Corporation, pulled a surprise and won the Region 5-B playoffs to earn a spot in the State Tournament. Mankato, which had joined the Minnesota River League in 1958, moved back to the Southern Minny to bring the league up to six teams.

The 1960 State Tournament was held in Springfield, which had made grandstand improvements and added bleacher seats to first and third baselines to prepare for the tournament. After three years in Class B, the town moved up to the now Class A Great Western League. Manager Norm Wilson had earlier driven down to the NCAA College World Series in Omaha to sign Gopher pitcher Howard Nathe. Unfortunately, Nathe had suffered a shoulder injury during the season. He wasn't able to pitch in the

Gophers NCAA Championship games and was limited mostly to outfield duty for Springfield.

Springfield won the Great Western playoffs. Wilson and pitcher Pat Davison were the only players with direct experience in Springfield's storied past in the Western Minny. Dave Gisvold and Bussie Wagner, though, had the pedigree—they were sons of Springfield legends Al Gisvold and Bassie Wagner. Hometown fans were disappointed, though, when the Tigers lost their first two games. St. Paul's Como Recreation, undefeated for the season, beat Bloomington, Mankato, and Minneapolis Twin Cities Federal to advance through the winner's division.

Bloomington won three straight in the losers' bracket to earn another shot at Como Rec.

The finals on Sunday, September 17, were rained out twice and were finally played on Saturday, October 1. This was definitely a break for Bloomington. Tournament MVP Wayne Tjaden, who won three games in the tournament, had pitched 8⅓ innings in an 8–4 victory

Action at second base at Springfield during the 1960 State Tournament. The championship games, delayed two weeks by rain, were not played until October 1. *Star-Tribune* photograph; courtesy of the Minnesota Historical Society.

over Mankato on September 16. When the finals were finally played, he beat Como Rec 10–2 in the first game and then pitched 2⅔ innings of relief in Bloomington's 8–4 victory in the championship game.

Class B had a new format for 1960—the tournament would remain single elimination until the semifinal round, when the four remaining teams would play double elimination. A review of the Class B entry list shows how much amateur baseball had changed in 10 years. Fergus Falls, 1950 Class AA champion, and Willmar, 1952 Class AA champion, were now playing Class B ball. Fairfax, the 1950 Class AA Western Minny champion, was also in the field. Defending champion Shakopee had once been a Class A powerhouse, and the 1958 champion, Pipestone, had been a member of the First Night League throughout its ascent from Class A to AA, and then its drop down to Class B. Norwood, whose string of five consecutive tournaments had been broken in 1959, was also back. They'd been runners-up in 1957 and 1958.

It was thought that Class B would be the refuge for small towns when it was created in 1948. In fact, its first two champions, the St. Cloud Moose in 1948 and Little Falls in 1949, were rather large towns. Lester Prairie (population 663) finally became the small-town standard-bearer when they won in 1950. Soderville's back-to-back wins in 1951 and 1952, followed by Rollingstone's triumph in 1953 and Milroy in 1954,

kept the title in small towns. However, as the decade closed, larger towns like Bemidji, Pipestone, and Shakopee started to dominate. What happened, of course, is that the large majority of teams—almost 90 percent of them—were now playing in Class B.

Pipestone, Norwood, Fergus Falls, and Shakopee made the semifinals. Pipestone's ace pitchers, Chuck Gageby and Don Bruns, were too strong for the rest of the field. Gageby had pitched for Pipestone in the 1954 Class A State Tournament, after two years in the New York Yankees farm system, and returned to Pipestone in 1960 after four years in the air force. Bruns pitched for Wanda in 1952 and then spent two years in military service. He pitched for Milroy in the 1955 Class A State Tournament and then spent four years in the Baltimore Orioles farm system, before returning to Minnesota in 1960. Bruns won three games in the tournament, while Gageby won two. Bruns beat Fergus Falls 5–0 in the finals of the winners' bracket on Friday night. He was pulled after seven innings to save him for possible relief in the championship game expected on Sunday. After the two-week rain delay, Bruns also started the final game, defeating Fergus Falls, 2–1, giving up only three hits while striking out 15.

The tournament drew 18,937 fans. It might have topped 20,000, but only 1,058 turned out for the rain-delayed finals. That was the smallest final-day crowd since before World War II.

CLASS AA: MINNESOTA'S BIG LEAGUES

IN 1945, AS IT HAD SINCE 1939, CLASS AA consisted of the Minneapolis and St. Paul city champions, and the St. Paul Suburban League and Southern Minnesota League playoff champions. The rules for Class AA and Class A teams were identical, except for the number of outside players permitted—two in Class A and three in Class AA. Based on that, the Minneapolis and St. Paul teams could have been designated as Class A, but the Association of Minnesota Amateur Baseball League put them in Class AA out of a sense of fairness. Similarly, the St. Paul Suburban and Southern Minnesota Leagues were placed in Class AA because of their larger towns.

Six additional leagues played Class AA baseball in the era. Two made only token appearances. The Southeastern Minnesota League, in 1946, and the Bi-State League, in 1948, were moved up from Class A because of teams using more than two outside players. (The Association of Minnesota Amateur Baseball Leagues punished the whole league even if only one team was guilty. They hoped that would encourage the leagues to police themselves.) The other four leagues elected to play in Class AA. They were driven by three factors: local fans who wanted a fast brand of baseball, businessmen and local leaders who were willing to help finance the more costly teams, and ego. Towns took a lot of pride in belonging to one of the state's "big leagues."

In 1947 the Western Minnesota League was the first new league to move up to Class AA. No one was surprised when the Western Minny made that move. They had long been considered the equal of the Southern Minny and had, in fact, won the Mythical State Championships over the Class AA champions four consecutive years, 1941–44. In 1948 the MABA moved the North Central League up to Class AA because of outside-player violations by Fergus Falls and Detroit Lakes. Neither team seriously protested the ruling, and the league decided to remain in Class AA in 1949. The West Central League elected to play Class AA in 1949, and down in southwestern Minnesota, the First Night League moved up to Class AA in 1950.

A look at Class AA league populations in 1950—the peak year, when there were eight leagues—shows a wide disparity in population within and between leagues. Remarkably, some

on the field," former Sleepy Eye outfielder Mel Cook said. "The crowd liked him, and when you put him and [Springfield's] Vandenberg on the field together, you could be certain of a crowd."

Baseball attracted crowds for many years, but possibly never more than when Nicklasson was running the show. In 1949 the Brewers averaged a record 1,817 fans per game and set an overall attendance mark of 39,521 for 26 home games in 1951. (The figures don't include attendance for the Millers, New Ulm's Class B team.)

The Minnesota Baseball Association held its State Tournament at Johnson Park in 1953 and 1958, with 31,031 attending in 1953. That attendance mark was third all-time, behind only the 35,318 who packed St. Cloud's Municipal Stadium for the 1950 tournament and 34,280 in Shakopee for the 1948 tournament.

Interest wasn't restricted to the community's men and boys. Women and girls were just as enamored by baseball. An article in the New Ulm paper the day after "The Game" was topped by the headline "Still Baseball Capital" and included an account of a mother's demand that her son not be late for supper because she had to get to the park by six o'clock.

After 1943, New Ulm would go 37 years without a state title, but the town would claim a major distinction in 1947 when it became the first outstate community in State Tournament history to qualify two teams, the Brewers finishing second in Class AA and the Millers reaching the quarterfinals in Class A. The tournament was played at Mankato's Tanley Field, only a short line drive from New Ulm, contributing significantly to the then-record attendance of 28,336.

The Brewers were 317–244 from 1945 through 1960, playing the majority of those seasons in the Western Minny, one of the state's toughest leagues. After a two-year break for World War II, the Millers, New Ulm's second team, resumed competition in 1946 and at the conclusion of the 1960 season owned a 142–101 record. The Brewers endured only two losing seasons in that stretch, the Millers three.

"On game days, baseball began at breakfast with coffee and a roll," Schaper said, "particularly for games against Springfield. That was possibly the most intense rivalry at the time."

New Ulm succeeded using a fair share of hired outsiders when it moved to Class AA, a cast including pitchers Bill Sherman, Lloyd Lundeen, Frank Pugsley, Jack Verby, and Gene Cooney, catcher Casey Dowling, infielder Bob Johnson, and outfielder Bob Knight. Homegrown talent, however, was available and helped keep the Brewer and Miller programs highly competitive. The program had a strong local influence—seven of the players who competed in "The Game" were products of New Ulm High:, Stan Manderfeld, Dick and Ron Spelbrink, Wally Ebert, Vic Eichten, Wilfahrt, and Loose.

Bill Horne (*left*), shown with Leavenworth native Mel Cook, gave up on a pro baseball career to come to Minnesota. Courtesy of Herb Schaper Historical Baseball Collection/*New Ulm Daily Journal.*

In the Johnson Park 50th anniversary program printed in 1989, *New Ulm Daily Journal* sports editor Jay Osmundson wrote: "Being a baseball player in New Ulm means more than simply getting an opportunity for exercise. The game, with all due respect to Abner Doubleday, belongs to this southern Minnesota hamlet."

Sleepy Eye won the 1945 Western Minny title at its first State Tournament appearance since 1932. *Front row, from left:* Ray Hollmen (president), Leo Pirsch, Louis Seesz, Don Eichten (draftee), William Groebner, Bud Seesz, Elmer Lehmert, John Tober. *Back row:* Henry Nicklasson (draftee from New Ulm), Clarence Litch, Marty Ledeboer, manager Bugga Stelljes, Ben Frank, Val Groebner, George Kober. Courtesy of Dode Wonson.

Sleepy Eye: Town Name Belied Spirit

Bill Horne, a native of Beloit, Wisconsin, jumped at the chance to play baseball in Minnesota when he got a call during spring training in Daytona Beach, Florida, in 1952. Horne was coming off five years in the minor leagues and was facing a Class C contract of only $125 per month. In addition, he had an eight-month-old daughter, and his wife wasn't too keen about the prospect of moving about the country every summer.

Burt Tracy, an old acquaintance from Tomah, Wisconsin, made the call on behalf of Sleepy Eye management, making an offer of $300 per month, plus a job. Horne and his wife started packing before the phone hit the receiver. On the drive to Minnesota they stopped to visit family in Beloit, who couldn't stop laughing about a town that called itself Sleepy Eye.

The Hornes, though, discovered what Minnesotans already knew about the community—it was a proud, well-to-do town (population 3,278 in 1950) with excellent public and parochial schools and several large employers, all situated in the middle of rich farmland. They also found that the town and surrounding Brown County had a rich baseball heritage stretching back to the late 1800s.

The Sleepy Eye Indians went toe to toe with the state's best as a member of the Western Minnesota League from 1945 to 1956. The 1945 season was particularly magical, as the Indians managed to knock off perennial powers Springfield and New Ulm in the Western Minny League playoffs. They qualified for the State Tournament thanks in large part to Harold "Chief" Wonson, a New Englander who was teaching at Blake Academy in Hopkins. Chief threw a two-hitter to beat New Ulm's ace, Gene Cooney, 2–1 in the league championship game.

Unfortunately Wonson was ineligible for the State Tournament because he had played a few games earlier in the year with the Minneapolis Millers, and the team lost in the second round to Mayer, the eventual second-place finisher. The summer of 1945 was a wonderful time for the town. By playoff time the war was over, and fans were free to celebrate baseball again with no guilty feelings.

Dode Wonson, Chief's wife, recalled how well the players and their families were treated. "I looked forward to the Sunday drives," she said. "The fans treated us like royalty. There were no reserved seats, but they knew where we liked to sit, and just left that part of the bleachers vacant until we got there."

But the magic of the 1945 season didn't carry over. The Indians won only two league games in 1946 and then struggled to a 113–166 regular-season record from 1947 to 1956, when the Western Minny played Class AA baseball.

Despite the town's limited population, Sleepy Eye fielded two teams for several years, the Indians and the Class B Warriors, and personnel was no problem for either club. The Indians had a variety of options in addition to spending a few dollars on talent: the town's public school system and St. Mary's Catholic school lured teachers with baseball talent, and the Del Monte canning factory and the city provided jobs. And both teams had some outstanding area talent from which to choose in nearby Stark, Comfrey, and Leavenworth. All three towns reached at least one State Tournament in the 1940s.

Mel Cook, a member of Leavenworth's 1949 State Tournament team and an Indians starter from 1950 through 1958, said that the country boys were committed to baseball, working out or playing several times a week after long days in the fields. He said that pitchers received up to $1,000 a month and some of the position players up to $300 a month. Cook received significantly less money than the outsiders, but he had no complaints.

"I can remember as a kid that my brother, Duke, and I picked sweet corn by hand," Cook said. "We received 50¢ an hour. So even a few dollars a game was good money."

Many former professionals were attracted to the town, including Dick Lanahan, who pitched in 56 games for the Washington Senators and Pittsburgh Pirates, catcher Casey Dowling, and Carm Cozza, a Miami of Ohio standout who pitched a season for Sleepy Eye before playing two summers of professional ball. One of the most memorable Indian stars was Harlan "Whitey" Felker, a right-hander who played service ball on the same team as Ted Williams and played one year in the minor leagues. Felker was nicknamed the "Iron Horse" after the 1951 season, when he pitched 24 of Sleepy Eye's 35 league games, 164 innings overall, both league records.

In one of Class AA's biggest upsets, the 1950 Fergus Falls Red Sox beat powerful Austin. *Front row, from left:* player/manager Jim McNulty, Don Blasius, Ed Piacentini, John Kelly, batboy George Sawyer, John DeWitt, Hal Younghans, Harley Oyloe. *Back row:* Fred Kroog, Rollie Harlow, Duane Baglien, Joe Colasinski. Mel Henson, a draftee from Detroit Lakes, was missing from the photograph. Courtesy of Harley Oyloe.

"He was a good pitcher, but I think he could have been a lot better if he hadn't had to throw so much," Cook said. "We really didn't have a rotation which would allow him a decent break. He'd pitch a game and then come back three days later."

A host of college players from Wisconsin and Ohio helped stock the team in the 1950s. In fact, Bill Horne was the most experienced player on the college-dominated team in 1953, and he was appointed manager. The team finished at 19–15, its only winning season in the Class AA era. When the Western Minny folded after the 1956 season, Sleepy Eye played one year in the Class B Indian Trails League but stepped back up to Class A in 1958. They won the Class A Minnesota River League playoffs but lost two straight in the State Tournament.

Fergus Falls: Success Discouraged Rivals

Fergus Falls fans flocked to baseball games after the war. They loved baseball and, not surprisingly, they loved winning baseball even more. To satisfy this desire, the baseball team got involved in a recruiting spiral that eventually got out of hand. They started out using Minnesota college athletes to supplement their local talent.

Then, under competitive pressure because other teams were also stepping up their recruiting, Fergus Falls started recruiting for college players from Texas and Pennsylvania. Finally they began to lure professional players from the lower minor leagues.

A combination of rising costs and decreased fan interest caught up with the team in 1950—the team's most successful season on the field. In the next several years, the club struggled to balance costs while maintaining a team in the state's tough Class AA leagues.

Fergus Falls native Ev Faunce, tailback on the University of Minnesota football team, helped recruit fellow Gopher athletes Buzz Wheeler, Duane Baglien, and Dick Durrell for the 1947 season. Fargo native Gordon Rothrock, who was playing baseball at Northwestern University, also joined hometown players Harley Oyloe, Mel Olson, Stan Banholtz, Harry Olson, and Ray Erickson to form a strong team. Fergus Falls defeated Detroit Lakes in the playoffs and then won the regionals and a berth in the State Tournament in Mankato. Behind University of Minnesota pitcher Bob Berglund—drafted from Detroit Lakes—the Red Sox beat St. Cloud in the first round, but then Don Zarling, a postseason draftee from Breckenridge, lost a tough game to Olivia 2–1.

In the off-season, local baseball officials, excited about attendance in 1947 and the team's success on the field, started making ambitious plans for 1948. They stepped up recruiting and got approval to build a $17,000 lighting system at the fairgrounds baseball field. Fergus Falls signed two additional University of Minnesota players—catcher Harry Collias and outfielder Jerry Smith—and the Red Sox team president Bob Allison made a trip to the NCAA College World Series and signed two Baylor players,

pitcher Fred Copeland and shortstop Hal Harris, the leading hitter in the Southwest Conference. They also lured Brooklyn native Jim McNulty, who was languishing in the Brooklyn Dodgers farm system, to Fergus Falls. He'd met Red Sox first baseman Dick Durrell in Japan after the war and jumped on a train when his old buddy called him about playing in Minnesota.

Fergus Falls didn't blink when the MABA, on Friday, August 20, right in the middle of the North Central League playoffs, bumped the league into Class AA for excessive use of outside players. Their supporters were thrilled to be in the state's "big show" and not disappointed in the team's third-place finish in the State Tournament.

Early in 1949, the MABA selected Detroit Lakes to be the host of that year's State Tournament. Fergus Falls officials knew that would give the Lakers even more motivation to stop the Red Sox's two-year run as North Central champions. Team officials did some more college recruiting in the off-season, and Jim McNulty was brought back during the year to become the team's player/manager. Fergus Falls won the pennant again and beat Detroit Lakes in three straight tense, well-played playoff games to claim the league title a third consecutive year. The three games drew an estimated 10,000 fans.

It had been a great season. The team was 41–7 overall and had drawn 38,400 fans to 29 home games. Merchants supported the team with jobs for players and prizes for special events. Players were sought out whenever they appeared on city streets by appreciative fans who offered to take them out for lunches or drinks—the nearest bar was in Foxhome, because Fergus Falls was a dry city at the time—or just wanted to talk about baseball. The ballpark was definitely the place to be in town. For Sunday-night home

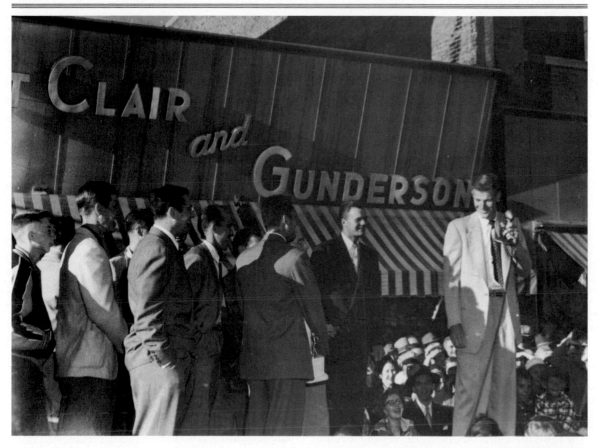

Outfielder John DeWitt *(right)*, a baseball and track star from Texas A&M, speaks downtown after a parade celebrating Fergus Falls' Class AA victory in the 1950 State Tournament. Courtesy of Harley Oyloe.

games, a steady stream of headlights could be seen on the highway leading to the fairgrounds as people returned from Otter Tail and other area lakes for the game.

Fergus Falls fell short again at the State Tournament, losing twice to Austin, 8–1 and 13–3, but they finished as runner-up. Manager McNulty knew he'd have to find some more players with professional experience if he expected to beat Austin in the future—six of Austin's starting fielders and all three of their pitchers had played in the minor leagues. He'd met Emil Scheid, too, and knew that the Austin skipper wouldn't be standing still in the off-season.

In 1950 team officials signed Ed Piacentini and Don Blasius from Northwestern University, and the school board hired Hal Younghans to teach. He had played shortstop in the Dodg-

ers farm system and with Waseca in the Southern Minny. McNulty also signed two former minor-league teammates, pitcher John Kelly and catcher Joe Colasinski, and unlike in 1948 or 1949, when the team didn't hit its stride until all the college players came on board, the Red Sox started strong in 1950 and got better. Fergus Falls won the pennant going away, with a 12–2 record, and easily won the playoffs.

The team had a 46–5 overall record. Attendance was 27,480 in 31 home games, down about 440 fans per game compared to 1949, but no one in Fergus Falls was worrying about that as the State Tournament began in St. Cloud. Hopes were high for the team after their third-place finish in 1948 and second place in 1949.

The team didn't disappoint this time. They advanced through the winner's bracket with three straight victories to set up another match with their old nemesis, defending champion Austin, which had been upset in the second round by Litchfield, 3–2. Austin beat Fergus Falls 5–1 to force one more game to decide the championship. Fergus Falls fans feared a repeat of 1949, but local pitcher Harley Oyloe, making his first appearance in the tournament, saved the day with a 3–0 shutout.

Team officials hardly had time to savor the huge victory celebration in Fergus Falls the day after the tournament. Despite extra fund-raising efforts during the year, the team was several thousand dollars in debt. Several local merchants signed notes for the team to pay off the debts, and new appeals for donations were launched.

The North Central was reorganized as a Class A league for 1951, as other teams were tired of the costs of Class AA baseball. Fergus Falls and Detroit Lakes attempted to join the West Central League but were turned down. The Red Sox, weakened by the loss of McNulty, Kelly, and several others who left for better pay elsewhere, struggled during the season, finishing in third place with a 14–10 record, three games behind first place Breckenridge-Wahpeton. However, they won the league playoffs for the fifth consecutive year. The MABA seeded them directly into the Class A State Tournament, where they were favored despite the return of 1950 champion Le Center. Fergus Falls beat Rollingstone 12–3 in the first round but then lost to eventual champion, Watertown, 4–3, in the semifinals.

Fergus Falls lost money again but was able to pay all its bills with another postseason fund-raising campaign. Undeterred, they applied once more to the West Central and this time were accepted in the Class AA league. They relied on college players in 1952 and 1953 and finished as also-rans in the league, with 17–18 and 17–19 records.

Fergus Falls stayed with the West Central League when it dropped down to Class A in 1954, and until it folded after the 1958 season, but did not make it back to the State Tournament until 1960, when it finished second place in Class B. By that time, Rollie Harlow was the only player remaining from the North Central League glory days of 1947–51.

Litchfield: Optimists for a Reason

If one were to describe Litchfield baseball during Minnesota's town team golden years, former Optimist outfielder Jim Hannan agreed that the term "meteoric" could appropriately be applied.

Like a comet, Litchfield's Class AA program streaked into the 1950 West Central skyline, emitted a brilliant glow in the next two seasons, and then gradually faded away. The 1950, 1951, and 1953 Litchfield teams qualified for the State Class AA Tournament, and the 1951 Optimists won the title. When the West Central League dropped to Class A in 1954, Litchfield moved its team to the Class AA Western Minnesota League. The team finished 14–14 that year, but caught fire at the end of the season, taking second place in the round-robin playoffs before losing to Fairmont in the championship series. The team struggled on the field and at the gate in early 1955 and was disbanded with 11 games to go.

"Yes, a lot of people still talk about those days, especially when they talk to me," Hannan said from his Litchfield home years later. "We had two outstanding managers in Pete Kramer and Dick Siebert [the esteemed Gopher baseball coach]. Pete was a foxy kind of manager who would try anything to win. Siebert was a take-charge guy who had the ability to get the best players available. They both knew their baseball backward and forward."

Litchfield, a cellar dweller in the Class A North Star league through 1947, had been without baseball for the 1948–49 seasons. But Dr. Jack Verby moved to town, and in addition to setting up a medical practice, he campaigned for a Class AA baseball team.

The movement started in November 1949, and by early 1950 the town had a team in the West Central League, an excellent player/manager in Kramer, and lights. The Optimists, a name selected through a contest won by a 14-year-old, started slowly but played a strong second half to finish in fourth place in the standings and then won the playoffs to qualify for the State Tournament.

The next season was to be one of the town's most memorable, with the Optimists winning the state tourney under the watch of Dick Siebert, who was hired as player/manager when Kramer went to Willmar.

The Gopher coach retained some players from the previous year, recruited some out-of-state pros, and added some college players. He assembled a particularly strong pitching staff. Bob "Pork Chop" Kinsel came back from the 1950 staff, and Siebert signed veteran Johnny Herr, a former Triple A minor-league pitcher, and Dick Donnelly, a star from Stetson College in Florida.

Siebert had the situation so in control that when Verby was drafted into the military midway through the season, the Optimists didn't miss a beat. They finished 27–8 in league play, three games ahead of Benson, and breezed through the playoffs into the State Tournament, where they opened with three consecutive shutouts and outscored the opposition 52–6 overall.

"I think we lost tonight to the best team we've met in a long time," Austin manager Emil Scheid said after his Packers lost to Litchfield.

Litchfield came within a heartbeat of qualifying again in 1952 when the Optimists lost in the last game of the best-of-five final playoff series to Willmar. Uncharacteristically, the savvy Siebert lost one game on a forfeit when he delayed putting his team back on the field after a heated argument with the umpires. The Optimists returned to the state tourney again in 1953, but that was the beginning of the end. Litchfield moved to the high-rent Western Minny league in 1954, and in 1955 the team folded with 11 games to go in the schedule. The players reportedly received every cent owed to them by the club, but the directors were left swimming in a sea of red ink.

"Everyone was trying to outspend everyone and [Litchfield] just couldn't keep it up, and

The 1950 Litchfield Optimists fired up the town by winning the West Central League in their first year of operation. *Front row, from left:* Larry Rosenow, Milt Olson, batboy David Beeker, Jim Hannan, Jerry Schaber. *Second row:* Jack Verby, John Garbett (draftee from Morris), Ralph Ruopsa, Pete Guzy, Casey Dowling, batboy Eugene McHugh. *Back row:* manager Pete Kramer, Bob Kinsel, Tom McCann, Wayne Abrahamson, Jim Madden, Gene Kelly (draftee from Willmar). Courtesy of Brian Larson.

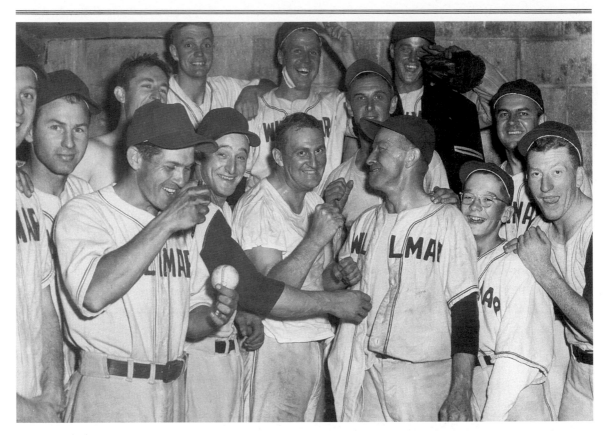

The Willmar Rails celebrate their 1952 Class AA State Championship. *Front row, from left:* Gene Kelly (partially obscured), Hal Younghans, Chub Ebnet, Byron Sharpe, Pete Kramer, Art Grangaard, batboy Cy Halvorson, Dick Naylor. *In back:* Max Ross, Duane Netland, Arnie Atkins, Howie Schultz, Hal Bergeson, Harley Oyloe. Courtesy of Mrs. Art Grangaard.

they went belly up," Hannan, one of the few year-round local players, said of a team he left after the 1953 season. "The Dassel manager offered me some money to play over there. I could see it was getting hairy [financially] in Litchfield and I was starting a family, so I accepted."

Willmar: Baseball Tradition Jumped Tracks

On the day after the conclusion of the Willmar Rails' 1954 season, the baseball faithful were mired in a gloom unlike any they had experienced in years. Their mighty Rails had struck out in the most unbelievable way, finishing 10–18 and anchored in the Western Minnesota League cellar. They were quickly eliminated in the playoffs. Never had a Willmar team traveled so far—an estimated 3,200 miles—to accomplish so little. The Rails finished with a .232 team batting average, slogged through a 21-inning scoreless malaise, and managed only four runs in their final 36 innings.

What a difference two years made. In 1952, Willmar dominated the West Central League and finished the season as Minnesota's Class AA champions. Even the brilliant pitching of Gene Kelly and Johnny Herr, lured away from neighboring Litchfield, couldn't maintain the Class AA momentum in 1954. Big-time state baseball was a faint memory in Willmar a couple seasons before Class AA ball was formally abandoned in the state.

Howie Schultz *(right)* receives a deserved hero's welcome after his grand slam home run in the 12–8 victory over Albert Lea in the 1952 Class AA championship game. Courtesy of Howie Schultz.

History, too, made this collapse even more enigmatic. Since Minnesota baseball officials established a championship series in 1924, Willmar teams had qualified for seven state tournaments, only one fewer than the record shared by six towns to that point. Among the more than 1,000 Minnesota towns that supported town team baseball through the years, Willmar was one of the state's front-runners.

The situation was certainly the last thing that Art Grangaard, a former professional football and basketball player, had in mind when he arrived in 1946 after completing a coaching career at Luther College in Iowa and St. Olaf College in Northfield, Minnesota. In his first season, he and Willmar qualified for the State Tournament and, before being eliminated in the second round, the Vets upset Delano 5–4, making its fifth state tourney appearance in seven years. Baseball once again was on the march in the agricultural and railroad community of Willmar, and Grangaard kept pushing to compete at a faster pace and higher level. He helped organize the West Central League in 1947 and certainly was a standard-bearer in the league's move to Class AA in 1949.

When the West Central League stepped up in class, Grangaard made certain that Willmar was prepared for the move. He recruited local stalwarts including Bird Island's Lefty Ranweiler, Willmar's Howie Peterson, and Lake Lillian's Gene Olson and Byron Sharpe. He also landed former major-league first baseman Howie Schultz, former Gopher and minor-league pitching ace Gene Kelly, and former Hamline University infielder Joey Hutton Jr.

He didn't rely on an inordinate number of out-of-state products as did many of the Class AA teams, but when Grangaard did shop outside of Minnesota, he acquired quality talent. One of his most extraordinary acquisitions was minor leaguer Arnie Atkins, who in 1952 combined with Kelly to give Willmar one of the state's top one-two pitching combinations. How good was Atkins, a full-time Rails pitcher in 1952 and

1953? Good enough that when he left Willmar, he resumed a minor-league career in which he reached Triple A before retiring in 1958. In his final five professional seasons, he was 47–39, highlighted by a 22–8 season with Shreveport in 1955, the second most victories in the Class AA Texas League.

"Art was a very good manager with a bright baseball mind, and I'm sure he could have managed professionally," Schultz said. "He did a great job of working with the locals and outsiders . . . we were a group of happy athletes."

Grangaard recruited the best he could find and supported them with his high-voltage competitive nature. He backed down from no one and could strike fear in an umpire's heart at the drop of a bat.

Willmar manager Art Grangaard (*right*) and Litchfield manager Dick Siebert meet with umpires at home plate. Grangaard lacked Siebert's credentials but was highly respected. Courtesy of Howie Peterson.

Ranweiler, who competed for Grangaard before becoming sports editor at the *West Central Minnesota Daily Tribune,* once offered a playful picture of his former skipper's competitive nature in a newspaper column. The anecdote had to do with one of Grangaard's responses to a controversial call during a game in which two Lutheran ministers, Rev. Johnson and Rev. Kildahl, were in the stands.

"Art came walking in from third base, using some of his flowery language," Ranweiler wrote, "and by the time he hit home plate he was in rare form. After a few minutes of this, Rev. Johnson reached over some fans and tapped Rev. Kildahl on the shoulder, commenting, 'One of your flock, isn't he?' "

Grangaard's leadership was never more apparent than in 1952, and not just because Willmar won the Class AA title. Despite a series of personnel losses to injury and the military draft, he found the resources and the guile to lead the Rails through a difficult West Central playoff series against Litchfield and an undefeated march through state tourney play. Grangaard announced his pending retirement before the tournament in which he was named MVP.

For Willmar baseball, the only thing that could have been more exciting was if the Class B Willmar Kernels had qualified for the State Tournament. The Kernels, led by veterans Dick Selvig and Tim Ray and supported by a group of promising youngsters, won the 1952 Corn Belt regular season pennant but were upset by Murdock in the playoffs. If the Kernels had qualified for the state tourney, it would have marked only the third time an out-state town qualified two teams for state competition.

Some might speculate that Willmar spent itself out of Class AA competition, but certainly the loss of Grangaard meant the loss of a major catalyst who had the respect of most opponents. "He was a fine person who loved the game, and he was also an excellent player," said Tom Petroff, a Michigan native who became an NCAA Coaches Hall of Fame member. "He continued playing the game, and he played it well while players much younger were giving it up."

In respect to the town's baseball tradition, it should be emphasized that Willmar didn't abandon baseball after the glory years. The Kernels resumed operation and, led by several former Rails including Ranweiler and Olson, qualified for the 1958 and 1960 Class B Tournaments. In addition, Willmar supported two other Class B teams for several seasons, the Cubs and an Air Force Base team in the Super Eight League.

With Grangaard retired, Ranweiler became the town's resident baseball celebrity, a true gentleman who played for the Kernels and faithfully covered them as the *West Central Minnesota Daily Tribune*'s sports editor. Lefty knew a lot about baseball, but it took the veteran outfielder time to develop journalistic objectivity. Consider his column "Portside Slants by Lefty" after a 4–3 victory over Perham in the 1958 State Tournament.

"I got thrown out of the ball game in the last of the fourth for telling the umpire he choked up," Ranweiler wrote. "They were continually out of position and had to be moved around either by our team or by the plate umpire. We had a man out by ten feet at third base, and the umpire called him safe.

Fairmont: Baseball with Professional Touch

Longer than many can remember, Fairmont has been known as "The City of Lakes," a catchphrase referring to the five bodies of water bordering the west side of the southern Minnesota town, settled in the late 1850s and stabilized when it became a regular railroad stop in 1878. The Amber,

Budd, George, Hall, and Sisseton lakes, named for some of the earliest settlers, developed into a major source of outside recreation for the locals and gradually became a tourist attraction.

But in the 1950s, approximately 100 years after the town was settled, Fairmont became recognized as a citadel for town team baseball, a designation established by the capable hands and resolve of Jim McNulty, a former marine who spent two seasons in the Brooklyn Dodgers organization before coming to Minnesota. The Brooklyn native led Fergus Falls to the 1950 Class AA state title and in 1952 was hired to manage Fairmont in the Class AA Western Minnesota League.

McNulty snapped the Martins to attention. "We needed some pitching and strength up the middle," McNulty said, talking about his plans for his first campaign. "I told them that I wasn't going to assure anyone a championship, but I did say we'd win our share of games and then

---

Fairmont took its baseball seriously under Jim McNulty but also had some fun. McNulty models his new jacket and hat to Milt Nielsen *(left)*, Ken Staples, and Gordy Figard before a game. The players bought the duds to pay off a bet they'd lost to McNulty. Courtesy of Jim McNulty.

maybe catch fire in the playoffs." Sure enough, fans who a year earlier supported a 13–22 team were soon rooting for Fairmont in the 1952 State Tournament.

Fairmont followed its 1952 playoff victory with back-to-back Western Minnesota pennants, qualifying for the State Tournament in 1953 and then winning the newly-organized Little World Series in 1954. Fairmont won the series, a best-of-seven affair against Southern Minny champion Rochester, four games to two.

Fairmont moved to the Southern Minny in 1955 and again won the Little World Series in three games of a best-of-five format. The fact that five Martins left town before the Little World Series against St. James, but the team was allowed to draft four replacements from the Southern Minny, alienated many players and fans. The Martins became a marked team that everyone loved to beat.

"I can remember the half season I pitched at Redwood Falls," pitcher Ron Tucker said. "I beat Fairmont one game, and they were ready to give me the key to the city. Oh, how they loved to beat Fairmont!"

But the marked Martins remained elusive targets. Fairmont continued to win after shifting to the Southern Minny, but as everywhere else, attendance began to flag. Attendance dropped from the thousands into the hundreds. In the 1960 season, the players were being asked to play for a share of the gate, and some of the best headed to towns that still paid reasonable salaries for the times.

During McNulty's tenure, fans were treated to some of the finest town team talent available because he had a pipeline to many professionals ready to settle down or escape the frequent travel. In a quick count, one can find more than two dozen professionals who played for the Martins, including former major leaguers such as Pittsburgh shortstop Grady Wilson and Cleveland outfielder Milt Nielsen. The heart of McNulty's 1955 pitching staff included Clyde DeWitt, Loyal Bloxam, and Harry Pritts, former professionals who had pitched at Class A or higher at a time when the minor-league classification system had six levels, from AAA to D.

Fairmont won the 1959 State Class A title with a four-game sweep in the seven-team, double-elimination competition, but most former Martins said that McNulty's teams in the mid-1950s had significantly more talent because of the major influx of professional players.

McNulty lured so many players from professional ball that he received a letter from George M. Troutman, czar of minor-league baseball. Troutman threatened legal action unless McNulty halted his campaign to recruit minor-league players. Team officials, however, gave him a vote of confidence, and he continued to recruit from the pros.

Troutman might have bothered McNulty no more, but financial pressures did. Not long after August 3, 1960, when McNulty managed his last game, he and his family moved to Minneapolis. He remained out of baseball and eventually moved back to his Brooklyn home. In the ensuing years, the tumult and the shouting at Martin Field—razed and replaced by a shopping mall—has been replaced by the roar of motorboats and Jet Skis in surrounding lakes.

Marshall: Baseball Found Home on the Prairie

Marshall sits in the southwestern corner of Minnesota, a prairie town located on the Burlington Northern main line, with a state university and strong commerce, surrounded by relatively flat, rich farming soil. This could also have been the setting for *Field of Dreams*, the classic baseball movie romanticizing a man's love of the game.

In fact, from the day when the town organized its first official team in 1929, town team ball flourished and, throughout the forties and into the fifties, became the most popular form of summer entertainment. Marshall teams never enjoyed the success of Pipestone, Springfield, New Ulm, Fairmont, and several other southern Minnesota communities, but the team received enough area support to field highly competitive teams.

Marshall didn't qualify for its first State Tournament until 1945, when Doc Henry led the 17–8 Southwestern Minnesota representatives to Albert Lea. In 1949, Marshall joined the First Night League. The league opted to play in Class AA in 1950 and 1951, and Marshall won the playoffs both seasons. They didn't have much luck in the State Tournaments, however, bowing out with 1–2 records both years.

But Marshall, which produced 11 consecutive winning seasons beginning in 1945, played one of the state's most family-friendly forms of

Marshall players' wives Mrs. Chet Wiener, Mrs. Marilyn Mills Christenson, and Mrs. Jack Whitaker cheer during an early-season game in 1955. Fans in the 1950s dressed more stylishly than their modern-day counterparts. Courtesy of Marilyn Mills.

ball, using a large number of college players and locals. Of the 18 Tigers listed in the 1954 *Western Minnesota League Media Guide* published by Don Gruening and Herb Schaper, 15 were college graduates or college students. Among those who later attained national prominence were Gopher star Jerry Kindall, future major leaguer and Hall of Fame college coach; Ohio State's Paul Ebert, later a world-renowned thoracic surgeon; and Fresno State's Jack Hannah, future Triple A professional player, California high school Hall of Fame coach, and cowboy singing star.

Mike Mills owned Mike's Coffee Shop, a 24-hour diner and truck stop along Route 23, a haunt for players and fans that became so popular that the owner had to expand his capacity of 13 stools. His daughter, Marilyn, remembered the late forties and early fifties with fondness because when Marshall stepped up to Class AA, the baseball board began bringing in young men from all over the country.

"No one came to Marshall to visit in those days. People either lived in town or were farmers who came to town," she explained. "Suddenly, we were getting people from all over the country, and they were treated like royalty. As for baseball, it was the only game in town—you could go to the Roxy to see a movie or you could go to the ball game, and most chose the ball game.

"I can remember my dad and I making up our work schedules so that we could leave the next shift in time for us to get to the ball games."

The team went 20–10 to win the pennant in the 1956 Western Minny season and won the playoffs to play in the Little World Series, but the playoff was canceled because the Southern Minnesota League championship was delayed and Marshall's players tired of waiting and left for their homes.

That was the end of pay-for-play baseball in Marshall. The parade of college men into town ended when the team dropped down to Class B for good in 1957.

De Graff, Benson, Atwater, and Lake Lillian: Davids against Goliath

Jerry Sullivan perched on a feed sack in a store along U.S. Highway 12, a road that runs through De Graff, a speck on a line that connects Willmar and Benson on a Minnesota map. He was discussing his favorite topic: baseball.

"Do you believe that at one time there would be 4,000 people over there for a ball game?" he said, swinging his arm toward the south side of the highway, shaking his head and smiling softly. "That's what we'd get at times when we'd play games with Willmar, Litchfield, or Benson, especially after we got lights. We used to play in the Corn Belt League, but once we got into the West Central all hell broke loose. After the 1953 season, it was gone."

Sullivan was the longtime guardian of De Graff baseball, the man who with his brother, Joe, farmed 550 acres, tended cattle, and still managed to build up the town's lofty baseball program. The reputation grew so large that when the Irish stepped into the Class A West Central League and held their own, *Minneapolis Tribune* baseball writer Ted Peterson described De Graff, a hamlet with a population of less than 300, as the "Biggest 'Little' Baseball Town in the State."

As a member of the Corn Belt League, De Graff qualified for Class A State Tournament four times from 1940 through 1945. They joined the West Central League in 1948 and jumped on the bandwagon in 1949, when the league moved up to Class AA. The tiny community had to invest $10,000 in lights to remain in the league. Class AA required Sullivan to begin to recruit high-priced outside talent. The team lost its local atmosphere, but few complained. In fact, the locals' love of big-time town team ball kept De Graff in Class AA longer than many had expected.

"Some people would give a hundred, a couple hundred dollars, which was a lot back then, and a lot of fans supported the team on the road," Sullivan said. "It was terrific for the town. We were alive. Everyone was thrilled. People weren't heading for the lakes in those days. There wasn't that much TV. Baseball was our activity."

After the 1951 season, rumors of financial problems began to surface in both Benson and De Graff. The *Swift County Monitor* reported that the two teams might merge. The two town team boards initially denied plans to combine, but when the 1952 season rolled around, the Benson Chiefs and De Graff Irish became the Benson–De Graff Irish-Chiefs. It was an odd alliance—the rivalry between the two towns had been as fierce as any in the state. Home games were split between the two towns, and attendance was rather solid, but not so good that the two towns could maintain the big-time pace.

The first season, Benson–De Graff had Jack Wilcox, John Mauer, Bob Mistele, Tony Jaros, and briefly former major-league slugger Rudy York on the payroll. Longtime Benson standout Roy Berens and veteran infielder Howie Peterson also received small salaries to compete. The team did well on the field, going 20–15, good for second place. In 1953 the Irish-Chiefs added some new salaried players, including Red Fischer and Ron and Howard Tucker, but finances became untenable, and the team folded in midseason, as did league peer Morris.

"It just got too much asking people who were 70 and 75 years old for money," Sullivan said emotionally. "We wound up selling the lights to Sibley, Iowa, and we sold the fence to a hog farmer who used it as a barrier. We got it done for a while. A lot of big names came through De Graff. But we had our hands full playing in that kind of league."

De Graff wasn't the only tiny town to try making it in Class AA during the West Central League's loftiest days. Atwater (population 880 in 1950) and Lake Lillian (358) also gave big-town baseball a go. Atwater put the squeeze on the community for money in 1949. Businessmen were approached and coffee cans were distributed along the main street to collect donations. The baseball directors hired Gopher football and baseball standout Harry Elliott, who starred the year before at Watertown, and supported him with some strong paid talent combined with area standouts such as Jim Hannan and Ole Hovey. Atwater was competitive, playing hub city rival Willmar almost even, but they couldn't keep up with the rest of the league. By 1950 the coffee cans were empty.

Lake Lillian tried Class AA in 1949. They had some quality locals, including the Flann brothers—Myron, Howard, Burton, and Newell—Byron Sharpe, and Gene Olson, and tried to get them to play for free to save money to be used for outsiders, but that plan backfired. Sharpe and Olson went to Willmar, and the Flanns spent as much time playing softball as they did baseball.

"One of the directors came to me one day and told me we were playing too much softball," Myron said. "I told him if they started paying us, we might think about it." The team lasted one season in Class AA. The team dropped down to Class A for a while, but the field eventually went to seed, and the lights were sold to cut the losses.

CLASS A: TOUGH COMPETITION

I N 1945, CLASS A CONSISTED OF EVERY team in the state outside of Minneapolis, St. Paul, and the St. Paul Suburban and Southern Minnesota Leagues. Teams ranged from ragtag collections of players who played on Sundays for fun to full-blown semiprofessional organizations actively recruiting and paying outside players. It was a situation ripe for complaints. State baseball officials bumped the Southeastern Minnesota League up to Class AA in 1946, and the Bi-State and North Central in 1948, but there were protests about other leagues and teams, too.

The Western Minnesota League was considered at least as strong as the existing Class AA leagues. In fact, it was—Western Minnesota teams beat the Class AA champions in the Mythical Championship Game four consecutive years, 1941–44. Sleepy Eye was upset in the second round of the 1945 State Tournament, ending that string. Although Springfield lost to Albert Lea in the Mythical Championship Game in 1946, the relative ease of the Western Minny team's wins in the Class A bracket led to more complaints. The Western Minny relieved many when it turned to Class AA in 1947. There would

have been protests from other towns in the region had the league not done so. The MABA took a big step when it created Class B in 1948. That provided a place for teams who simply wanted to play ball on Sundays and did not want to recruit and pay salaries. The board made the ruling in April 1948 and left it up to the individual leagues to determine what class they wanted to play in. There wasn't much time to decide, but 47 leagues—and 339 teams—elected to play Class B the first year.

Three leagues dominated Class A in the first ten years of the era—the Minnesota Valley, North Star/Wright Star, and Minnesota River Leagues.

MINNESOTA VALLEY LEAGUE

The Minnesota Valley League consisted of the growing suburbs of Bloomington, Hopkins, and St. Louis Park, as well as close-in towns Chaska, Excelsior, and Shakopee. Jordan was a member from 1945 to 1947 but left to join the new Minnesota River League in 1948. The Minnesota Valley was close to Minneapolis and its rich source of players and could offer shorter driving times to hired players who might also be considering playing for teams in southern or western Minnesota. There were also an abundance of college players in the Twin Cities area. League teams Excelsior (1945 and 1949) and Chaska (1947) won State Championships, while Shakopee took third place in 1948.

Excelsior: Hamline West

Excelsior cruised through the 1945 State Tournament. The team was a mix of veterans and young players, led by 29-year-old slugger Al Litfin, who had once played with the House of David touring team. Sixteen-year-old second baseman Joe Hutton Jr., son of the famous Hamline University basketball coach, and shortstop Dick Kartak anchored a slick-fielding infield. Vern Bruhn, a coach at New Prague and a former University of Minnesota athlete, and Jesse Schwartz provided strong pitching. Manager Steve Eddy drafted pitchers Roger McDonald of Jordan and Ed Poppitz of Chaska for the State Tournament, as well as Jordan catcher Gordon Gelhaye.

Bruhn shut down Clear Lake 16–2 in the first game of the tournament. (Johnny Dellwo pitched the last two innings.) Litfin hit a three-run home run in the bottom of the first inning, and a solo blast in the second to lead the rout. Clear Lake's two runs were the last scored off Excelsior pitching in the tournament. Schwartz gave up only two hits in five innings in the quarterfinal 16–0 win over Ashby. Poppitz gave up no hits in the last two innings of the game, which was shortened to seven innings. Bruhn won his second game of the tournament in the semifinals with a three-hit shutout of De Graff, 5–0.

Postseason draftee Roger McDonald won the championship game over Mayer 4–0 with a no-hitter. He walked only one batter, but hit two and

struck out 11. McDonald, whose family lived in Tacoma, Washington, was a star athlete at St. Thomas College—where he quarterbacked the football team, played on the baseball team, and won four first-place medals in the 1944 Minnesota Intercollegiate Athletic Conference track meet—and had just transferred to the University of Minnesota's U.S. Navy V-12 Officer Training Program.

Al Litfin, who went 8 for 19 with three home runs, was voted the tournament's MVP. St. Louis Cardinal scout Jack Ryan said that Litfin, although he was 29 years old, might be offered a professional contract. Ryan thought that Litfin was good enough to hold his own immediately in the American Association. Drafted catcher Gordon Gelhaye was passed over in the MVP balloting but actually hit better than Litfin. Although he didn't bat in the first game of the tournament, he went 7 for 11, with two home runs, in the next three. Perhaps the voters favored a regular roster player over a postseason draftee, or maybe it came down to a beauty contest—the 305-pound Gelhaye, a former St. Thomas College football and baseball star, didn't fit into the idealized image of the toned and muscled athlete.

Excelsior lost to Shakopee in the first round of the playoffs in 1946 and by 1947 had an almost completely new team. Five current or former Hamline athletes were on the team, including Rollie Seltz, who played basketball with Anderson, Indiana, in the National Basketball League. He had also played baseball four years in the minor leagues but grew tired of the 12-month grind of playing two professional sports.

After a lackluster year in 1947, the team showed some improvement in 1948. They eliminated defending State Class A Champion Chaska in the first round of the playoffs but lost to Shakopee in the finals. They built a powerhouse for 1949, however. The team, now with Seltz as manager, finished 15–5 and tied Shakopee for first place in the regular season.

The team featured an all-Hamline infield—Dick Mingo at third base, Joe Hutton Jr. at shortstop, Seltz at second base, Don Eliason at first base, as well as Einer Anderson at catcher. Veteran pitcher Gene Cooney, who'd been with Bloomington the past three years, was the number one starter, but Rich Weigel, fresh out of St. Cloud State, and St. Paul high schooler Joe Cammack also had clutch victories in the playoffs. Cooney won two games in the State Tournament—he beat Fulda 8–4 in the first round and then won the championship game 7–2 over Winnebago. Weigel was the winner in an unexpected 17–1 rout of defending champion Winsted in the semifinals. Rollie Seltz was selected as the Tournament MVP.

Chaska and Shakopee bolted the Minnesota Valley for the Minnesota River League in 1950, hoping to draw better crowds with teams farther out of the Minneapolis suburban area. The Minnesota Valley couldn't recover in time to reorganize and actually shut down for one year. Excelsior and Hopkins moved to the Twin Cities Suburban League, where the Lakers edged out Soderville for the pennant and then won the playoffs.

Don Eliason broke his leg in the last league playoff game, a 4–3 win over Soderville. Seltz appealed to TC Suburban League officials for a replacement, as was a common practice at the time. He brought Buffalo first baseman Dick Siebert to the first regional playoff game with Minnesota River champion Le Center. Siebert went 4 for 5 to the protests of LeCenter partisans. Former teammate Rich Weigel, who was drafted from Monticello, went the distance in a 14–3 win. To quiet Le Center, which was appealing to the MABA state directors, Seltz agreed

to drop Siebert for the rest of the series. Region 1A directors permitted him to draft Elk River first baseman Don McPherson instead. It probably didn't make much difference, as the Lakers pitching fell apart, and Le Center won the next three games, 13–5, 6–5 and 16–5, to capture the regional title.

Excelsior was back in a new four-team Minnesota Valley League again in 1951, along with Hopkins, Bloomington, and Shakopee Kopp's

Gene Cooney, shown with Twin City Ordnance Plant in 1944, pitched for eight State Tournament teams from 1945 to 1953. Photograph by Lefty Evans; courtesy of Don Evans.

Realty—Shakopee's number two team. The league members had agreed to cut back on player expenses, and it showed. Excelsior won the league playoffs and then lost two straight to Le Center, 25–10 and 9–0, in Region 1A playoffs.

The team's next chance to make the State Tournament was in 1955 when they went undefeated in league play and playoffs but were upset by Twin Trails League champion Hutchinson in Region 3A playoffs. Joe Hutton Jr. was back after his hiatus at Willmar and military service. The team featured two former University of Minnesota pitchers, Dale Engstrand—a veteran of the state's Class AA leagues—and Don Streeter. Former Gopher Whitey Skoog, now with the NBA Minneapolis Lakers, joined the team in 1953 and was an occasional starter.

The team had been handicapped somewhat over the years by the lack of lights at their home field at Excelsior Commons. They frequently rented lights to play "home" games at Chaska, Shakopee, or Anoka. They dropped down to Class B when the Minnesota Valley League folded after the 1957 season.

Chaska: The Miracle Cubs

The Chaska Cubs won their last regular-season game with Jordan in 1947 to take fourth place in the Minnesota Valley League and just squeak into league playoffs. Then they caught fire and beat St. Peter and Bloomington to win the league championship, and followed that with series victories over Burnsville and Kenyon to win the Region 11A berth in the State Tournament.

The stretch drive was made possible by a late season "acquisition." Excelsior was going nowhere —having been all but mathematically eliminated from achieving a first-division finish to qualify for the playoffs—and agreed to release pitcher Don

Anderson so that he could sign with Chaska before the July 15 signing deadline. St. Peter protested Anderson's eligibility during the playoffs, but he had played in three regular-season games for the Cubs, which met MABA rules.

Shortstop Bill Schalow and center fielder Roy Eder, who had brief minor-league seasons before WWII military service, were the team's leading hitters. For the State Tournament the Cubs drafted St. Peter catcher Bill Wettergren and two pitchers, Vern Bruhn from Excelsior and Gene Cooney from Bloomington. The postseason draftees played key roles in Chaska's sweep through the State Tournament Class A field.

Don Anderson and Gene Cooney combined on an unusual no-hitter in a first-round 1–0 victory over Maple Lake. Anderson had given up no hits for 8 ⅓ innings when he had to be removed because of a large blister on the index finger of his pitching hand. Cooney relieved and got the two remaining outs to complete the no-hitter. He picked up the win when Wettergren scored the game's only run on a throwing error in the bottom of the ninth inning. He had reached first base after a third-strike wild pitch by hard-luck loser Johnny Garbett.

Bruhn beat the New Ulm Millers 3–2 in the next game, and Gene Cooney stopped tournament-favorite Olivia 5–4 in the semifinals. Anderson started the championship game against the Rochester Queens but was wild and was relieved by Cooney in the fifth inning. Cooney picked up his third win in the tournament—two of them in relief. The Cubs knocked tournament MVP Gread McKinnis out of the box early in the game. Cooney and McKinnis had each pitched a complete game the previous day, and McKinnis was attempting his third start in four days.

Chaska lost to Excelsior in the playoffs in 1948 and 1949 and then moved with Shakopee

Chaska won the 1947 Class A state title, defeating Rochester and tourney MVP Gread McKinnis in the final. Batboys, *from left:* Ray Tschimperle, Jerry Lubansky, Vic Schlefsky, Tom Lubansky. *Front row:* Don Anderson, Bill Wettergren, Joel "Sparrow" Dressen, Matt Riesgraf, Hauser Lano, Gene Cooney, Vern Bruhn. *Back row:* manager Oscar "Candy" Gnan, Wally Lahl, Bill Schalow, Roy Eder, Clarence Soley, Earl "Scrubby" Engelhardt, Roger Riesgraf, Eddie Poppitz. Courtesy of Chaska Historical Society.

Delano, Glencoe, Howard Lake, Hutchinson, Maple Lake, Waverly, and Winsted, and a few others who were members one or two years. Winsted had an ambitious baseball program and dominated the league. They won the State Tournament in 1948, took third in 1949, and second in 1950. Glencoe took third place in 1947. In 1951 the North Star League split up over financial issues, as several teams wanted to cut down on the schedule and reduce spending. As a result, Winsted, Maple Lake, Watertown, and Delano withdrew from the league and joined with Buffalo and Monticello to form the Wright Star League. Watertown won the playoffs and the State Championship in 1951.

to the Minnesota River League in 1950. The two teams were the only towns in the Minnesota Valley League with significant fan followings, and they hoped to develop better rivalries with Belle Plaine, Jordan, Le Sueur, New Prague, Montgomery, Prior Lake, St. Peter, and Le Center—the other teams in that strong league. After two years, though, Chaska dropped out of Class A ball. Their Class B team made the State Tournament in 1952, where it beat Red Lake Falls 12–10 before losing to Kensington 10–8.

NORTH STAR/WRIGHT STAR LEAGUE

The North Star League was composed of smaller towns a little farther from Minneapolis than the Minnesota Valley teams—Brownton, Cokato,

Winsted: A Shooting Star

Winsted serves as a good exemplar for the ambitious, baseball-mad small towns in Minnesota in the late 1940s. The Winsted Warriors started up after the war in 1946. The team was unashamed about recruiting outside players and was a strong contender right out of the box. Their key acquisition in 1946 was St. Thomas College freshman pitcher Alex Romanchuck, who promptly became the ace of the North Star League.

Local manufacturer Millerbernd, Inc., installed lights on the team's bandbox field in 1946. Dimensions were 315 feet to left, 425 to center, and 269 to right. A 12-foot-high, 40-foot-long fence stood on a hill rising from the playing field and extending from the right field foul line toward center field. Millerbernd was contacted by so many towns who came to take a look at the installation that it soon became the leading supplier for lights all over the state. Attendance for Sunday-afternoon games had been high before the lights were installed, but midweek night games seemed to pick fan enthusiasm up another notch.

Romanchuck nearly caused his team a nervous breakdown in early August when he was chosen to represent Minnesota on a National Youth All-Star team that would play a three-game series with a group of Brooklyn All Stars at Ebbets Field, home of the Brooklyn Dodgers. While Romanchuck was being wined and dined at New York City nightclubs and visiting Madison Square Garden and Rockefeller Music Theatre, his Winsted mates were preparing to start the league playoffs. The club sent a congratulatory telegram to him at the St. George Hotel in Brooklyn but also asked if he would be home by Sunday.

Romanchuck did return in time, but the Warriors lost to Glencoe in the finals of the league playoffs. They lost to Glencoe again in 1947, but things turned around in 1948. Winsted went 12–2 to win the North Star League pennant by three games over Glencoe and Delano. University of Minnesota pitcher Lloyd Lundeen and Minneapolis cop and catcher Fred Wallner were the two

Alex Romanchuck, second from left, and his 1946 World All-Stars teammates were treated to a night on the town at Jack Dempsey's restaurant in New York. Courtesy of Alex Romanchuck.

outside players permitted by the MABA rules for Class A teams. Most of the other players on the team were from outside Winsted, as well, but established residency in town by April 1 and were provided jobs by Pure Milk—the team's major backer—and by Green Giant, Coast-to-Coast, Keating's Furniture, and George Rauf's Dray Line.

Pitchers Lundeen, Alex Romanchuck, and Vern Wroge were paid $50 per game (when they pitched) and Wallner $25. Most of the other players got $5 or $10 per game. The team payroll was about $150 per game. Crowds were great all season, with several estimated at between 3,000 and 3,500. At one hot Sunday afternoon game with archrival Waverly, Winsted sold out its 440-case supply of beer and had to make a run to Lester Prairie and New Germany for new supplies. The $2,640 in gross sales from 10,560 bottles—beer was 25¢ a pop at Winsted in 1948—certainly helped to pay some of the team's expenses.

Winsted swept Glencoe in two games in the first round of the playoffs, then beat Waverly three straight for the league championship, and followed that up with two-game sweeps over the

Winsted's field was a left-handed hitter's delight. The fence, which sat on top of a small incline, was only 280 feet down the right-field foul line. Courtesy of Herald-Journal Publishing, Winsted, Minnesota.

Tomahawk League champion New Ulm Millers and Martin County champion Ceylon in the Region 3A playoffs.

Winsted beat Worthington in the first game of the State Tournament, 8–3. Lundeen pitched eight shutout innings but weakened in the ninth. John Boller, a postseason draftee from Glencoe, came on in relief to finish the game. Boller and another postseason draftee, Delano pitcher Bob Hendrickson, combined to defeat co-favorite Shakopee and ace pitcher Gene Cooney 5–4 in 10 innings in the semifinals. Lundeen won his second tournament game by shutting down Belle Plaine, the other co-favorite, 6–4 in the championship game. He struck out 16 and gave up only six hits as Winsted beat another storied pitcher, Lefty Johnson. Winsted broke the game open with three runs in the fifth inning, highlighted by back-to-back home runs by Wallner and Lundeen.

The North Star League increased the schedule to 28 games in 1949 as teams sought to replace the steady diet of exhibition games that had been played in the past two years. Winsted cruised into the State Tournament favored to repeat. They started out well. Romanchuck beat Melrose 5–3 in the first round, but the Warriors were routed by Excelsior 17–1 in the semifinals. They returned again in 1950, losing a heartbreaker 4–3 to Le Center in the championship game.

Winsted played in three consecutive Class A State Tournaments from 1948 to 1950, winning the championship in 1948. *Front row, from left:* Bob Kasper, Cy Seymour, Pat Williamson, Art Hokenson, Ken Norman, Vern Wroge, Bud Seymour. *Middle row:* Dick Neumann, Jerry Hahn, Ken Keating, Alex Romanchuck, John Boller, Bob Hendrickson. *Back row:* Gordon Kubasch, Lloyd Lundeen, Herman Peschken, Bill Hasse, Fred Wallner. Batboy is Gene Heigl. Courtesy of Brian Larson.

rivalries. Delavan and Kiester (population 541) fans just loved to beat their larger rivals—Winnebago (2,127) and Blue Earth (3,843).

But they managed to be comrades once the games were over. Just before the State Tournament in 1953, for example, George Krohn and Gilbert Olson, owners of Blue Earth Monument Co., treated members of the Blue Earth and Delavan teams to a chicken dinner at the Legion Hall to thank the teams "because they played such good ball during the season." Blue Earth manager John Haase was the master of ceremonies, and the Blue Earth players—who had just lost to Delavan in the league playoffs—wished Delavan good luck in the State Tournament. Earlier in the year, several Delavan play-

Delavan players celebrate after the final out in the 1953 Class A championship game. Courtesy of Herb Schaper Historical Baseball Collection/*New Ulm Daily Journal.*

ers had tried to upstage a preseason celebration in Blue Earth, where team members were being introduced and honored. They put a large sign on a black hearse—"Bury the Blues"—and drove back and forth past the crowds. They also fueled barroom talk by claiming they'd signed Satchel Paige to pitch for Delavan that season.

Winnebago won the league playoffs five times—they were runner-up to Excelsior in the 1949 State Tournament and lost in the semifinals in 1951—while Delavan won three times, and Kiester once. Delavan's team became a contender when the school board hired Rich Weigel for the 1950–51 school year. Weigel was a St. Cloud State graduate who'd pitched for Excelsior's 1949 Class A champions. Delavan lost to Winnebago in 1951—which had recruited Southern Minny veteran pitcher Hank Nowacki—but won the league playoffs in 1952 and advanced to the State Tournament. They lost a tough 4–3 decision to St. Paul Kohl's in the first round of the tournament. Weigel, who'd had some arm problems during the year, had to leave the game after the eighth inning with a 3–2 lead.

Delavan went 11–1 in the league in 1953, four games ahead of Winnebago and Kiester, and then beat Winnebago and Blue Earth in the playoffs. The only significant problem that new manager Bill Murry seemed to have was the lack of a home field. Delavan played on a field at the high school that was torn up in early July for the construction of a school addition. For the next year and a half, Delavan played its home games at Winnebago. Actually, this wasn't much of a problem, as the team had used the lighted field at Winnebago for midweek exhibition and playoff games for several years, and it was only seven miles away.

Delavan beat Fillmore County League champion Preston to reach the State Tournament. Weigel beat Jordan ace and State Tournament veteran Johnny Garbett 1–0 in the first round and then came back to beat Minneapolis DeVac's 5–2 in the semifinals. In the championship game 5–3 win over Little Falls, Delavan broke the game open with three runs in the third. Starter Hank Nowacki, a postseason draftee from Winnebago, ran into trouble in the seventh and gave way to Weigel, who pitched 2⅔ innings of scoreless relief to preserve the victory. Weigel earned the tournament MVP award for his efforts.

It was to be Delavan's last trip to the State Tournament. Four key players did not return in 1954. Weigel left for a teaching and coaching job in Little Falls, his wife's hometown, and catcher Marv Hardy moved to Illinois. First baseman Ron Hall decided to play with his hometown, Estherville, Iowa, and outfielder Jim Murry—manager Bill Murry's younger brother—was called into military service. Southern Minny veteran pitcher Rollie Marquardt did a good job pitching, but Winnebago beat Delavan in the 1954 league playoff finals.

Sadly, by the early 1960s, the team folded when the veterans of the early 1950s had all retired and not enough young men could be found to field a team.

TOWNS MOVING DOWN FROM CLASS AA

Class AA peaked in 1950 with eight State Tournament entries, but by 1954 there were only two, and the class disappeared after 1957. From 1952 to 1958, four Class A State Championships were won by former Class AA teams in their first year of Class A competition—Cannon Falls in 1952, Benson in 1954, Waseca in 1957, and Austin in 1958. In addition, Fairmont won in 1959 in their second year in Class A.

Cannon Falls: Bears Move Down to Win a Title

West St. Paul had won the St. Paul Suburban League playoffs three of four years since the war when three new players arrived in Cannon Falls in 1949: pitcher Gail Mayo, who pitched Albert Lea to its fourth consecutive State Class AA championship in 1947; Dr. Jack Verby, once a power pitcher, but now a power hitter who had led the Southern Minny in hitting with a .404 average for Mankato in 1948; and Pete Kramer, an all-around athlete and center fielder for the Southern Minny's Waseca Blue Jays in 1948. The Bears won the 1949 league playoffs and went 2–2 in the Class AA State Tournament, with the last game a tough 3–2 loss to the eventual champion, Austin.

Verby and Kramer departed for Litchfield in 1950, but Cannon Falls kept building its team behind new manager Dick McCardle. Star pitcher and outfielder JeRoy Carlson started with the team in 1951 when he was hired as a teacher/coach by the high school. The Bears won the league playoffs again in 1950 and 1951 but were quickly eliminated in the State Class AA playoffs.

Cannon Falls' Bob Pagel is embraced by a teammate after a second-inning grand-slam home run in an 8–6 victory over the St. Paul Kohl's in the semifinals of the 1952 Class A tournament in Austin. *Star-Tribune* photograph; courtesy of the Minnesota Historical Society.

The St. Paul Suburban League, which had been Class AA since 1940, moved to Class A in 1952. Cannon Falls, with eight players back from their 1951 team, and with five with the team since 1949—Lou Davisson, George Goudy, Gail Mayo, Art McKinley, and Bob Pagel—won the league again and entered the State Class A tournament as favorites.

They didn't disappoint. They rolled over Twin Trails champion Brownton 13–1 in the opener, with Mayo and Ernie Mechelke, a postseason draftee from West St. Paul, splitting the pitching duties. JeRoy Carlson beat St. Paul Kohl's 8–6 in the semifinals to set up the dream championship match with Minnesota River League powerhouse Belle Plaine. Cannon Falls took an early lead, but Mayo ran into trouble in the eighth inning, giving up two runs on successive hits by Rollie Seltz, Gene O'Brien, and Bob Meyers. Mechelke came on in relief to stop the rally. Cannon Falls won the championship in the bottom of the tenth inning, when catcher Kelly Roth, who had hit into a triple play earlier in the game, drove in Mayo with the winning run in the exciting 5–4 game.

When Mayo, who was universally admired by

The Cannon Falls Bears won the 1952 Class A championship the year after the St. Paul Suburban League moved down from Class AA. *Front row, from left:* Art McKinley, Louis Davisson, George Goudy, John Burch, Don Stenhaug, manager Dick McCardle, batboy Jerry Wedin. *Back row:* Bob Pagel, JeRoy Carlson, Gail Mayo, Kelly Roth, Ernie Mechelke, Francis Penfield, Jack Holt, Pat Ryan, Max Mohr. Courtesy of Pat Ryan.

teammates and foes, decided to retire at the end of the season, some feared the team would lose its desire. However, they won the league championship again in 1953 but lost in the semifinals to Little Falls, 5–4, in their last State Tournament appearance in the era. The team dropped out of the St. Paul Suburban League after the 1956 season, played one season in the Class A Goodhue-Wabasha League and then the next three in the Class A Century League.

Waseca: Good-Bye to the Southern Minny

Much of Minnesota baseball lore revolves around the David versus Goliath story. We delight in the tales of a small rural town going head-to-head with a larger foe, or—better yet—taking on a large regional center or Twin Cities team. We have got feel-good stories to relish, like Delavan (population 302 in 1950) beating Minneapolis DeVac's (520,000) and Little Falls (6,717) on its way to the 1953 State Class A Championship. Or Milroy (population 268), the 1954 Class B State Champion, beating Benson (3,398), the Class A Champion, for the Mythical State Title and then, in 1955, beating Marshall (5,923) for the championship of the Class A First Night League.

Waseca (population 4,927) could also make a claim to the David role. By far the smallest town in the Southern Minny League—Owatonna, at 10,191, was the next smallest—Waseca battled evenly against its much larger rivals. As a matter of fact, in the heyday of the Southern Minny, from 1948 to 1954, the Waseca Braves' cumulative record was a third-best 151–119. They won the pennant outright in 1953 and tied for first with Austin in 1950 but never managed to win in the playoffs.

Waseca's struggles to field winning teams in Minnesota's top Class AA league illustrate the problems many teams faced all over the state as pressures to win forced teams to spend more and more money to compete. In 1948 the Southern Minny played a 28-game schedule. Waseca averaged about 1,300 fans for league and playoff games and managed to be competitive while breaking even financially. Player salaries were $8,089 (about $66,000 in 2005).

In January 1949, Waseca voters, by an overwhelming 992–179 margin, approved the expenditure of $15,000 to install lights at the community baseball field. This made it possible for the Southern Minny to go to a three-games-per-week, 35-game schedule. Waseca and Faribault had been the only teams in the league without lights in 1948, but both now had them installed for the 1949 season.

In theory, the extra games would bring in ex-

Arleigh Kraupa *(right)*, shown with catcher Gene Farrell in 1946, was a fixture in Waseca until his retirement in early 1954. Courtesy of Waseca County Historical Society.

tra revenues and, since most players were paid by the month, wouldn't increase payrolls. However, competitive pressures drove up the bidding for out-of-state college and professional players. By 1950, Waseca's payroll was up to $14,746 (after taxes). Rochester topped the league at $24,598. At a net $0.50 per ticket (ticket prices were $0.60, but $0.10 went for federal amusement taxes), Waseca needed an additional 13,314 in attendance just to pay for salaries in 1950 compared to 1948.

Waseca managed to do that. They drew 36,926 fans—an average of 1,846 per game for 20 league and playoff games—and topped the 1948 total by 13,326 fans, but other expenses, like umpires, transportation, and social security and withholding taxes, also drove up costs. Despite donations of over $3,000, the team wound up $748 in the red. The baseball association discussed withdrawal from the Southern Minny at its annual meeting in late October but decided to continue in the league. They planned to raise $5,500 before the start of the 1951 season to pay off the 1950 debt and to provide a cushion to begin the new year.

The next four years offered no relief, however, as local fans and merchants were forced to raise up to $10,000 each year to field the team. Waseca joined with nearby Owatonna to field a joint team, the Twins, in 1955 and 1956. The change seemed to make things worse. Merchants in both towns still had to raise a lot of money to support the team, and somehow performance on the field took a nosedive. Waseca and Owatonna had each finished 22–22 in 1954, tied for fifth place. The Twins finished in the cellar with a 16–33 record in 1955 and were on their way to a similar record in 1956 when the towns threw in the towel and folded the team. Ostensibly, the cause was the Pete Deem incident described in part 1 of this book, but supporters in both towns were simply tired of the constant fund raising.

Field manager Warren Dunn, in uniform, holds the 1957 Class A championship trophy, while to his right his father and team business manager Dutch Dunn looks on proudly. *Dispatch–Pioneer Press* photograph; courtesy of the Minnesota Historical Society.

Waseca baseball supporters had no thoughts at all about rejoining the Southern Minnesota League in 1957. They were unanimous in the desire to support a baseball team, however, and entered the Braves—the nickname of their former Southern Minny team—in the Class A Minnesota River League. Their Class B team, which had been a fixture in the Four County League, was dropped.

Dutch Dunn, a local businessman, was appointed manager of the team, and he pulled in players from around the area. Pitcher Vern Edmunds, who owned a grocery store in Waseca, was the only carryover from the 1956 Waseca-Owatonna Twins. Dutch's son Warren and Don Schmudlach were signed from Owatonna's 1956 Class B Four County League State Tournament team. Schmudlach, a five-year minor-league veteran, pitched for the Twins and Rochester in the Southern Minny in 1955 and started the year with the Twins in 1956, but he was released and signed up with Owatonna. Dunn also recruited two teachers from Owatonna—Roger Anderson (who played on the Gophers team in 1954 and 1955) and Merle Knoll—and New Richland basketball star Roger Edgar, who was also playing baseball at Luther College. The rest of the team was from Waseca. However, Owatonna and New Richland were less than 15 miles from Waseca and met the requirement for "local" players.

Waseca, which finished 12–6 in the regular season, lucked out when New Ulm, 16–2 with four wins over the Braves, lost to St. Peter in the first round of the playoffs. Waseca won series victories over Le Sueur, St. Peter, and Belle Plaine to capture the league championship. Fred Bruckbauer, a postseason draftee from New Ulm, beat Bloomington, the Minnesota Valley champions, 4–3 in the first game of the Region 4A playoffs. Then, on Labor Day, Edmunds, pitching on one day's rest—he had beaten Belle Plaine 3–2 on

After years in the tough Class AA Southern Minnesota League, Waseca stepped down to Class A in 1957 and immediately won a state title. *Front row:* Bob Gigeay, Swede Swenson, Warren Dunn, Bob Sandburg, Mike Gray, Jimmy Howard, and Pinky Yess. *Back row:* John King, Don Schmudlach, Roger Anderson, Vern Edmunds, Bob Johnson, Roger Edgar, Merle Knoll, and Shyde Krause. Courtesy of Waseca Historical Society.

Saturday night in the final game of the league playoffs—shut out the powerful Bloomington team 1–0 to advance to the State Tournament.

Edmunds almost single-handedly won the State Class A Tournament. He shut out Minneapolis Kopp's 2–0, on three hits and 17 strikeouts, in the team's opening game on Saturday, September 7. Then on Thursday he pitched a one-hitter, with 13 strikeouts, to beat Kiester 2–0. St. Paul Briteway Cleaners made things difficult by defeating the Braves 5–1 on Friday night. Starter Fred Bruckbrauer gave up three runs in the first inning and was replaced by Otey Clark (a postseason draftee from St. Peter) without getting an out.

The Class A tournament now had three teams with one loss, and officials decided to draw names out of a hat to determine the opponents for the next game. Waseca got the long straw and sat back and watched Briteway eliminate Kiester 11–2 at a game starting Sunday noon. Edmunds wasn't as sharp as he had been earlier in the tournament, but he beat Briteway in the championship game Sunday night 6–4. He gave up six hits and struck out 10, but he also walked six. For the tournament he had three wins and 40 strikeouts,

gave up only four runs in 27 innings pitched, and was voted the Most Valuable Player. Edmunds also shut out Class B Champion Braham 8–0 the following Sunday in Waseca to win the Mythical Championship game.

The Braves returned to the Minnesota River League in 1958 but struggled all year. Edmunds got a sore arm and didn't pitch after June. The team finished in a tie for last place with St. Peter and was swept by Sleepy Eye in two games in the first round of the playoffs.

Waseca moved to the Class A Century League in 1959, but the change of scenery did not do much good. Edmunds was still unable to pitch—in fact, he asked to be released in late July—and when Owatonna also fielded a team in the Century League, Owatonna players formerly with

Waseca went back home to play. (Owatonna had only a Class B team in 1957 and 1958.) The Braves were competitive when veteran Whitey Felker pitched—he was 9–7 with a 2.09 ERA—but the team lacked offense. They finished with a 10–16 record, good for fourth out of five in the Century South Division, and attendance was poor all year. The low point came in a game against last-place Rochester on Sunday, August 9, when only 134 fans showed up. Interest in baseball had gotten so low that no one got organized in time to enter a team in a league for 1960. In mid-June a group of players got together to form an informal team, and they played exhibitions the rest of the season, mostly with teams from the Four County League, which had seven teams, and, consequently, one with a bye each week.

A NEW ERA

When the Minneapolis Teamsters won the 1956 Class A State Tournament, it marked the first time a Twin Cities team had won a State Championship since 1943. It also marked a developing trend that had veteran metropolitan area players coming home and younger players staying home to play baseball. There were simply fewer out-state teams paying for players. Class AA was down to two leagues, and the Western Minny rookie rule further limited the number of roster spots available. Class A teams all over the state were also cutting back on expenses. Most now only paid salaries to pitchers and catchers. Bloomington assembled a team full of veterans of the state's Class AA leagues, and was a threat to win the State Championship every year from 1956 to 1960.

Gopher coach Dick Siebert left Litchfield, where he had been player/manager for four years, to form the Minneapolis Kopp's Realty team in 1955. Composed mostly of young Gopher baseball candidates, Kopp's won the Park National League playoffs but lost two straight in the State Tournament. In 1957, Siebert started a Gopher development team in Edina and entered it in the Minnesota Valley League. The Twin Cities Federal team, managed by future Minnesota Twins executive Don Cassidy, won the Park National playoffs in 1959 and 1960 with a roster stocked with current and former Gophers. The young stars were a little overwhelmed in the 1959 State Tournament, managing only one hit in two games while losing to St. Peter 3–0, and Bloomington 4–0.

Minneapolis Teamsters: Bums Regain Respect

Manager Hank Nash blended a bunch of veterans with a few youngsters to field a team that snuck up on everyone to capture the 1956 Class A State Tournament championship. His leading pitchers were young St. Mary's College star Dave Theis, and veterans Gordy Crichton, who was appearing in his third State Tournament, and Bob Gormley, who had played one year of minor-league baseball in 1952. Leading hitters were North High's Dick Cassidy, who had played for several out-state teams, and Len Feriancek, who had four seasons in the minor leagues, interrupted by two years of military service. Feriancek was one of nine brothers who played with Blackduck at various times. Four brothers were in the starting lineup for Blackduck's 1946 State Tournament team.

The Teamsters were not even mentioned in the lists of pretournament favorites in 1956, and they didn't help their image by losing to Little Falls 12–6 in the first round. However, they won three straight to set up a rematch with Little Falls, also at 3–1, in the championship game.

Little Falls hometown fans, sensing a title after finishing in second place in 1953 and 1954, and third place in 1955, were loud—and unmerciful, calling the Teamsters "Washington Avenue Bums" and reminding them of the thrashing they received by the Red Sox in the earlier game. Little Falls hoped to be the first tournament host to win a State Championship since Albert Lea in 1945. Their jeers were silenced in the fifth inning when a run-scoring single by Feriancek and a three-run home run by Cassidy gave the Teamsters a lead they never relinquished. Theis won the game with 7⅓ innings of solid relief pitching. Crichton won one other game, and Bob Berglund, a veteran drafted from Kopp's, won two games in the tournament, one a clutch two-inning relief performance to beat St. Paul Lorence Rec 6–5.

Nash moved to Minneapolis Kopp's in 1957.

Minneapolis Teamsters won the 1956 Class A title to become the first Minneapolis or St. Paul team to claim a title since 1943. *Front row:* Bob Kammerer, Frank Litecky, Duane Peterson, Bob Gormley, Duke Snider, Jim Diedrich. *Second row:* Larry Shobe, Kenny Kirberger, Lenny Feriancek, Pete Guzy, Leo Schleisman, W. C. Duffy. *Back row:* Bill Campbell, Dick Cassidy, Jim Bednarczyk, Lenny Johnson, Dave Theis, manager Hank Nash, Teamsters Local 544 principal officer Fred Snider. Courtesy of Dick Cassidy.

He brought Gormley, Cassidy, and Crichton with him and added Gophers Woody Erickson, Skeeter Nelson, Pete Badali, Doug Gillen, and Bill Sandback to form another strong team. Kopp's won the Park National League playoffs but lost to eventual champion Waseca 4–0 in the first round of the State Tournament. They beat West Central champ Breckenridge-Wahpeton 6–5 in their next game, but then were eliminated by Kiester, 5–2.

Bloomington: Twins' Home Wins
State Championship

The peaceful, small-town suburb of Bloomington grew from 3,647 in 1940 to 9,902 in 1950. Then it really began to grow; it finally threw off its village form of government in 1958, and its population hit 50,498 in 1960, when it was selected as an "All-American City." Bloomington was selected for the site of Metropolitan Stadium, which opened in 1956 and for five years was home to the Minneapolis Millers of the American Association. It became a big-league city in 1961 when the Washington Senators moved to Bloomington and became the Minnesota Twins.

Bloomington's rise as a power in state amateur baseball seemed to mirror the growth of the city. The Bloomington Athletics played in the strong Class A Minnesota Valley League throughout its existence. Its Class B Red Birds, originally formed as a joint team with Richfield in 1948, went on their own in 1950 and made the State Tournament. The Athletics were also-rans in the Minnesota Valley until 1956 but fi-

From left: Jack Preston, Gene Elder, Jim Carroll, Buster Radebach, Paul Scanlon, and Jim Sticka played Class AA ball before sharing in Bloomington's 1960 Class A title. Elder, Radebach, and Scanlon also were former pros. *Star-Tribune* photograph; courtesy of the Minnesota Historical Society.

nally won the playoff championships in 1956 and 1957.

The Athletics' success had more to do with the demise of Class AA baseball than with the city's rapid rise in population, however. With only two Class AA leagues in the state, there were fewer opportunities for players to earn good money by playing summer baseball. Class A leagues had also cut back, and most were paying only their catchers and pitchers. Consequently, men who lived in the metropolitan area and wanted to continue to play baseball turned more and more to local teams.

Bloomington Manager George Thomas Sr. built a powerhouse in 1956. He signed veterans like Gene Olive, a coach at Richfield, who played three years in the minor leagues and then seven with Waseca in the Southern Minny; Paul Scanlon, who had two years in the minors and five years in the West Central, Southern Minny, and Western Minny; and Jack Preston. Gene Elder, a former University of Minnesota player, who played three years in the West Central, was just coming back to Minnesota after a two-year try in the minor leagues. Current Gopher George "Tommy" Thomas also signed with the team. Tommy was manager George Sr.'s son. George's other son Jerry pitched the NCAA Little World Series championship game for the Gophers in 1956 and was pitching for St. James in the Western Minny. (Scanlon, who moonlighted as a scout for the Detroit Tigers, signed both brothers to professional contracts in 1957.)

The Athletics unseated defending Class A champion St. Peter, the repeat Minnesota River League playoff winners, in the regional playoffs, and were co-favorites with Little Falls at the State Tournament in Little Falls. They beat St. Paul Lorence Rec 5–1 in their opening game and then upended Little Falls 6–4 on an erratic pitching performance by Tommy Thomas. He gave up only two hits, struck out 13, but walked 13. Bloomington was eliminated when they lost two straight, 8–7 to Pipestone in 11 innings, and 8–3 to the eventual champions, Minneapolis Teamsters.

The Athletics won the Minnesota Valley League playoffs again in 1957 but were upset in the regional playoffs by Minnesota River champion Waseca, which went on to win the State Championship. The Minnesota Valley League folded after the 1957 season, and the team joined the newly formed Century League. They won the

Bloomington's Wayne Tjaden was no slouch at the plate, but it was his pitching that earned him 1960 MVP honors. Courtesy of Don Evans.

playoffs and beat St. Paul Park, the St. Paul Suburban League champs, in the regional playoffs, only to be disqualified by a protest. St. Paul Park was given the state tournament berth when the MBA ruled that Bloomington had three outside players on its team, while Class A rules permitted only two.

Bloomington's quest for a state title was derailed again in 1959, but this time on the field. They won the Century North championship—the league was split into two divisions, with each winner going to the State Tournament—but ran into the Fairmont buzz saw, losing 11–5 in the second round and 14–2 in the final game.

The Athletics won the Century League playoffs—only one team going to the State this time—again in 1960 and finally, after a five-year quest, won the State Class A Championship. Their lineup included six veterans with many years of state Class AA experience, two former University of Minnesota players, and pitcher Wayne Tjaden, a native of Des Moines, Iowa, who spent three years in the Chicago Cubs farm system. They were upset by undefeated St. Paul Como Rec in the opening game 6–3, but roared back through the losers' bracket with three easy wins—7–1 over host Springfield, 5–0 over Stillwater, and 8–4 over Mankato—to earn another shot at Como Rec.

The finals, scheduled for Sunday, September 18, were delayed two weeks by rain, which was a lucky break for Bloomington—ace pitcher Wayne Tjaden pitched eight innings in the Mankato game on September 17. With two weeks' rest, Tjaden went 8 innings to beat Como Rec 10–2 in the first game and then came back to pitch 2⅔ innings in relief to preserve the 8–4 victory in the championship game. Tjaden, who started and won three games and relieved in two others, was selected as the tournament MVP.

CLASS B: SMALL TOWNS WITH BIG DREAMS

CLASS B WAS CREATED BY THE MINNEsota Amateur Baseball Association in 1948 in response to complaints about creeping—rampant, some claimed—professionalism by many of the state's existing Class A teams. The decision was an immediate hit; 339 teams, just over 50 percent of the state roster, chose to play in the new class. In 1950, when the MABA hit an all-time high of 799 teams, 73 percent of them were in Class B, and by 1960 the figure was 90 percent.

The rules for Class B were simple: teams must have no outside players and pay no salary whatsoever. Class A teams were permitted two outside players, while there were no restrictions on salaries in either Class A or Class AA. Some Class B teams found ways to dance around the rules, but for the most part Class B was amateur baseball in the strictest sense.

School boards in some towns, for example, helped the local town team by hiring teacher/coaches who were also good baseball players. Other towns were able to attract college players with summer jobs and "establish" a local residency for the athlete before the MABA deadline, although this practice was much less frequent in

Class B than in Class A. Still other towns worked around the salary restriction by treating the team treasury as a nonprofit organization and distributing the excess funds at the end of the season. By the end of the era, however, very few teams had excess funds.

Although Class B was known as the "small town" division, membership was not based on a community's population. In fact, the St. Cloud Moose—a team fashioned from a city with a population of 28, 410—won the first Class B title in 1948. Little Falls (population 6,717) won the 1949 Class B crown, and in the late 1950s champions included Bemidji (9,958) in 1956, Pipestone (5,324) in 1958 and 1960, and Shakopee (5,201) in 1959.

Some of the growth in the division was the result of former Class AA and Class A cities electing to move down to avoid the expenses of continued competition in those divisions. Willmar, the 1952 Class AA champion, dropped to Class A from 1955 to 1957 but eventually wound up supporting three Class B teams—the Kernels in the Corn Belt League, and the Cardinals and Air Force Base in the Super Eight. The Kernels qualified for the

1958 and 1960 State Tournaments, the city's first postseason appearances since 1952. Many leagues bounced around in classifications. The First Night League sent teams to the State Tournament in all three classes. Fergus Falls and Springfield, as well as Willmar, hit the trifecta by sending their primary teams to the State Tournament at least once in each of the three classes during the era.

Crow River Valley League champion Lester Prairie (population 663) gave the State Tournament a small-town charm by winning Class B in 1950, as Doug Dibb shut out the Duluth Teve's, a team from a city with a population of 104,511. The 1953 championship game triumph of Rollingstone (population 315) over Holdingford (458) was the small-town dream game. Tiny Milroy (268) gave the class bragging rights when it defeated 1954 Class A champion Benson in the Mythical State Championship game.

From 1948 to 1960, Class B provided the tournament some of its most memorable events—some of them days of triumph, others days of sadness. There was the joy for the many first-time teams such as Inger, a group of Chippewa Indians from the Leech Lake Reservation, who won the hearts of fans at the 1953 State Tournament in New Ulm. There was also Warroad, a perennial Cinderella team, qualifying for 10 consecutive state tournaments and 11 times in 12 years, but rarely making it past the first round. There was sadness for Lake Henry in 1959, playing in its first State Tournament game ever only hours after burying its left fielder, accidentally killed at work one day after the team qualified for the tournament.

St. Cloud: Big Town Wins First Small-Town Tourney

St. Cloud has always been a hotbed of baseball interest. Over the years the city usually had two or more teams entered in leagues affiliated with the MBA. In addition, many local players drifted out to play in surrounding towns such as Clear Lake, Luxemburg, St. Stephen, and Rockville. In 1948, the St. Cloud Sportsmen, St. Cloud Vets, and Waite Park played in the Class A Big Town League, while the St. Cloud Moose Lodge moved to Class B. The Central Minnesota League had voted to move to the newly created Class B, and the Moose—the 1947 league playoff champions and State Tournament entrant—decided to stay with the league.

The roster was a mix of St. Cloud Cathedral and Technical High School graduates. Although the team didn't attract much attention at home—crowds were sparse—*Star Tribune* columnist Ted Peterson and the *Pioneer Press*'s Bob Schabert picked the Moose as the Class B favorites. In truth, no one really knew what to expect in the popular new class.

Rudy "Cobby" Saatzer pitched a two-hitter, and Don Winter hit a home run to beat Dalton 8–1 in the team's opening game of the State Tournament in Shakopee. Saatzer, who had played briefly earlier in the year with Enterprise, Alabama, in the Class D Alabama State League, had three brothers who also played in the minor leagues. He later became a major-league scout and worked for the Minnesota Twins. Bob Kinsel, a postseason draftee from Kingston, started the next game against Lester Prairie. Saatzer came on in relief in the eighth inning, when Lester Prairie scored two runs to tie the game. He drove in a run in the bottom of the 12th inning to win the game 6–5.

Neil Rengel, a 45-year-old veteran, started the championship game against the Springfield Cubs and was leading 9–0 after six innings and had given up only two hits. However, he ran into trouble in the seventh, giving up five runs. Saatzer

came in to relieve again and shut down the Cubs the rest of the way as St. Cloud won easily, 12–5.

The Moose dynasty only lasted one year, as several players departed to pay-for-play teams. Saatzer and Kinsel wound up back in the 1949 State Tournament with Class A Winsted. No other St. Cloud teams made the State Tournament in the 1945–60 era, although many individual players were on the rosters of teams that did.

Lester Prairie: Success without Hired Help

In the foyer of Lester Prairie's town hall, the 1950 Class B state championship trophy is prominently displayed near a team photo and a scuffed, muddy

The 1948 St. Cloud Moose were the first champions of the newly created Class B. They had been first-round losers in Class A in 1947. *Front row, from left:* Jerry Becker, Sev Hagen, Ray Jaeger, Bing Miller, Vern Winter, batboy Ronny Raeder. *Back row:* Don Winter, manager Speed Winter, Bud Streitz, Rudy "Cobby" Saatzer, Junie Weisbruck, Gene Rengel. Photograph from the collection of the Stearns History Museum, St. Cloud, Minnesota.

baseball. Welcome to the town the *Minneapolis Tribune* sportswriter Ted Peterson once described as the "state's amateur baseball capital."

Although town team ball vanished from the summer calendar long before the turn of the century, the small exhibit represents a major achievement in a special period. At a time when small towns went on spending sprees to build a winning program, Lester Prairie succeeded without hired help.

"We had a lot of good athletes around here then," former Lester Prairie regular Bruce Birkholz said. "Some forget that in 1941, this town with a population of around 450 qualified for the Minnesota state basketball tournament, and that's when there was only one classification and eight teams. We also had some excellent pitching. We had five players who were capable of getting the job done."

In addition to the basketball crowd, young Lester Prairie athletes developed baseball skills through the 1940s, including players such as Doug Dibb, a precocious left-handed pitcher who would become one the state's premier Class B pitchers. Everyone on the roster lived well within the mileage range required to qualify as a local; in fact, the town's talent pool was so large that some good players were forced to play elsewhere. Once on the roster, commitment was a

Lester Prairie pitchers gave up only three runs in four games to win the 1950 Class B State Tournament. *Front row, from left:* batboy Roger Emich, Gordon Kubasch, Wallace Dibb, Arden Lung, Elton Klaustermeier, mascot David Kopischke. *Middle row:* Orland Kruschke, Louis Jenneke, Douglas Dibb, Oscar Rolf, Bruce Birkholz, Bill Ernst. *Back row:* Earl Machemehl, Bert McCarthy, Walter Wichelmann, Edward Hoese, Duane Meyer, Orval Birkholz, manager Everett Kuhlmann, scorer Milo Schultz. Courtesy of Doug Dibb.

prerequisite. The team played 52 games one season despite not having a lighted field, and practices were frequent and well attended.

Not that baseball wasn't fun. "We would celebrate [winning], but we weren't out on Saturday night before the game partying . . . never. No sir," Doug Dibb said. "Sunday was a big day for all of us, and we played hard while we were there."

The experienced players and youngsters combined to make Lester Prairie a perennial Crow River Valley contender, and the town's team reached the state tournament four times between 1948 and 1953.

Some didn't expect to reach the tournament in 1950 when the town finished behind undefeated Norwood in the regular season. But the team made a resolute move through the playoffs and upset the regular-season champions. Then, after drafting pitchers Bert McCarthy from Green Isle and Ed Hoese from Mayer, they wound up playing the opening game of the 1950 State Tournament at St. Cloud.

Lester Prairie beat Ulen 8–1 in that opener, the start of one of the most overwhelming sweeps in state tourney history. Manager Everett Kuhlmann's team outscored four opponents 21–3 in four games, and three Lester pitchers allowed only 15 hits in four complete games—Dibb giving up 7 hits in two victories, and McCarthy and Hoese each allowing 4 in their decisions.

This was a triumphant season for fans in this tiny community. They loved baseball and faithfully attended games, and many even showed up for practices. Baseball was a family affair in summers back then.

"Those were the good times," Arlene Dibb said, looking back. "You'd pack up the family and go to the games. All the players' kids were about the same age, and they'd have a ball. It was our life every Sunday of every summer for a long time."

Soderville's Dave Spencer gets a lift from teammates after a 1–0 victory over Scarles in the 1951 Class B championship game. Longtime Soderville baseball booster Iver Soderquist is on the left. *Star-Tribune* photograph; courtesy of the Minnesota Historical Society.

Soderville: The Outlaws Repeat

Soderville was an unincorporated village, just a dot on the intersection of U.S. 65 and Crosstown Boulevard in the northern part of current-day Ham Lake, yet it had a powerhouse team from the late 1940s through 1958. The Outlaws—the team took the name when they successfully fought several player eligibility protests in 1952—won consecutive Class B State Championships in 1951 and 1952 but were also competitive in Class A before and after those triumphs.

Iver and Albert Soderquist, who were sons of the village's Swedish founders, John and Anna Soderquist, were the men behind the baseball team. They operated a general store, and Iver doubled as the village postmaster. Iver also worked tirelessly for the Soderville Athletic Association, the sponsor for the team, and he and Albert donated the land for a new baseball field built in 1951.

The team began to gel in 1946, when returning World War II veteran Dick Johnson joined the

team. He and new friend—and old competitor—Quint Peterson built up the team initially by recruiting friends in Columbia Heights and the surrounding areas. Although Soderville itself consisted of about 30 residents, the MABA 15-mile recruiting radius extended into Columbia Heights, and toward Anoka and Forest Lake. In later years, up to five University of Minnesota players were on the roster—some who established summer residency in Soderville to become eligible for the team.

Led by Johnson, who caught and hit third for the team, Soderville won its first title in 1947, when they beat Anoka for the playoff championship of the Class A Independent Central League. They played in the Class A Twin Cities Suburban League from 1948 to 1950. They lost to defending State Class A Champion Excelsior in a tough three-game playoff series in 1950.

Soderville stayed with the league when it voted to move down to Class B in 1951. Johnson, now the manager, retained six players from the 1950 squad and handily won the league and regional

Soderville, a township near Minneapolis, won the 1951 Class B title, relying heavily on college players. *Front row, from left:* Milt Gregoire, Dave Spencer, Dan Anderson, Bill Marchiniak, Quinton Peterson, John Norton, batboy David Williams. *Back row:* Jerry Meyers, Jim Faust, Leo Schleisman, Dick Johnson, George Masko, Larry Winkler, Arnie Oss. Courtesy of Verna Lee.

playoffs. Dave Spencer, one of the holdovers, was selected as the State Tournament MVP. He no-hit Pengilly 17–0 in six innings in the first round and threw a one-hitter to defeat Searles 1–0 in the championship game. Seven players on the team were from Columbia Heights.

The team was strengthened for 1952 by the pickup of Gopher pitcher Norb Koch and outfielder Frank Larson and easily won the State Class B Championship again, topping Verndale 14–3, Bemidji 9–2, Kensington 12–3, and Pine City 15–5.

The MBA had been disturbed all season by eligibility questions raised about the team, but no protests had been made to stick. Nevertheless, the MBA told Soderville to find a Class A league in 1953. They joined the Minnesota Valley League and, strengthened by the additions of Gophers Chuck Bosacker and Jerry Kindall, won the league playoffs, but were beaten in the Region 2A playoffs by Little Falls. The 1954 team made it into the Class A State Tournament, but they lost two straight.

The Outlaws stayed in the Minnesota Valley League for two more years and then moved to the St. Paul Suburban League for the 1957 and 1958 seasons. Fan support had declined gradually since the early 1950s, and Soderville did not field a team in 1959 and 1960.

Rollingstone: A Charmed Year

A Sunday afternoon game in Rollingstone (population 315 in 1950), nestled in the Mississippi bluff country just northwest of Winona, was the quintessential Minnesota baseball experience in the 1940s and 1950s. The hometown Merchants team made the State Tournament four times—

A lazy Sunday at Rollingstone field, nestled in the bluffs near Winona and the Mississippi River in southeastern Minnesota. Courtesy of Jack Rader.

1951 in Class A and 1952, 1953, and 1955 in Class B—and was the focus of the town's social calendar in the summer.

A new field, with grandstand seating for 500, had been built in 1948, but many fans watched from an adjoining park, where there were picnic facilities and a pavilion, or from their cars, which could be parked along the left-field foul line. Some fans wandered back and forth from the field to the park during the game. There was no fence to cordon off the park from the baseball field, but someone from the team would walk through the park to collect donations.

Town merchants were originally planning to install lights, like their archrival Lewiston, but Bob Rader, who was responsible for pulling the post–World War II team together, talked them out of it. He argued that most small-town lights were inadequate, poorly maintained, and would eventually be too costly to sustain. The team could rent lighted fields at Gabrych Park in Winona for $40 per game, or in nearby Lewiston or Alma, Wisconsin. The team had no problem drawing fans to these distant "home" games. In 1954, for example, 1,812 fans attended the Hiawatha League playoff finals on a Wednesday night in Gabrych Park to see Lewiston beat Rollingstone 9–2.

The team really didn't need lights. They resisted the temptations of many other teams in the era and stayed with Sundays-only leagues.

Rollingstone outscored the opposition 51–16 in four games to capture the 1953 State Class B championship—and they did it without draft choices. *Front row, from left:* Dewey Clinkscales, Jack Maus, Bob Schmit, Bob Rader, Johnny Harper, Steve Rader, batboy Jack Rader. *Back row:* Coach Cyril Schmit, manager Dick Rader, Joe Weis, Bart Weaver, Erwin Ehmke, Roy Wise, Myles Vaughn, Joe Drazkowski. Courtesy of Herb Schaper Historical Baseball Collection/*New Ulm Daily Journal.*

That's not to say that they weren't serious competitors, however. The team held hard practice sessions on Tuesday and Thursday evenings during the season.

Baseball certainly was a Rader family pastime. By the early 1950s, Steve and Dick Rader joined Bob on the team. On Sundays, the boys would go to church and then after breakfast do field maintenance—dragging the field, spraying down the dirt, and chalking the baselines—before going home to dress for the game. By the late fifties, after Bob left for a job in Michigan, younger brother Jack, a batboy in the early fifties, joined his brothers on the town team.

The team started to build strength in 1948 and 1949, when they played in the tough Class A Bi-State League. The MABA bumped the Bi-State into Class AA because of outside players used by other teams, but Rollingstone had always relied on its own home players. Rollingstone ran into another MABA ruling in 1951, when they won the Class B Hiawatha League playoffs, but found themselves in a Class A regional when other teams in the league were found to be illegally using outside players. State rules at the time punished the whole league if only one team were found to be in violation. The Merchants took the decision in stride and beat Fillmore-Houston League champion Spring Grove to advance to the State Tournament, but found themselves matched against defending Class AA champion Fergus Falls, who had moved down to Class A, and lost in the first round, 12–3.

Rollingstone returned to the State Tournament in 1952 and lost in the first round to Pierz in the Class B bracket, but things came together for the team in 1953, the magical year. The team played its usual Sunday schedule during the summer, going 9–2 in league play, and 1–1 in exhibitions. The Merchants had two strong left-handed pitchers in Dick Rader and Dewey Clinkscales, and the batters hit their stride in the league playoffs, scoring 54 runs in three winning games.

The team couldn't find another pitcher in the league to draft who could make the regional playoffs and State Tournament, but felt they were strong enough with Clinkscales and Dick Rader. They were right. Merchants hitters stayed hot, and the team won three straight Region 5B playoff games by a combined 26–5 margin. Then they beat Inger 17–2 and Park Rapids 21–11 in the first two rounds of the State Tournament. They almost stumbled in the semifinals but rallied with two runs in the seventh inning and three in the eighth to beat Ada 6–2.

In the championship game against Holdingford, Dick Rader gave up a run in the first but pitched shutout ball the rest of the way. The game was tight. Holdingford pitcher Lefty Ebnet was trying for his fourth tournament win, but Rollingstone broke the game open with three runs in the sixth inning and three in the seventh to win 7–1. There were a lot of Merchants hitting heroes in the tournament, but Joe Drazkowski came through with a five-for-seven performance in the tough games against Ada and Holdingford.

In 1954 the team lost to Lewiston in the Hiawatha League playoffs, but in 1955, bolstered by the addition of two players from the Winona Chiefs of the Southern Minny—submarine-ball pitcher Hugh Orphan and first baseman Norm Snyder (who had purchased a tavern in Rollingstone)—the team cruised into the State Tournament as the favorite in Class B. They won their first two games, 15–4 over Wheaton and 1–0 over a tough Bagley team on a three-hitter by Dewey Clinkscales, but were upset by Granite Falls in the semifinals, 3–1.

Rollingstone continued to be a charming

place to watch baseball, and the team did return to the State Tournament in 1962 and 1965, but they were never again able to capture the magic of that wonderful 1953 season.

Two "Little Giants" walk into Cold Spring's stadium, perhaps dreaming of one day playing for the Springers. Photograph from the collection of the Stearns History Museum, St. Cloud, Minnesota.

Cold Spring: Little Giants Grow into Champs

Cold Spring established a baseball history when it was one of the eight towns represented in the inaugural 1924 Minnesota state baseball tournament. The town quickly developed a fan base in this small central Minnesota community, nestled in the state's Chain of Lakes Region. Not only were townspeople faithful to a program that produced State Tournament teams in 1939 and 1950, but they donated money and manpower to produce one of the state's finest ballparks. Men and women organized a volunteer construction crew that helped sculpt the field, put up fences, install lights, and slap on coats of paint wherever needed. In 1950 they participated in the construction of Cold Spring Athletic Field's towering grandstand area.

What Cold Spring didn't have for many years was a youth program. The town's baseball success was attained in large part through outside players, some paid and others hired to work in the area's granite quarries. Enter Pete Bell, one of five Bell brothers who played in the early days, the father of three sons and an uncle of several nephews. He fashioned a makeshift baseball field on farmland a half mile west of the existing ball-

park and formed the "Little Giants," named after his favorite major-league team. The fledgling
program was simply sandlot ball, but his efforts
evolved into a recreation program guided by Red
Soltis, a Cold Spring teacher and ballplayer.

Eventually, Cold Spring teams had more of
a local bent, and when the Springers won the
1955 Class B championship, the Little Giants
were prominently represented on the team. "My
dad was a good athlete who played all sports and
knew a lot about baseball," Dave Bell said. "He
knew what he was doing. Everything was well
organized. We even had T-shirts that had 'Little
Giants' written on them. He worked a lot with us,
and our mother even umpired some of the time.
Then along came Red Soltis from Holdingford.
He was the school's industrial arts teacher, but
he also worked with the town recreation department. He was my hero [as a player and coach]."

Cold Springs dropped down from Class A in 1955 and
won the State Class B Championship, thanks to four
pitching gems by Dave Perl and Jack Hoppe. *Front row,
from left:* Mike Bruner, Jack Hoppe, Dave Perl, Tom
Bell, Gene Schreifels, Ronnie Thelen, Dave Bell, Jesse
Phillips. *Back row:* manager Sal Theis, Don Fuchs, Tom
Sauer, Don Rehkamp, Hal Salzl, Russ Reiter, Harvey
Heurung, Hal Roske, Diz Meyer. Courtesy of Tom Bell.

With Soltis and Don Athman directing the
recreation program, the Cold Spring youth began to play an intercity schedule. Meanwhile, the
1950 Cold Spring town team became the town's
first state tourney team in 11 years. The Springers defeated the Red Wing Aces 7–0 in the opening round before being summarily drummed out
of the tournament by Le Center, 12–2. Le Center
went on to win the Class A title.

Cold Spring played four more Class A seasons, two in the Great Soo League and two in the

Big Dipper, but they rejoined the Great Soo in 1955 when the league dropped to Class B. And what was almost exclusively a local club went on to enjoy a banner season, one in which Cold Spring would win its first state championship. The Springers were young, particularly in the infield, which included Tom and Dave Bell at first and second, Russ Reiter at third and shortstop Gene Schreifels, the unit's elder at age 23. For Dave Bell, a high school player, this was the first season he donned a town team uniform. The only outsider was left-hander Dave Perl, an Austin resident, but a student at St. John's College in Collegeville, a city within the 15 miles allotted college players for local eligibility away from their home town.

Cold Spring breezed through the Great Soo League season and the Region 14B playoffs. One of the two regional victories came against Waite Park, whose starting pitcher was Soltis, the young Springers former coach and hero. Perl went 12–2 for the season and was unhittable at times. The 26–5 Springers strengthened their pitching staff by drafting Jack Hoppe from Paynesville. They received media mention as a major contender. Halstad, loaded with many members of the town's 1952 state high school championship team, was 31–7 and was also deemed a major contender.

"I thought we had a pretty good chance of winning because of our pitching," manager Sal Theis said. "We knew that Halstad had all those kids from the '52 championship, and we figured that they'd be tough. And we did wind up having a very tough game against them."

After defeating Redwood Falls 6–2 in the opener, Cold Springs and Halstad met in a scintillating pitching matchup between Perl and Halstad's Hugh Schoephoerster. They each pitched seven scoreless innings, but with two out in the eighth, Cold Spring scored all its runs in a 4–0 victory that snapped Halstad's 15-game winning streak. The

Jack Hoppe, a Paynesville draftee, receives the 1955 MVP trophy from Clarence Lee, MBA director from Fergus Falls. *Dispatch–Pioneer Press* photograph; courtesy of the Minnesota Historical Society.

eighth-inning surge was started by Tom Bell and Tom Sauer, who hit back-to-back singles, and highlighted by Jesse Phillips's two-run home run. Halstad had one of the state's top pitchers on its team, but Rod Oistad—who a year earlier pitched Benson to the State A title—was recovering from an arm injury and played in the outfield.

Cold Spring completed one of the most convincing state championship marches in history, defeating Stewartville 7–0 and Granite Falls 11–0 in the final two rounds. The town hadn't experienced that much baseball pride since 1949, when Joe Schleper beat Little Falls 3–0 with a perfect game. Hoppe was named the tournament MVP, but Theis said that Perl was maybe more deserving. "[Perl] pitched that outstanding game against Halstad, but he wasn't that sharp in the championship game [against Granite Falls]," Theis explained. "He struggled some and complained a lot to the umpires. I think that hurt his MVP chances."

Cold Spring went on to play in the Mythical State Championship without catcher and

St. Joseph's postseason draftee Hal Roske, who broke his leg in the second inning of the Class B final against Granite. They almost lost Tom Bell to the military, but they made an appeal to the draft board, and he was granted an extension to his induction date. The Springers, though, lost 7–3 to Class A Champion St. Peter.

Pipestone, eliminated by Braham in the 1957 Class B semifinals, came back to win the 1958 championship. *Front row, from left:* Wallace Melby, Larry Brugman, Bruce Michels, Pete Spawn, Butch Raymond, Jim Klassen, Lane Johnson, batboys John Le Breen and Rodney Lee. *Back row:* manager Ken Kielty, Marv Heinrichs, Dave Roesler, Dick Hellmer, Roy Ring, Del Koopman, Loren Grage, Jack Kelly. Courtesy of Ken Kielty.

Pipestone: Good Sports Became Two-Time Champs

At the 1958 pretournament meeting in New Ulm, a Class B team manager petitioned to use a nonroster player, but as soon as Pipestone player/manager Ken Kielty heard the request, he adamantly declined. Kielty calmly explained that the Indians had received the State Tournament's Sportsmanship Trophy the year before, and his team did not return for another friendly pat on the back.

Kielty said that four previous Pipestone teams had played in the tournament, and each came away empty, and the 1957 sportsmanship award did nothing to assuage the Indians' disappointment after their semifinal loss.

"We returned [in 1958] with the goal of nothing less than to win it all," Kielty said of the First Night League champions. "We probably had a better team the year before, but let it get away in the semifinals. We didn't want to win the tournament at *any* cost, we just wanted to win it straight up, and we expected no less from the rest of the field."

Kielty's philosophical stand was the beginning of a championship mission in Pipestone's second season in Class B. The Indians, who were beaten

5–0 by Braham in the 1957 semifinals, won the four consecutive games to earn the championship. They completed their bid with a 5–3 victory over Norwood, a perennial Class B contender making its fifth consecutive state tournament appearance. The four tournament victories that completed the Indians' 31–6 season matched the combined total of the four previous state tourney teams.

Del Koopman, a postseason draftee from Fulda, was the winning pitcher against Norwood, but he had relief from Lane Johnson and Dick Hellmer, the Indians' ace in the regular season and a winner of two tournament games. Six Pipestone regulars hit above .300 during the season, and Jack Kelly was the team's tournament slugger going 8 for 15 with 10 runs batted in. In defeating Norwood, Pipestone outdistanced three of the state's outstanding Class B pitchers: Lefty Graupman, Vern Wroge, and Bert McCarthy, all draft picks from the Crow River Valley League.

"It was great that we finally got one [a state title], but I felt badly that Jack Kelly wasn't named the tournament MVP," Butch Raymond said of an award that went to Austin pitcher Jim Lawler. For Marv Heinrichs it was a bittersweet triumph. He'd been the player/manager for Pipestone's 1954, 1956, and 1957 teams but had to savor the 1958 championship as a postseason draftee from Fulda, where he'd moved for business reasons.

Pipestone repeated in the 1959 First Night League and made it through region play, but despite having basically the same lineup, and the addition of veteran pitcher Chuck Gageby, the Indians were unable to repeat. An outstanding regular season came to an abrupt end when Pipestone lost in the first round to eventual champion Shakopee, 5–2. This marked the second time in three seasons that Pipestone was eliminated by the eventual Class B champion, and in 1956 they had been eliminated in Class A by the champion Minneapolis Teamsters.

Kelly, Kielty, and Lance Johnson were not on the 1960 roster, but the local sportswriter Len Hart predicted that this Pipestone team was possibly the best ever to represent Pipestone on the diamond. The youngsters from Harold Boelter's junior program had matured into seasoned tournament players, veterans Pete Spawn, Butch Raymond, and Chuck Gageby were back, and the team now had Don Bruns, a quality pitcher and solid hitter with five years of minor-league experience. Hellmer returned briefly and left, but Dave Roesler became a quality spot starter and reliever.

Pipestone breezed through the First Night League season, at one point owning an 11-game winning streak, and the biggest scare they received in the postseason came from Tracy, which pushed the Indians the distance in the playoffs and might have prevailed if Roesler hadn't been so steady in relief.

"I honestly believe that Pipestone and Tracy were the two best [Class] B teams in the state that season," Spawn said. No one in the State Tournament seriously challenged the Indians, who outscored their four opponents 46–5, including an 18–1 romp over perennial contender Norwood.

"We had some good players from our area, and Boelter's junior program probably did a lot of good for our younger players," Spawn said. "And remember, we really hadn't come down from Class A until after the 1956 season and we still had some of the players who played in Class A. We had some excellent pitching from guys like Gageby, Bruns, and Hellmer, and we had some excellent position players such as Jack Kelly, Butch Raymond, and Marv Heinrichs."

As for Kielty, he wasn't around for the second state title because he made a decision far more difficult than the one he made before the

1958 tournament. After developing a quality Edgerton High basketball program from 1955 through 1959, he accepted a teaching position at West High in Minneapolis. Edgerton lost in the district finals in 1959, squandering a second-half lead, but under Rich Olson the team won the 1960 Minnesota title when the state still had only one division.

Kielty said he had no regrets because he knew that in some way he had played a role in the team's development, and he also knew that moving to the Twin Cities was a sound career move. He was quick to praise Olson's job of taking a talented team the rest of the way.

Braham: Caught a Major Break

The consensus is that good pitching generally beats good hitting, and Braham was no exception when the Pirates won the 1957 Class B state championship in Cold Spring. Former Pirates second baseman Carl Hellzen emphasized, however, that catching depth helped the Pirates develop a pitching staff for the tournament. With an abundance of home players who could catch, Braham was able to draft three pitchers after winning the Eastern Minnesota League playoffs.

"We had four or five guys on our team who could catch and we had a good stopper in Bob Westerlund," Hellzen said. "We had a good team overall, with a bunch of us having played a long time together, but I don't know if we could have won it all if we hadn't so many good pitchers, particularly Fred Brandt."

Braham selected Hinckley's Brandt and Lyle

Braham manager Art Johnson accepting the 1957 State Class B championship trophy from *St. Paul Pioneer Press* writer Bob Schabert. *Dispatch–Pioneer Press* photograph; courtesy of the Minnesota Historical Society.

Mortenson and Rush City's Virg Johnson after the Pirates defeated Hinckley in the league playoffs. Westerlund beat Norwood 3–1 in the title game, but postseason draftees Brandt, Mortenson, and Johnson figured in three Braham tourney victories. Braham and Brandt beat Verndale 11–3 in the opener, Mortenson's 4⅔ innings of relief gave him the victory in a 6–4 decision over Morris, and Brandt shut out Pipestone 5–0 in the semifinals.

Brandt, a former Brooklyn Dodgers minor-league pitcher, showed MVP mettle in his two complete games, giving up only six hits and striking out 17 batters in his two complete games. He took a no-hitter into an eighth inning against Pipestone.

"Fred was an excellent pitcher," Hellzen said of Brandt, who was edged by Waseca's Vern Edmunds in the MVP vote. "He always had an outstanding fastball, but he developed a very good curve. I'm surprised that he didn't go further in professional ball, but . . ."

Braham almost didn't have Brandt. The pitcher, who a year earlier had left professional ball in time to help pitch Hinckley to the 1956 State Tournament semifinals, began the 1957 season with high expectations. So when Braham defeated Hinckley in the 1957 league playoffs, Brandt was less than delighted by Braham's postseason invitation.

"Someone from Braham came up to me after the game and asked me if I'd pitch for them, and I told 'em, 'There ain't no way in hell I'm going to pitch for you,' " Brandt said. "But I cooled down after a bit, and when they called me three days later I told them I would pitch for them."

Hellzen's respect for Brandt's pitching by no means overshadowed his respect for his team's overall 1957 success. In the 1954 and 1955 State Tournaments, Braham had gone one and out, but they won four straight games in 1957. Bobby

Winfield did a yeoman's job after replacing Braham's regular catcher Stan Walberg midway through the first game when Walberg struggled to handle Brandt. Winfield, a high school junior who was used sparingly during the regular season, played like a veteran during the remainder of the tournament.

Warroad: More Than a Hockey Town

In an edition of a Warroad newspaper, circa 1950, a Lutheran minister wrote a playful commentary that might have seemed irreverent, but many had to admire his divine sense of humor. "God must've been a real baseball fan," the good reverend wrote, "because the Holy Bible starts out, 'In the Big Inning God created . . .' "

The lighthearted commentary expressed the sentiment of the times in Warroad, a city nestled against the Lake of the Woods, only eight miles from the Canadian border. Warroad is best known for its hockey, fishing, and winter recreation, but through the 1950s, baseball was the summer talk of the town. You won't find a state baseball championship trophy adorning city hall, but beginning in 1949—the year after Warroad helped form the Lake of the Woods League—the town began a record run of 10 consecutive state tournament trips. While the streak was broken by Baudette in 1959, Warroad returned the next three years before baseball lost its footing in the tundra.

"The first trip in '49 was exciting, an adventure," longtime Warroad baseball supporter Jack Marvin said. "We were glad to be there, but we also weren't intimidated." Warroad had dominated the area in 1947 as an independent, led by Oliver Accobee's pitching acumen.

Warroad finished third in a 14-team field in its first appearance, defeating Duluth Gary VFW 6–3 and Ulen 8–5 before being outslugged by La Crescent 11–10 in the semifinals. Accobee pitched a three-hit command performance in the opener but was chased early in the loss to La Cresent, leaving the team with a 24–3–1 record for the season.

Official mileage statistics are not kept by the Minnesota Baseball Association, but Warroad must have set the record in 1952 when they drove 450 miles to reach the State Tournament in Austin, only to lose 4–3 to Kingston in the first round. They reached the semifinals in 1954, defeating Sauk Rapids 6–2 and Ada 6–3, but were ousted from the tournament by Milroy 19–3, in a game that went only seven innings. They compiled a 7–11 record in their 11 State Tournament appearances in the era.

Perhaps the team might not have reached the state tourney as many times if they hadn't landed

In 1956 Warroad qualified for an eighth consecutive State Tournament berth. *Front row, from left:* Dave Thompson, Bob Johnson, Roger Ganyo, Dan McKinnon, Jim Ploof, Erling Olimb, Jack Stoskopf, batboy David Ganyo. *Back row:* manager Tony Stukel, Jim Hodgson, Bob Evenson, Joe Koenig, Ken Reitan, Del Hedlund, Earle Sargent, Bernie Grover, Bob Kofstad. "Badger Bob" Johnson, a first-year teacher at Warroad, went on to become a legendary hockey coach at the University of Wisconsin and for the U.S. Olympic hockey team. Courtesy of Warroad Heritage Center.

North Dakota youngster Bob Evenson in 1956. Warroad had a fine collection of pitchers throughout the years in Jim Fish, Accobee, and Lorne Lien, but Evenson was the team ace from his opening season, when he went 8–3, striking out 152 and walking 47. He also lost some heartbreakers; in fact, Warroad might have made the tournament for an 11th consecutive year, but Evenson lost two games to Baudette in a best-of-three series when his defense committed four errors in each game.

Warroad was the state's Cinderella town and twice received the tournament's Brennan Sportsmanship Trophy. Through the first seven years, Warroad compiled an 89–3–1 league record and was rarely forced to go the distance in Region 12B playoff games against the likes of Grygla, Hallock, Carpenter, Lancaster, and Karlstad. The town's perennial league challenger was Baudette, the town that ended Warroad's 47-game league winning streak in 1952 and seven years later ended Warroad's record string of state tourney trips. Ken "Lefty" Knutson, who pitched for Le Center's 1950 state Class A champions, was Baudette's mainstay for several years and pitched the 3–0 victory that ended Warroad's 47-game streak. Knutson's feat was no fluke, for he also pitched a perfect game against league rival Williams.

Warroad was so dominant that before the 1953 Lake of the Woods League playoffs, Roseau agreed that if the first game against the Lakers was too decisive, it would concede the remaining playoff games. Warroad had earlier thumped Roseau 19–0 during the regular season. Irate about Warroad's recruiting practices, Roseau withdrew from the league following the 1956 season.

One local writer was apparently bored by the romps and suggested editorially that Warroad form a northern Class A league, but the idea never flew, perhaps in part because travel would be financially prohibitive.

But most Warroad fans seemed to enjoy winning. The team not only had a large following home and away, but the townspeople also helped raise money to provide lights, helped install them, and helped groom the field before and during the season. And being a fan did not require major travel. Warroad installed lights in 1952, giving the community one of the few lighted fields in the region. Consequently, Warroad hosted many regional playoff games, and other teams flocked to the field to play midweek exhibition games.

Emil Schultz was the team's first manager, and Pallie Martin was the club's first president, later to become the manager. But it was catcher Tony Stukel, a St. Cloud State Teachers' College recruit, who became the program's mainstay. He joined the team in 1951 and after the 1953 season was named the team's player/manager. By the 1955 season, Jack Hodgson was the only remaining member of Warroad's inaugural state tournament team, but Stukel—with the cooperation of city businesses and the school system—recruited the region's best players to keep the team competitive.

Norwood: Homegrown Success

Bob Zellmann spoke proudly of Norwood's town ball reputation in the 1950s, emphasizing that six state tournament appearances between 1950 and 1960 were secured exclusively by homegrown talent. As one of Norwood's most celebrated players, Zellmann explained that the team never relied on school board or civic hiring policies to bring ringers in. "We grew up together, learned to play together, and we stuck together," he said emphasizing each phrase. "We played by ourselves all the time; that's how we learned. We had a Legion team, but no midget or peewee programs until much later."

Norwood did spend some of the World War II days combined with Green Isle, Young America, and Hamburg because of manpower shortages. But the towns parted ways in 1946, and Norwood spent three seasons in the S-C-S (Scott-Carver-Sibley) League before moving into the Crow River Valley League in 1949.

Success did not come quickly. Norwood failed to reach the Class B tournament until 1954, but once the boom period began, the tiny farm community became a state force. Of its six trips to the State Tournament, Norwood placed second twice and third on two other occasions. The 1957 team lost to Braham 3–1 in the final, and the 1958 club lost the title game to Pipestone 5–3.

Norwood was undefeated in league play in 1950 and 1959. Eventual state champion Lester Prairie upset Norwood in the 1950 league playoffs, ending the town's 20-game winning streak. In 1959, undefeated Norwood—playing with only three players born outside the town—survived the league playoffs but lost in the Region 7B tournament. The six Norwood state tournament teams were a collective 12–7, with four of the losses being by two runs or less.

Four Feltmanns and two Zellmanns, along with longtime town ball regulars Keith Braunwarth, Willy Willemsen, and LeRoy Miller, helped lay the foundation for the decade of dominance. One of the latecomers was pitcher Bert McCarthy from Green Isle. He had pitched for Norwood earlier as a draft selection, but in the late fifties he moved his dental practice to Norwood and became a local. He was an outstanding addition.

I think he was one of the best amateur baseball pitchers there was at the time," said Willemsen, a highly respected pitcher in his own right. "He was tough. He never had a sore arm in his life, and he could go at least nine innings with no trouble. He had a good knuckleball and he could

for a few seasons. But even before settling on a Class B philosophy in the second half of the fifties, the fearsome foursome and West served the town well, particularly pitchers Hochsprung and Lyle Katzenmeyer. Hochsprung never got a shot at professional ball, saying he was just looked upon as a gangly left-hander who wore glasses, but the right-handed Katzenmeyer did spend a brief time with the St. Louis Cardinals organization before getting homesick and returning home.

Brownton didn't win them all with its two aces, but the team won far more than it lost. Lyle Katzenmeyer once was 26–0 over two seasons, but he smiled when reminded of his success. "I did a lot of managing back then," Katzenmeyer said. "So I'd give Gerry the tough ones and save some of the others for myself."

Brownton's 1958 team was particularly strong, taking a 27–2 record into the state tournament with a starting lineup that included five

Brownton veteran Gerry Hochsprung slides safely into third base as Norwood's Don Feltmann leaps for the ball in a 1958 State Tournament game at New Ulm. Courtesy of Herb Schaper Historical Baseball Collection/*New Ulm Daily Journal.*

farm products including teenage shortstop Dick Peik, son of an area farmer. Brownton won its first two games, 6–0 over Little Falls and 8–2 over Warroad, but was eliminated in the quarterfinals by Norwood 8–2.

Peik demonstrated that those from farming stock were not only competitive but tough. On a Thursday of tournament week, he was beaned in the fourth inning but remained in the game and the next night played football for his high school team, scoring two touchdowns and two extra points in a 14–13 road victory over Sacred Heart. Peik scored the winning TD and extra point with 10 seconds left in the game, after returning a punt 55 yards.

The 1958 Brownton Bruins reached the State Class B Tournament, led by a cast of veterans. *Front row, from left:* Delbert Klabunde, Bob Robinson, Max West, Neil Katzenmeyer, Bruce Hakes, Tom Janke, Bob Bandemir, batboys Thomas Alsleben and Armon Fischer. *Back row:* manager Lyle Katzenmeyer, Norm Gehrke, Jiggs Westergard, Gerry Hochsprung, Hank Loncorich, Joe Janke, Bob Werner, Dick Peik. Courtesy of Chuck Warner, former editor-publisher of the *Brownton Bulletin*.

Perham: Fireball Started Ball Rolling

When the winds of World War II began to sweep the nation, towns began to put baseball on hold, sometimes for lack of players, sometimes for financial reasons, and sometimes simply out of respect for men in uniform.

Perham was one of those towns, for whatever reason, and while many teams hauled out the equipment when the war ended in 1945, Perham—a town nestled in the lakes region approximately 200 miles northwest of the Twin Cities—waited until 1949 to resume play. No one seems able to explain why this town with a baseball history stretching back to the late 1880s waited so long, but once back in action the team quickly bounced back behind pitcher Roy "Fireball" Martin, an area farmer.

Martin said that he never threw a baseball during the eight-year break because he simply had too much farmwork, and even when he started competing again, the awkward-looking pitcher with the sizzling fastball and unique sidewinder motion didn't have the luxury of practice. "I still was working hard and didn't have any time," Martin explained. "My only practice came in the games; in fact, I hardly had a chance to throw a ball until the games began."

Fireball hadn't lost his competitive fire, and as one Perham fan put it, "Perham reached the 1949 Class B State Tournament on Roy Martin's right arm." The *St. Paul Pioneer Press* baseball writer Bob Schabert picked Perham as a contender for the title because of Martin. Fireball pitched the opener for Perham, and the Pirates defeated Cass Lake in 11 innings, 4–3. By the

Baseball was a family affair in Perham. Roy Martin, in uniform, kneels with young Buck Burgau. In back row, left to right, Buck's parents Don and Lila Burgau and Roy's wife Elsie Martin and their two daughters look on. *Star-Tribune* photograph; courtesy of the Minnesota Historical Society.

time Martin came in to relieve starter Bee Hertel in the next game against La Crescent, the damage was done, and the Pirates lost 7–3.

Martin went 36–12 in the 1949–51 seasons, but then damaged a tendon in his throwing arm while dehorning cattle. He was forced to give up pitching, but continued to play outfield for the team into the 1960s, and was consistently one of the team's top hitters.

Perham returned to the Class B State Tournament four more times in the era, in 1954, 1956, 1958, and 1959. The school system and local businessmen supported the team with their hiring practices. Jack Wilcox and Al Stigman were two classy pitchers recruited from other towns— Wilcox was hired away from the Staples school

system to coach basketball at Perham, and Stigman lured from New York Mills with a higher-paying job. Brothers Don and Ray Burgau were two more outstanding players recruited with the promise of employment.

Bill Bauck, a longtime Perham resident who played an administrative role on the baseball board after returning from the service in 1952, said that Perham abided by the rule that required teams to use players within a specified distance from the town, but he admitted that teams found means to fudge on the rules. "Everybody just sort of winked when it came to eligibility," he said. "We had a Stanford University pitcher named Al Dunn for several years. He didn't have any ties to the area except his parents had a summer place on Star Lake. Wadena and Verndale had an air force base in the area, which fell in the 15-mile radius, so they got some players that way."

Al Woessner was the first postwar manager, but the team really began to move when Perham high school coach Ted Mienhover took over the team. The 6-foot-8 former University of North Dakota all-everything athlete, who played semiprofessional baseball for the Bismarck Phantoms, didn't play an inning with Perham, but he masterminded the teams of the mid- and late fifties.

Except for a 5–0 first-round loss to Little Falls in 1959, the Pirates were competitive in every tournament. They gave the 1954 State B champion Milroy team its toughest tournament test, a 2–0 decision. They won two games in 1956 before losing 3–2 to Bemidji, who went on to win it all.

Just as impressive as Perham's competitive record was the team's fan base. While this town, named for Josiah Perham, the Northern Pacific Railroad's first president, was a recreational Mecca surrounded by myriad lakes, the Pirates received major support. The rivalries between Perham and nearby towns including New York Mills, Verndale, and Frazee often attracted full houses.

Perham was host site to the 1949 Region 9B tournament and again in 1953 and 1954 when attendance for each tourney topped 5,000 fans. According to the *Perham Enterprise-Bulletin*, the 1954 regionals, in which Perham was entered,

attracted 5,434 spectators and earned $3,288.05. Not bad for a village whose 1950 population was a shade below 2,000 residents.

Inger: Baseball Becomes Chippewa Legend

Frank Rabbit brought official amateur baseball to Inger in 1948, responding to the suggestion by his good friend Art Frick, a Grand Rapids businessman, who was also the MABA regional commissioner. Frick promoted and ran up to five leagues based around Grand Rapids, many consisting of teams that had no satisfactory home fields.

Rabbit, a Chippewa Indian who had played baseball since he was a kid, decided that it was a good idea and began recruiting a team for the settlement on the edge of the Leech Lake Indian Reservation in northern Minnesota. Frick provided some of the financial support, but Rabbit also embarked on a major fund-raising drive in Deer Creek and surrounding areas. A $10 payment bought Inger a league affiliation, and town team baseball started along the banks of the Bowstring River.

Under the guidance of Rabbit, Inger quickly emerged as a perennial league contender and in 1953 Rabbit and his cast of Chippewa players won the league and defeated Taconite and Lawrence Lake to win the Region 13B title. Soon after beating Lawrence Lake 3–0 on the pitching of David Cloud and Roger Wakonabo's home run, the team was its way to New Ulm, a 270-mile bus ride from Inger, a tiny community that included a general store, a post office, a shaggy ball field, and a small residential area. Unfortunately, Inger was abruptly eliminated in their opening game 17–2 by Rollingstone, which went on to win the Class B title. Inger didn't score until the fifth, and

Shanty Dolan in 1945, when he was piloting
the Albert Lea Packers to their second of five
consecutive Class AA championships. Photograph
by Lefty Evans; courtesy of Don Evans.

two unassisted triple plays while playing for
Tracy in a game in 1925 against Lamberton.

In 1938, Dolan and his large family—he had
five sons and three daughters—moved to Albert
Lea from Estherville, Iowa. Shanty thought he
was ready to quit baseball and settle down when
he arrived in Albert Lea. He turned down an invitation to play with a team in Emmons, a small
town south of Albert Lea on the Iowa border.
But then he heard a radio broadcast of a game
between Emmons and Austin and got the itch
to play again. With the blessing of his wife, who
came from a baseball-playing family in Marshall,
Dolan unretired and suited up with Emmons.

Albert Lea had a fairly strong baseball tra-

dition—they'd won the State Tournament in
1929—but didn't have a team in 1938. Local businessmen led by Len Kelly and Ray Moulton organized a team the next winter and talked Shanty
into becoming its player/manager. That turned
out to be one of the best decisions the businessmen ever made. The team was admitted to the
Southern Minnesota League and finished the
1939 season in fifth place. Things came together
in 1940 when the team won the pennant and
playoffs and followed up by winning the State
Class AA Championship. Southern Minny rivals
Owatonna and Austin won the state championships in 1941 and 1942, but Albert Lea began a
six-year run as Southern Minny playoff champions in 1943. They lost the State Championship
2–1 to Minneapolis Mitby-Sathers that year, on
a two-run home run in the 13th inning.

Dolan built the team around a nucleus of veteran players. He lost some players to the draft
during the war but managed to keep enough of
his "Ol' Dandies," as they were called by fans and
critics alike, together to keep winning. Dolan,
Jimmy Delmont, Spike Gorham, Gordy West,
and Bob Hill played on the 1943–45 teams,
while Bob Carter, Walt Menke, and Chet Chap-
man played on two of those three teams. After
the war, Dolan blended experienced players like
Don Blanchard, Russ Schmidthuber, Herb Terhaar, Don Opperman, Red Hougard (who'd also
played in 1943), and John Menke (who'd been
the MVP of the 1940 State Tournament) to the
mix and kept on winning.

The 1948 season was to be the last hurrah
for Shanty's Ol' Dandies. The league expanded
the schedule to 28 games that year, and Albert
Lea finished in fourth place with a 17–11 record, three games behind first-place Mankato.
The team had solid pitching but was getting a
little old. Shanty didn't play much until the play-

offs, but his addition of Jack LaVelle and Mel Harpuder, two refugees from the minor leagues, added some punch to the lineup. Albert Lea upset Mankato in the first round of the playoffs and then beat Austin in an exciting three-game series to win the team's sixth consecutive berth in the State Tournament. Earl Mossor, a drafted pitcher from Austin, won two games in the State Tournament, while his brother Wandel, also from Austin, and Don Opperman each won one game as the team went undefeated in the double-elimination tournament. Spike Gorham won the MVP award at the tournament, joining three other Packers winners during Dolan's championship run: John Menke (1940), Jimmy Delmont (1944), and Walt Menke (1946).

Austin caught up with Albert Lea in 1949. Shanty was injured much of the year and didn't play much. Age took its toll on other players, as well. Blanchard, West, and Terhaar were gone, and to make things worse, LaVelle and Harpuder defected to Austin. Shanty's son, Bobby, just out of high school, became a regular on the team. Albert Lea barely made the playoffs, finishing in fourth place again, with a 17–18 record, 11

Shanty Dolan tags a Fergus Falls runner at third base during a game in the 1948 State Tournament at Shakopee. *Star-Tribune* photograph; courtesy of the Minnesota Historical Society.

games behind first-place Austin, who beat them three games to one in the first round. Shanty resigned at the end of the season, citing both personal and business reasons.

He was out of amateur baseball during the 1950 season but did some scouting for the Pittsburgh Pirates, who were trying to sign his son Bobby, regarded as a top major-league prospect. Southern Minnesota was ripe with rumors all year, though, that Shanty was anxious to get back into action. In December the Faribault Lakers announced that they had hired Dolan to manage the team in 1951. He was put in complete charge of the team and given a free hand in hiring players. He started the season with Johnny Blanchard, a Minneapolis Central High School star, and his son Bobby, now at St. Thomas College, in the starting lineup. However, both were gone by mid-June, when Blanchard signed with the Yankees and Bobby with the Dodgers.

Faribault finished the 1951 season at 22–20,

tied with Albert Lea for fourth place, and seven games behind the first-place Owatonna Aces. The Lakers upset Owatonna three games to one in the first round of the playoffs but lost by the same margin to Austin in the finals. However, on the field, it was the most successful season in Faribault since 1931, the last time the team made the State Tournament. Financially, though, the team had a rough time. Attendance averaged 1,812 per game in 21 home games, compared to 2,345 in 1950, when there were 18 home games.

The team started slowly in 1952, and attendance was significantly lower than in 1951. In late July, with the team in fifth place at 14–14, the Faribault board of directors released Dolan and three players in an economy move. The board felt it could no longer afford Dolan's (estimated) $3,000 salary. In fact, Austin's Emil Scheid was the league's only remaining nonplaying manager. Mankato had already released bench manager Ed Buckley earlier in the season.

It didn't take Shanty long to find another job. In late August the *Mankato Free Press* reported that the Dolan family was planning to move to Mankato. Shanty said that there "was no connection between Mankato baseball and my decision to settle down here." He said that he and his wife wanted to move to a larger town in the southern Minnesota area and chose Mankato after he was offered a job as manager of a service station. The family planned to move immediately to get their children enrolled in their new schools.

Of course, Southern Minny baseball fans were skeptical about Shanty's intentions and grew even more so when he was invited to a Key City Community Enterprises (KCCE) board of directors meeting. This organization was set up in the early 1940s to purchase Tanley Field from its founder, Bill Tanley, and had hosted the State Tournament in 1947. About 700 local citizens

and firms were stockholders in the closed corporation. Earlier in the year, KCCE had purchased the Southern Minny baseball franchise from the Mankato Baseball Association. No one was surprised in mid-October when KCCE announced it had signed Dolan as manager.

Shanty led the 1953 Mankato Merchants to their first winning record since 1948. The team fell to fifth place with a 16–19 record in 1949 and then had three dismal seasons in a row. Their 1950–52 records of 8–27, 9–33, and 13–29 earned two eighth-place and one seventh-place finishes. Dolan's 1953 Merchants improved to 23–21, good enough for fifth place. However, the team was popular and was in the running all year for a playoff spot, which they missed only with a loss on the last game of the season. The team led the Southern Minny in attendance with 2,080 per game and finished with a $2,937 surplus.

The 1954 Merchants led the league out of the gate and were in first place almost all year. However, they lost their last six league games and finished with a 24–20 record, two games behind pennant-winning Albert Lea. Then they were swept in three games by Albert Lea in the first round of the league playoffs. Although attendance dropped off at the end of the season, the team averaged 2,027, just a little down from 1953, and once again led the league. The team did manage to break even financially, however, thanks to preseason fund-raising.

In 1955, Dolan's Merchants started slowly. They played .500 ball but looked like they were contenders for the first division and a playoff spot. Average attendance at the end of June was down 20 percent from 1954, but Mankato was still leading the league. Crowds dropped off significantly, though, as the team lost seven of eight at the end of June and early July, and the Key City Enterprises board was worried about finances.

To cut payroll, Shanty trimmed his roster to the starting eight position players, one reserve catcher, and three pitchers. That only slowed the red ink. Key City officials estimated they'd need to average 1,600 fans for the rest of the season to break even—compared to just over 800 for their last four home games.

Shanty was given a vote of confidence by the Key City board, and before a special meeting called by the board on July 18, he offered to manage the rest of the year without pay. At that meeting, however, Dolan said he could not afford to manage without pay. The board released Dolan, expressing regret, but said they could not afford his $3,000 salary. The Merchants had been 14–16 under Dolan and went 6–13 for the rest of the season to finish in a distant fifth place, 9 games behind fourth-place Albert Lea and 13 games behind pennant-winning Faribault.

Shanty's son Bobby was home recovering from a beaning in pro baseball and was signed to finish the season in Mankato. Shanty stayed around Mankato to watch him until the end of the season and then moved his family to California, where he lived until his death in 1995. It's tempting to consider Shanty's fate a sad and ignominious ending to a long career. But it's not clear that Shanty would have thought that way. More than once during the season, he'd said that 1955 would be his last year in baseball. Friends felt he had already planned to move to California.

The Southern Minny was a tough business by 1955. Pressures to win had pumped up player salaries, and all teams were having financial troubles. When that happens—as modern major-league managers quickly learn—the manager often becomes the target for change. Shanty was even more of a target at Mankato because he was a bench manager, a rarity in the league. Most teams had player/managers. His $3,000 salary was 10 to 15 percent of the payroll budget, and by the time Key City Enterprises gave Dolan his release, they'd already had to dip into a Tanley Field capital improvement fund to pay player salaries and said they had no alternative. Shanty was just a victim of the times.

But what times they were! Old-time fans will never forget the championship run of the Albert Lea Packers. As player/manager, Shanty was a shrewd judge of talent. He molded a close-knit team that played well together and always found some way to win when the chips were down. Shanty had the knack for importing the right player, like pitcher Gail Mayo in 1947, to fill a gap that had emerged in the team. Initially this was with players from Minnesota and Iowa, but by 1948 he saw the trend toward recruiting players from the professional ranks, and he brought in pro refugees Mel Harpuder and Jack LaVelle to help win the team's fifth consecutive Class AA championship.

Dolan's efforts at Faribault and Mankato were certainly not unsuccessful. At both places, he revived the teams' fortunes on the field. A testimonial to his reputation was the number of out-of-state players who contacted him for advice and help in finding a team to play for in Minnesota. Shanty, when he couldn't use a player himself, often referred the player to a competitor in the Southern Minny.

Shanty Dolan was a great player, manager, and feared competitor—one of the giants in the glory days of post–World War II Minnesota baseball.

Emil Scheid: The Man Opponents Loved to Hate

Emil Scheid became manager of the Austin Packers in 1947, and for the rest of the era he was the key mover and shaker of the Southern

Minny League—alternately hated and loved by both friends and foes. He developed contacts in college and professional baseball and used them to bring baseball players to Austin, and he shamelessly poached players from other clubs in the league, attracting them with jobs at his own plumbing and heating shop, at Hormel, or at local schools and businesses. He also worked tirelessly to promote the Southern Minny League, offering to dig into his own pockets several times to help out a franchise in trouble.

Scheid had established a plumbing business in Waseca in 1929. He moved the business to Austin in 1941 but worked at Hormel during the war. He managed the Austin Merchants—the town's second team—of the Cedar Valley League

Emil Scheid in 1950. His powerhouse Austin Packers were upset by Fergus Falls in the State Tournament. Courtesy of Larry Scheid.

in 1946. The team's average age was only 20, but they had a magical run at the State Tournament that year. They pulled three upsets before losing to the veteran Springfield team 9–1 in the Class A championship game. Scheid was appointed manager of the Austin Packers, the town's Class AA Southern Minnesota League team, in 1947. The venerable Southern Minny was never the same after that. Scheid left his fingerprints on every aspect of the league.

He was a relentless competitor, on and off the field. During games he would argue, file protests, demand that umpires inspect pitchers' clothing, stomp around, stall, and do anything he could to distract opponents. He got into some fierce shoving matches. One night in Austin he chased an umpire after a game, shouting, "I'm gonna kill him!" Emil's wife stood up in the bleachers, imploring him to stop. "Don't do it, Emil," she screamed.

Emil was fiercely loyal to his players. He provided loans to many in addition to helping them find good jobs. Bob Bartholomew recalled that Scheid gave him a load of heating coal when he moved to Austin in late 1951. He gave encouragement to teams struggling to make ends meet, and was always making suggestions for improving the league. He subscribed to the local newspapers of the other teams in the league to monitor what they were saying about him and his team, and often wrote scathing letters back to them, setting them straight and correcting their "mistakes."

His high profile and his team's success made him an inviting target. Opposing fans filled the third baseline bleachers and delighted in jeering at Scheid as he assumed his customary spot in the third-base coaching box. Emil had a chronically dry throat and chewed on pieces of lemon to keep from coughing. Opponents had a blast with this affectation. "Lemon sucker!" they yelled constantly. He had a slow, somewhat slouching gait as he walked to the mound. Opposing fans would shout "pip, pip, pip . . ." as he walked to the mound, timing their yells to his cadence. An old injury made it difficult for him to throw or swing a bat. His own team had to hold back laughter on occasion when he had trouble hitting ground balls during infield practice. Of course, Austin's opponents and their early-arriving fans took delight in these shortcomings.

In short, Emil was a little larger than life, and he was the guy that opponents and their fans loved to hate. However, there is no evidence that he was ever bothered by it. He actually delighted in the attention. Years later, the Rochester sports columnist Ben Sternberg, who had managed against Scheid, wrote that Emil was actually a perfect gentleman off the field. He recalled that they would fight furiously during the season but would enjoy each other's company in the off-season. The fights and arguments were just part of the game.

Scheid began recruiting players right away in 1947, determined to topple the Albert Lea dynasty. He plucked pitcher Earl Mossor and out-fielder Ray Riley out of the Class D Tobacco State League. The team went 9–5 and tied for second place, and lost out in the playoffs. In the off-season, Scheid campaigned for a 42-game schedule in 1948. He was convinced that six teams would have lights by the start of the season, and that a three-games-a-week schedule would be possible and popular with fans. The league compromised with a 28-game schedule. The league ultimately went to 35 games in 1949 and 42 games in 1950. It reached its peak at 49 games in 1955.

For 1948, Scheid picked up Wandas Mossor (Earl's brother), an eight-year minor-league veteran, and Minnesota college stars Dick Seltz

(Hamline) and Duane "Red" Lindgren (Augsburg). Seltz and Lindgren had played two years of minor-league ball and were coming off .300 seasons in the Northern League. Lindgren's .348 average was fourth in the league. Austin came within one out of beating Albert Lea in the playoffs—Albert Lea was trailing 7–6 with two outs in the top of the ninth inning when they launched a two-run rally to win the game and the playoffs.

Austin finally broke Albert Lea's string in 1949 when they ran away with the pennant and won the playoffs and the Class AA State Championship. Scheid helped himself by talking Mel Harpuder and Jack LaVelle into jumping from Albert Lea. He also signed minor-league pitchers Sam House and Bob Kuhlman, as well as veteran minor-league catcher Billy Campeau.

Austin had another powerhouse in 1950. Scheid picked up pro pitcher Roman Bartkowski, University of Minnesota slugger Harry Elliott, and Bill Skowron, a college hitting sensation from Purdue. The Packers were a prohibitive favorite at the State Tournament but stumbled in the second round, losing 3–2 to Litchfield. They fought back through the loser's bracket of the double-elimination tournament but were forced to play five games in the final two days. They beat undefeated Fergus Falls 5–1 in their second game on Sunday to force a final game that night. Fergus Falls' crafty veteran Harley Oyloe shut out Austin 3–0 on a four-hitter to win the championship. This was the first time a team outside the Southern Minny won the Class AA title since 1943.

Billy Campeau performed a truly Herculean feat by catching all five games played on the final two days. Skowron, who had signed a $30,000 contract with the New York Yankees just before the tournament, went on to have a great major-league career. Harry Elliott also turned pro. A World War II vet and 28 years of age, he was a

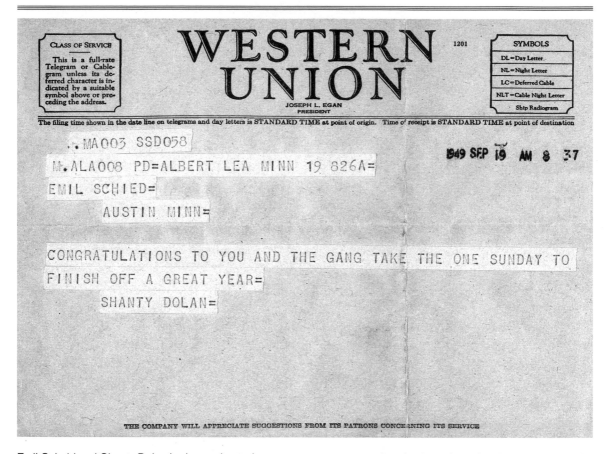

Emil Scheid and Shanty Dolan had many heated arguments on the field but shared a mutual respect for each other. Even though Austin ended Albert Lea's string of Southern Minny playoff championships in 1949, Dolan sent this telegram of encouragement to Scheid during the State Tournament. Courtesy of Larry Scheid.

little old to be starting a pro career, but his hitting attracted a few scouts.

Meanwhile Scheid went back to work. His 1951 team fell to second behind pennant-winning Owatonna but won the playoffs. The Packers lost again in the second round and were forced to come back through the losers' bracket. They beat St. Paul Nickel Joint 16–0 and Springfield 6–1 to force a showdown with Litchfield. Austin won the first game 4–2 but lost the championship game 10–2.

Austin finished in fourth place in the tight 1952 Southern Minny pennant race, only two games behind first-place Albert Lea. Austin lost in the first round of the playoffs to the other Packers, who finished in second place in the State Tournament.

Austin snapped the three-year string of second-place finishes for the Southern Minny by winning the Class AA State Championship in 1953. There were only three Class AA leagues left in the state by this time. The Packers lost their first game to Litchfield 3–2 but then won three consecutive games, including an 8–1 victory in a return match with Litchfield in the championship game.

Things had not been that smooth for the club during the year, however. Attendance fell off significantly—to 1,409 per game, down 32 percent from the 1952 season, even though the team was doing well on the field. The *Austin Daily Herald* conducted a write-in poll to get feedback from fans. Responses included charges that tickets were too expensive. Some blamed Scheid for not hiring good enough ballplayers or not managing well. In particular, they criticized him for not being aggressive enough in sending runners from his third-base coaching box and for not pulling starting pitchers soon enough when they got into trouble. It might not have been possible to guess that the team was in the thick of the pennant race by reading the comments. Many cited poor weather, but most ominous, perhaps, were the suggestions that television was keeping people at home.

The next year was even worse. The 1954 Packers finished in seventh place and, at 20–24, fell below .500 for the first time in Scheid's reign. Attendance fell to an average of 1,044. Scheid couldn't do anything right on the field. He brought in three players from the NCAA champion Missouri team, including the future Washington Senators bonus baby Dick Schoonmaker. To make room for the collegians, he cut longtime Packer favorites Billy Campau and Red Lindgren. This move made a lot of fans unhappy, especially when it didn't improve the team's record.

The Austin Baseball Association fired Scheid at the end of the season, proving what a tenuous job being a baseball manager can be—two state championships and two second-place finishes in eight years weren't enough to earn a second chance after a single bad season. Scheid was hopping mad and didn't hesitate to manage at Winona—the only team that finished below Austin in 1954—when Chiefs officials called to offer him a job. Scheid took five Austin players with him, driving them to games in one of his plumb-

ing shop's two Buicks—he rotated them to even out the mileage. He also picked up Jerry Kindall, who was coming off a good year at the University of Minnesota, but the team didn't do very well. They finished in sixth place at 19–30, compared to 12–32 in 1954. If there was any consolation, the Chiefs did finish one game ahead of Austin. Scheid said he was tired of the constant traveling and resigned at the end of the season.

He didn't stay retired very long, however. Waseca and Owatonna, the two smallest towns in the "old" Southern Minny, combined to form one team for the 1955 season. That opened up the spot for Fairmont, which transferred to the league from the Western Minny. The Wasetonna Twins finished in the cellar with a 16–33 record and were the only team in the league to draw average crowds less than 1,000. Scheid had ties to Waseca dating back to the days when he had a plumbing shop there, and it didn't take too much talking to convince him into managing the 1956 Twins.

Financially, the Twins were in worse shape than Scheid had imagined, and businessmen in Waseca and Owatonna were tired of subsidizing the team. Therefore he signed younger players and cut overall salaries by about one-third compared to 1955. He even purchased new uniforms for the team out of his own pocket, with the provision that the team would pay him back if it finished in the first division. Unfortunately for Scheid, there was little danger of that happening, as the team seemed mired near the bottom of the league.

Attendance was poor, and the team was losing money despite Scheid's budget cuts. Then, at a game in Owatonna—the Twins rotated games between Owatonna and Waseca—Faribault manager Pete Deem punched umpire Pete Bedor during a violent argument and knocked him un-

(**ABOVE**) Emil Scheid accepts the 1958 Class A
championship trophy. The Southern Minny, now a
Class A league, returned to the State Tournament for
the first time since 1953. Courtesy of Herb Schaper
Historical Baseball Collection/*New Ulm Daily Journal.*

(**RIGHT**) Emil Scheid *(right)* posed before
the 1959 Southern Minny season opener with
Rochester Yankees manager Bob Balance and
Austin mayor Charles "Baldy" Hansen. Scheid
sponsored both teams. Courtesy of Larry Scheid.

conscious. In the complaints and protests that
followed, Wasetonna team officials withdrew
from the league. Scheid wouldn't let the team
die, however. He personally assumed control of
the team for the rest of the year. The Travelers
played all remaining games on the road. Their
play didn't improve much, but their overall 17–
25 record was a modest improvement over 1955,
and they finished in a tie for sixth place.

Mason City, Iowa, replaced the Travelers for the 1957 season and selected Scheid as
manager. The Southern Minny decided to go
to a split schedule that year, with the first-half
champion playing the second-half champion for
the league championship. (The Southern Minny
was now the only remaining Class AA league in

the state.) At the end of June, with Mason City at 10–5 and one game out of first place, Scheid dropped a bombshell with the announcement that he was resigning to take over as manager of the Austin Packers. Austin was 6–12 at the time. The team finished in eighth place in the first half, at 6–15, but improved to 12–9 under Scheid for the second half, good enough for a fourth-place tie.

During the off-season Scheid worked hard to keep the Southern Minny alive. Rochester was flirting with professional baseball and ultimately decided to purchase a franchise in the Class B Three-I League. Several other teams were ready to throw in the towel on Class AA baseball. Scheid felt that fan interest could be rekindled by dropping to Class A and competing once again in the State Tournament. He couldn't prevent several teams from bolting to other leagues, however. The proud Southern Minny went down to a four-team Class A league in 1958—Austin, Fairmont, Albert Lea, and Mason City.

Scheid's Packers finished in third place at 18–17 but won the playoffs and the State Class A championship. They did it in typical Austin fashion—losing in the first round but coming back through the losers' bracket to win five consecutive games. Pitcher Jim Lawler went 3–1, pitching 36 innings, and won the tournament's MVP trophy.

Following the tournament, the city of Austin finally paid a tribute to Scheid, hosting a banquet to thank him for his years of service promoting the city and baseball. It was a fitting tribute, and an emotional one for Emil. During the dark days of 1954, he probably never could have imagined it.

But his work wasn't done. He had to save the Southern Minny once again in the off-season. He did it by getting Rochester and Winona to re-

join the league. Rochester was reluctant. They'd already decided to sponsor a Class A team, the Rochester Red Caps, in the Century League, but Scheid brokered a deal where he would sponsor a Rochester team—renamed the Yankees—in the Southern Minny and share dates at Mayo Field with the Red Caps. Bancroft and Estherville, Iowa, also joined, to bring the league back up to eight teams.

Dick Siebert: Gopher and Town Team Icon

Dick Siebert left a Lutheran seminary because he wanted to play professional baseball, not because he lost his faith. He left major-league baseball in 1946 because he didn't want to play for the St. Louis Browns, not because he lost his love for the game. Siebert seldom did anything without good reason. He had obviously seen enough of Missouri early in his career, and never saw too much of Minnesota. He would see all parts of his native state over the next several decades.

Dick Siebert, who excited Minnesota baseball fans when he announced that he would be playing for the Shakopee Indians in 1948, examines his glove with catcher and University of Minnesota assistant coach Max Mohr. *Star-Tribune* photograph; courtesy of the Minnesota Historical Society.

Dick Siebert, who started on the mound, covers home after an overthrow in Shakopee's opening-round 5–4 win over Lanesboro in the 1948 Class A State Tournament. *Dispatch–Pioneer Press* photograph; courtesy of the Minnesota Historical Society.

Upon his return to Minnesota, Siebert—a 1928 graduate of St. Paul's Concordia High—became a Twin Cities radio celebrity on WTCN, but his hiatus from active baseball was only brief. In the fall of 1947, the man who had played professionally for the St. Louis Cardinals and Philadelphia Athletics agreed to coach a flagging University of Minnesota baseball program. He spent the next 31 years building a college dynasty and making a solid foundation for amateur baseball within the state even stronger.

When all was said and won, the former major-league first baseman had 754 victories and three College World Series pennants, the three NCAA titles claimed in 1956, 1960, and 1964—what his former ace shortstop and later assistant coach Jerry Kindall refers to as "Election Year Championships" for obvious reasons. Throughout the twentieth century, only five universities had won more than two NCAA baseball titles, and Minnesota was the only one from outside the Sun Belt to attain the distinction. And to make things even sweeter, Siebert did it using primarily Minnesota talent. All 19 players on the 1960 tournament roster were from Minnesota, and 16 of 18 on the 1956 squad.

"I always wondered how a team in Minnesota could keep winning the Big Ten," Carm Cozza, a football coaching legend who played several summer baseball seasons in Minnesota, said. "But I realized he did it by coaching them while playing with them. He was smart."

Tom Petroff, a good friend and American Baseball Coaches Association Hall of Fame peer, said that the Gopher coach had an exceptional baseball mind. Petroff added, however, that Siebert had the advantage of having little major college competition for players. Wisconsin, Iowa, and Iowa State, the biggest and closest universities, were still a comfortable distance beyond Siebert's turf.

Petroff, who spent several seasons in Minnesota as a town team player, would never accuse Siebert of taking any advantage for granted. Siebert tirelessly worked the state, making friends and believers in a baseball program that even Siebert once admitted he initially considered only to be a stepping-stone for a business career.

"No one in the world could have convinced me [in his first year as the Gophers' coach] that I would have been here 31 years later," Siebert said late in his career. "But I love it, working with great young men and staying in the best form of baseball I know . . . the college game."

Siebert became a major advocate and consummate organizer in Minnesota amateur baseball, encouraging the top college players from the state to play summer ball at home. He scouted and conducted clinics throughout the state, using state high school and college coaches as his assistants. He was quick to spot talent and demonstrated an innate ability to recognize potential, and he was relentless in his quest to squeeze the most out of everyone's potential. He wrote books that received acclaim from coaches throughout the nation, and the conventional wisdom within the state became "If it's good enough for the University of Minnesota, it's good enough for us." A dream for many coaches was to have one of their players make the Gopher team, but Siebert did not bow to political recruiting.

Bob Streetar, a former Grand Rapids coach who played freshman baseball at the University of Minnesota, remembers a particular visit by Siebert to the Iron Range. When informed that Esko had a hard-throwing prospect, Siebert expressed an interest, so someone tracked down the pitcher and brought him to the Gopher coach.

"The kid hummed about three pitches in and suddenly Dick hollered, 'Enough,'" Streetar said.

"He told the kid, who had sort of a plump build, 'Well, you've got a nice arm, but taking one look at you son, you're lazy. Nobody your age should be in that shape and say that he's serious about baseball. I'll tell you what, you want to come to the university, come on, but I've got no money for you.'

"He knew what to watch for and how to fine tune things . . . chink, chink, chink. He'd say, 'Kid, you swing like Ted Williams, but you aren't Ted Williams, so we're going to have to make changes.' And he knew everybody. When he'd come up here to Grand Rapids, he knew exactly the people he had to see. He loved sitting around the bar having a few beers with the area folks."

Siebert knew the right people because he hawked the state as a coach, clinician, and competitor. Two years after abandoning his major-league career, he resumed competition as a player. He played the 1948 and 1949 seasons at Shakopee, and his pitching and hitting factored in the team's 1948 third-place finish in the State Tournament. He went to Buffalo in 1950 and followed that brief stay with a four-year tour in Litchfield. Pete Kramer, a friend and former teammate of the team's cofounder Jack Verby, managed the 1950 Optimists, but Siebert accepted the job in 1951 when Kramer moved 25 miles farther west to Willmar.

Second baseman Jerry Schaber, a product of a relatively firm disciplinary system at Hamline, returned to the Optimists for his second season in 1951 and found the new manager's style of leadership to be significantly more liberal. He was introduced to Siebert's laissez-faire approach during a ride with the coach and a couple of Gopher players from Litchfield back to the Twin Cities. In Howard Lake or one of the small towns on Route 12, he pulled over to a tavern and suggested that they have a beer.

"I asked one of the guys, 'What's the deal?' " Schaber said. "They told me, when 'The Chief'— that's what they called him—took them to Texas on the spring trip, he put the captains in charge. His rule was that they could have a couple beers, but no whiskey."

Streetar also found Siebert's casual approach to be fascinating, and on one occasion, gratifying. One day he and three of his Iron Range buddies skipped freshman practice to attend the Minneapolis Millers' opener at the Met. They were having a grand time until they heard a voice from behind them: it was Siebert.

"He said, 'You're enjoying this, aren't you?' " Streetar said, smiling. "He told us, 'You Rangers never change, do you?' The next day at practice, all he said to us was 'Well, at least you were at a ballgame.' I'm sure that he realized that we were a bunch of guys who had never seen more than ten people together in one place."

Unusual or unorthodox as Siebert's approach might have seemed, he consistently demonstrated his ability to lead, and his Litchfield ten-

ure was no exception. In his first season, the Optimists won the 1951 State Class AA title and qualified again for the 1953 Class AA Tournament, where they finished second. Individually, he was Litchfield's starting first baseman and finished among the West Central League's leading hitters every year, winning the batting title in 1951. From 1951 through 1954, three seasons in the Class AA West Central League and another in the Class AA Western Minny, Siebert hit .380, .372, .328, and .340.

Litchfield joined the Western Minnesota League in 1954, when the West Central returned to Class A, and the Optimists qualified for the playoffs and lost to Fairmont in the final round of the playoffs. Siebert decided to stay in the Twin Cities in 1955, where he established Kopp's Realty, a team comprised mainly of Gopher freshmen and sophomores. The team got off to a slow start but, under Siebert's deft leadership, finished third in the Minneapolis Park National League and won the playoffs and a ticket to Chaska for the State Class A Tournament.

Siebert's contacts as a coach, manager, and organizer served him and his University of Minnesota program well. When he couldn't use one of his players in the town where he was managing, he found a manager in one of the Class AA or Class A programs to use them. When his competitive days ended, he continued to work tirelessly with college coaches to maintain the quality of summer ball. The Midwest Collegiate League of the 1960s was the fruit of his labor, and with that league and his clinics, he continued to enhance Minnesota's amateur baseball reputation. Whether it was town team or his University of Minnesota program, he always recruited outstanding aides, and Glenn Gostick, a former Gopher assistant, said that Siebert was never too proud to accept a suggestion.

Dick Siebert *(left)* developed contacts throughout the state. Here he is talking in a dugout during the 1955 State Tournament in Chaska to potential recruits Dave Lesar and Bob Streetar, who were playing with Grand Rapids Riverview. *Dispatch–Pioneer Press* photograph; courtesy of the Minnesota Historical Society.

Jim Dimick, a longtime St. Olaf baseball coach, said that part of the state's baseball success can be attributed to the rural nature of the state, where for years young men didn't have direct major-league baseball exposure to distract them from playing the game. But he was quick to add, "I think that Dick was the number one reason why Minnesota plays tremendous high school baseball."

Before his death in December 1978, he emotionally expressed what his Minnesota coaching and teaching career had meant to him. He had an outstanding playing career in the major leagues, fashioning a .290 batting average and starting on the 1943 American League All-Star team. That didn't earn him a spot in Coopertown's Baseball Hall of Fame, but his college success did earn him a place in the American Baseball Coaches Association Hall of Fame and a special spot in Minnesotans' hearts.

He was a college coach who sits among a cast of Minnesota sports icons including Bud Grant, Paul Giel, Bronko Nagurski, and any of the greatest Twins and Vikings who have passed this way. "Dick was the cornerstone of Minnesota baseball, and not just at the university," Siebert protégé Jerry Kindall said of his former coach and boss.

Obviously he wouldn't have had it any other way. The St. Louis Browns' loss back in 1946 was both Siebert's and Minnesota amateur baseball's gain.

Jim McNulty: Minnesota Adopted the Brooklyn Kid

Jim McNulty arrived in Minnesota in the summer of 1948, a refugee from the minor leagues, and within less than a decade Minnesota town team baseball had acquired a distinct Brooklyn accent. Not only did the former member of the Brooklyn Dodgers organization play second base with the grace of Fred Astaire, but he was a gifted teacher, an intuitive organizer, and an enthusiastic leader who over the next 13 years would play an integral role in Minnesota town team ball. He spent three summers in Fergus Falls, and after the 1951 season with Estherville in the Iowa State League, he began to fashion a dynasty in Fairmont. In 12 seasons in Minnesota, all but one as a player/manager, he shared in five state championships—the first with Fergus Falls in 1950 and then with Fairmont in 1954, 1955, 1957, and 1959—and more than 300 victories.

As the player/manager at Fairmont from 1952 through 1960, he won 197 regular-season games and six pennants and five playoff championships in the Western Minnesota and Southern Minnesota Leagues, the state's two premier leagues. McNulty's legacy should be measured not strictly in wins and losses but also by the men he attracted to Minnesota. In his tenure, he recruited heavily from baseball's professional ranks—several with major-league credentials, including Pittsburgh shortstop Grady Wilson and Cleveland outfielder Milt Nielsen—and he educated many future leaders in his clinics.

McNulty's baseball days began on the streets of Brooklyn, New York, where he played a form of stickball they called "sewer-to-sewer ball." He became a baseball star at Grover Cleveland High, and earned all-city and all-state recognition in soccer.

At the time when McNulty was beginning to seriously entertain a professional baseball career, his timetable was drastically altered by World War II. He quit high school, enlisted in the Marine Corps, and in 1945 wound up in the Pacific, preparing for the invasion of Iwo Jima instead of graduation day. He participated in

players and they didn't know or didn't care how good Austin was. We played an outstanding tournament and Harley Oyloe pitched a great game to clinch the championship."

Unfortunately, the North Central League collapsed, and the owners of the Red Sox, unable to fashion a Class AA schedule, were forced to drop to Class A in 1951. Although he now had a full-time job in Fergus Falls and had moved there year-round, McNulty feared that

Player/manager Jim McNulty accepting the 1950 Class AA championship trophy from MABA president Tom Mallery after upsetting the highly favored Austin Packers. Courtesy of Harley Oyloe.

the team would abandon its pay-for-play policy. McNulty's reputation, though, had flourished throughout Minnesota and surrounding states, and he accepted an offer to manage Estherville in the Iowa State League. Oyloe and others in Fergus Falls were disappointed to see McNulty go. "He was an inspirational guy with a good baseball sense," Oyloe said. "If he could have hit, he probably would have made it to the majors. He definitely should have been a professional manager."

McNulty spent only one year in Iowa. The Fairmont Martins, disappointed by a 13–22 record in their first season in the Western Minnesota League, lured McNulty back across the border. He signed a contract to become the player/manager for $300 per month—on a twelve-month basis—and was given a sporting-goods sales position at a popular local store. He eventually purchased a bar and restaurant he named the "Martin's Nest." He wasn't playing in Ebbets Field or the Polo Grounds, but he was enjoying life at a lofty and comfortable level.

Using his minor-league contacts, McNulty quickly began to sculpt a state dynasty by recruiting more than two dozen professional players, many with some major-league or Triple A experience. In the mid-1950s, his team was anchored by seven players with professional Class AA or better experience.

McNulty's 1952 Fairmont team finished 15–20, but only because the Martins had to forfeit 10 victories for the inadvertent use of an ineligible player. The Martins, however, won the Western Minnesota playoffs to qualify for the State Tournament, where they went 1–2 in the double-elimination competition.

The Martins won the next two Western Minnesota titles, qualifying for the 1953 State Tournament again and winning the 1954 Little

World Series title, a playoff between the Western and Southern Minny champions. In 1955, Fairmont moved to the Southern Minnesota, a move some detractors deemed to be folly, but the Martins hardly missed a beat.

They won the 1955 Southern Minny pennant, playoffs, and Little World Series. After an "off year" in 1956, when they finished in second place and lost in the playoffs, they won the 1957 Southern Minnesota title when it was the only remaining Class AA league in the state. In 1958 the Southern Minny dropped to Class A. Fairmont won the pennant but lost to third-place Austin in the playoffs. The Martins won the Southern Minny pennant again in 1959 and this time followed up by winning the playoffs. The Martins returned to the State Tournament for the first time since 1953 and walked away with the Class A trophy.

The 1960 Martins finished 16–14, third in the Southern Minny behind Austin and Mankato, rounding out McNulty's nine-year record at 224–142. As player/manager for Fergus Falls and Fairmont, he won nearly 300 games and brought each town state titles.

"Dick Siebert told me that the 1955 Fairmont team was the best he'd ever seen," former Martins pitcher Myron Hoffman said of a team that finished 33–16 and swept St. James in three straight in the best-of-five Little World Series.

"We had some awfully good teams, but I guess the 1955 team was the best, definitely better than the team that won the State Tournament in 1959," McNulty agreed. "By 1959, the caliber of competition had diminished a great deal from the early years. By the 1960 season, no one was making any money. The players that season wound up playing for a share of the gate. I knew that it was over."

McNulty, who had bought and lost a bar while living in Fairmont, packed up and headed to the Twin Cities with his family during the off-season. He remained in Minnesota for three more years but, confronted by financial woes, returned to Brooklyn, where he drove a taxi for several years before establishing a limousine service.

From his home in the Poconos, where he and his wife, Millie, settled after his retirement, McNulty conceded that he didn't handle his money very well in his Minnesota days, but insisted that he had no regrets. And Durrell, his former wartime buddy and teammate, takes pride in having been the one to introduce McNulty to Minnesota baseball.

"He was dynamite, a holler guy who also knew the game well. Fundamentally, he had it all," Durrell said. "The fans thrived on him. He was unique. He was a guy with a New York accent, but he wasn't a wheeler-dealer type . . . just a nice guy, a good citizen. He served Minnesota baseball well."

When McNulty left Fairmont for the Twin Cities after the 1960 season, he left behind many of his former players who had become integral members of the community. But while gone, the personable player/manager was not forgotten. He left an indelible impression. Don Dahlke, a former infielder who became a school administrator and coach in Fairmont, remembered his former manager just as vividly as he did the Martins' best season.

"We had a good time while it lasted, but then nothing lasts forever. Things change," Dahlke said. "But I think the most memorable part of the era was playing for such a great manager as Jim McNulty."

MINNESOTA'S MAJOR-LEAGUE ATTRACTIONS

W HEN VETERAN FANS TALK ABOUT Minnesota's state baseball glory days, Bill "Moose" Skowron's name is frequently among the first to be mentioned because he went on from playing Southern Minnesota League ball to become the New York Yankees' starting first baseman.

Skowron, who played for Austin in 1950, the year he signed with the Yankees, is one of the most prominent Minnesota town team players to have played major-league baseball, but he is not the lone member of the state's big-league alums. Minnesotans, even those who lived in the era, might be surprised at how many men played town team ball before or after their major-league days. Some were Minnesota products such as Dick Siebert, Howie Schultz, Hy Vandenberg, Paul Giel, Jerry Kindall, and others. Among those from the outside were Herb Score and Gordy Coleman, teens when they played at Brainerd, Sam Jones, and Rudy York, a tragic figure who enjoyed major-league all-star status before his self-destructive lifestyle brought him down.

Ironically, York and Vandenberg met in the 1945 World Series, York with Detroit and Vandenberg with the Chicago Cubs, seven years before competing in the same Minnesota town team season. York spent a season at Benson–De Graff and St. James, Vandenberg with several towns.

Henry "Hy" Vandenberg: Clown Prince of Town Baseball

Two years after one of the most significant weeks of his baseball career, Henry "Hy" Vandenberg was pitching in Springfield, Minnesota. This was a quantum move from the big leagues and Chicago, where he pitched for the Cubs in the 1945 World Series, but the lanky right-hander never seemed to express any regret.

He remained highly competitive, going 39–11 for Springfield in the Western Minnesota League from 1947 through 1950. He also established a reputation for "Hy" drama and comedy before, during, and after games.

He once stopped to tie a shoelace after rounding third base and then feigned confusion after being tagged out. He would sometimes applaud

Hy Vandenberg, in his old Minneapolis Millers jersey, has some fun with New Ulm's Hank Nicklasson in an old-timer's game in 1956. As a Springfield Tiger, Vandenberg was noted for his clowning and flamboyant antics. He and Nicklasson clashed often on the field. Courtesy of Herb Schaper Historical Baseball Collection/*New Ulm Daily Journal.*

when an opposing batter would get a hit. He'd pick up a stone from the mound, admire it, and announce to the crowd that he'd found an arrowhead. He talked to fans, both admirers and detractors, and even surprised the detractors by smiling and extending a friendly hand. He baited and taunted umpires unmercifully. Once he addressed a corpulent umpire saying, "Hey fatso, how many are you going to miss tonight?" He'd tease opponents, informing some what he planned to throw and delivering as promised.

His raucous routine seemed to have no limits. Dick Mingo, an infielder who played with Vandenberg at Olivia, remembered a 1951 game in which Vandenberg served up a fat pitch to Willmar's Howie Schultz, who sent the ball well beyond the outfield boundaries. Vandenberg, flashing either his panache or his frustration, chased Schultz around the bases yelling, "You SOB, there is no way you can hit that pitch like that."

Vandenberg often upstaged his prowess with his pranks, but Casey Dowling never disputed the eccentric pitcher's ability. He lauded Vandenberg's tricky curve, his baffling screwball, his ability to hit the spots, and his capacity to read each hitter's strengths and weaknesses. Dowling was an accomplished catcher and Vandenberg's friend, but the five-foot-nine catcher was not immune to the pitcher's mischievous nature.

"When I was catching for Sleepy Eye and we'd face Springfield, he would often get down on his knees to pitch to me," Dowling said. "Another favorite of mine was when someone would hit a high fly in the infield. Hy would stagger around seeming to be trying to find the ball that would wind up in the first baseman's mitt."

Vandenberg was no stranger to Minnesota when he donned his Springfield uniform in 1947. In addition to having spent his formative years in Minneapolis, according to the *Springfield Advance-Press,* he pitched town team ball for Sanborn at 16 years of age under the alias of Harold Stetler. He also pitched all or parts of three minor-league seasons for the Minneapolis Millers and played a season for the Minneapolis Park National Mitby-Sathers in 1943 when he took a leave of absence from professional baseball to work in a war plant. "I was the catcher on Mitby-Sathers that season, and so I caught Hy," Casey Dowling said of the 1943 season. "Hy pitched some fantastic games, and he was a darn good hitter, too."

Twin Cities Ordnance put together an all-star team that included Milt Bruhn, a Minnesota football star who later coached the University of Wisconsin football team, and several outstanding pitchers including Gene Kelly, who pitched for the University of Minnesota and later was an outstanding pitcher in the West Central League.

"We beat [Twin Cities Ordnance] at least a couple times," Dowling said. "I think Hy beat Kelly 1–0 in one of those games. But Hy couldn't play in the State Tournament because of the state association rule that anyone coming down from Class A ball or higher had to wait 13 months to be eligible."

The six-foot-four pitcher returned to professional baseball in 1944 and played consecutive seasons with the Chicago Cubs, compiling a 13–7 two-year record, but after the 1945 World Series adventure, he was sent down and finished the last season of his 15-year professional career with the Oakland Oaks in the Pacific Coast League. He was 41 years old when he arrived in Springfield, where in the Class AA Western Minny he was a tremendous success. Former National League pitcher Les Munns was unbeatable in 1944, and Claire Strommen was outstanding before he was sidelined by illness after the 1946 season, but Vandenberg more than held his own against their reputations.

Vandenberg left Springfield after the 1950 season, resurfacing at Olivia in 1951, but finished the season at Fairfax. The move inspires curiosity. According to former Springfield offensive star Art Marben, the former major-league pitcher was respected and liked by his teammates.

Not every opponent or opposing fan appreciated Vandenberg's irreverent behavior, but even his detractors must have been amused by his antics. Tom Mee, a former town team player for Redwood Falls and several other Minnesota teams before joining the Minnesota Twins ad-

ministrative staff, saw Vandenberg's vain side on a car ride late one afternoon from the Twin Cities to Redwood Falls. Mee said that all the way out to Redwood, where he played infield for the Redbirds and Vandenberg pitched for the Tigers, Vandenberg spent much of the time talking about Vandenberg.

"I was the leadoff hitter for Redwood in that game, and I hit a home run in the bottom of the first," Mee said. "Hy wound up still winning the game something like 5–3, but he didn't speak to me during the entire trip back to the Cities."

Dave Gisvold, son of former Springfield manager Al Gisvold, said that Vandenberg's clowning in tense situations was strategic. His shenanigans distracted opponents and kept them off guard. After leaving Springfield, Vandenberg pitched some excellent games for Olivia, Fairfax, and Wanda, begging the question why the Tigers let him get away. Mike Schwaegerl, a former Springfield resident and Tigers fan addressed this question in a retrospective article years later.

"It was probably because people were kind of tired of him. He was sort of a high-maintenance player who demanded and got quite a bit of attention," Schwaegerl wrote, "but he was fun to have around."

Hy Vandenberg may have been a person whose feet seemed to be planted firmly in mid-air, but he was definitely a well-grounded athlete when he was pitching and the game was on the line.

Rudy York: Troubled Slugger Struck Out

Rudy York was cheered by millions during his major-league career. He was an American League All-Star seven times. He set a handful of major-league records while with the Detroit

Five years after the last of his seven major-league all-star games, St. James's Rudy York *(left)* was a 1952 Western Minnesota League all-star, along with Fairmont's Sid Langston and Ted Beck. Courtesy of Jim McNulty.

Tigers, some that have survived throughout the twentieth century. From his rookie season in 1937, when he hit 35 homers and drove in 103 runs, he was lauded. But when the good times ceased to roll, York began a rapid downward spiral that led him to Minnesota in 1952 at age 39. He played briefly for Benson–De Graff in the West Central League and then finished the season with St. James in the Western Minnesota League. Although a celebrity wherever he played that summer, he was unable to help either team.

York batted .258 at Benson–De Graff (8 for 31, with two home runs) before joining St. James, and although he made the league all-star team, it was more of a box office ploy than for his play. He finished with a .263 batting average for the last-place Saints, with just two home runs in 57 at-bats. It wasn't as if Jerry Sullivan, the Benson–De Graff manager, hadn't warned York about the league's strength.

"I told Rudy, 'I'm not going to give you any lectures on baseball because you're miles ahead of me on baseball,'" Sullivan said, " 'but I'm gonna tell you one thing that you're going to find out quickly. They can stick it up your butt in this league, and they will if you don't report in reasonably good shape for a guy your age.'

"I told him that I knew that he wasn't the fastest guy in the world and that he wasn't a great fielder. I said, 'I want you for your power.'"

Sullivan didn't ask York for a pledge of sobriety, but he hoped the slugger would temper his nocturnal lifestyle. Sullivan said York's intentions were good when he arrived, but his resolve was weak. His teammates quickly became agitated, and Benson's Roy Berens received the task of telling Sullivan that York was spending too much time playing the wrong games. If York didn't go, Berens warned Sullivan, the manager might lose his team, and on June 19, Sullivan dismissed York. The decision was painful for the competitive but soft-hearted Irish-Chief manager.

"He never hurt anyone but himself . . . never," Sullivan said. "When he left, he left as a friend who understood. I only wish that things had worked out better for both him and our team. But at least he found himself, and no one was happier to see him than I was when he returned to Minnesota years later [as a coach] with Boston."

York caught on with St. James shortly after leaving Benson–De Graff. Former Saint James player John Ness said that York assured management that he would behave, and he caused no problems during his stay. Even so, opposing fans, and even some unhappy St. James supporters, were less than sympathetic with York's plight and taunted him while watching him struggle in a league light-years from where he used to be a star. Ness said that York got along well with his teammates, and he emphasized that the slugger never just went through the motions. York even became involved with instruction in the town's youth baseball program.

Although the slugger did little for the Saints, he provided Western Minny fans major entertainment during batting practice. Phil Hall, a Truman High School teacher with a baseball background, made it a point to go early to Saints games just to see York take his pregame swings. The former Detroit Tigers star, who once hit a major-league-record 18 home runs in a month, may have lost some of his keen batting eye, but he still possessed much of his power. Hall said that when York made contact, the sound was explosive, and the flight of the ball was like a moon launch.

At some point after leaving Minnesota, York received a second chance in major-league baseball, perhaps through his good friend and former Tigers standout Hank Greenberg, who is believed to have helped York financially on occasion while York was in Minnesota. He briefly scouted for the Yankees, was a Boston Red Sox coach from 1959 through 1962, and even spent one day as the Red Sox manager between the firing of Mike Higgins and the hiring of Bill Jurges.

York returned to Minnesota when Boston came to town, and Jerry Sullivan remembered a trip he made to Bloomington to talk to York before a game in Metropolitan Stadium.

"I went down by the dugout and got his attention and he came over, and we talked," Sullivan said. "I told him that I wouldn't bother him long . . . that I just wanted to say hello. I told him that I didn't want to embarrass him or anything in front of the fans. But he told me, 'Don't worry about them,' and said he was glad to see me. We talked for a fairly good length of time."

Herb Score: Florida Teen Brought the Heat

Herb Score's arrival in Brainerd for the 1951 town team season created fanfare and curiosity among the locals. An article in the local paper announced that a teenager with major-league potential was coming to town to pitch for the Braves, a town team with no league affiliation but a rugged independent schedule. Little else was known about the young left-hander, but that's the way Cy Slapnicka liked it. The Cleveland scout with a summer home in this resort area brought the 17-year-old Score from Lake Worth, Florida, to northern Minnesota to hide the hard-throwing youngster from the rest of the baseball world until his graduation the next spring.

Word of the teen with a sizzling fastball gradually made its way around the state. His high school record included four no-hitters and one victory in which he had 24 strikeouts, but despite his amazing statistics, it was hard to imagine that he could throw as hard as rumored. You had to see him to believe him, according to several who batted against the six-foot-two left-hander, and many said they discovered Score was faster than rumored—faster and wilder.

As for Brainerd baseball fans, the moment the 1,400 spectators watched Score throw his first missile against the House of David in Brainerd's Memorial Park on June 13, it was love at first sight.

Gordy Coleman, 17, another Slapnicka prospect and future major-league player, led the team in hitting at .344. Whitey Skoog, a home-town Gopher basketball great who had recently signed an NBA Lakers contract, hit .321 and gave the team defensive versatility. Dick Cook, a local from nearby Nisswa, hit 10 home runs and .323. Frank O'Rourke, a nationally acclaimed author, offered a trifle of baseball prowess and plenty of panache. And finally there was minor-league veteran Wayne Stewart, who went 10–4, including a victory over Fergus Falls the year after the Red Sox won the Minnesota Class AA title.

It was a dream team of sorts, though Score was unquestionably the team's marquee player

In 1951, the year before he completed high school, Herb Score pitched for the Brainerd Braves, an independent in Minnesota town team ball. Four years later the hard-throwing lefty was pitching for Cleveland in the majors. Courtesy of *Brainerd Dispatch*.

with his dazzling speed. The dynamic teen made 19 appearances, carving out a 12–4 record despite missing several games during an eleven-day layoff because of a sore arm. He allowed 49 runs off 65 hits and 81 bases on balls, but any runs, hits, or walks were forgiven in light of his 176 strikeouts. Score defeated Foley 8–0 in mid-August, a no-hitter in which he notched a season-high 19 strikeouts—along with eight bases on balls.

Among his other victories, Score defeated Willmar 6–5, a talent-laden team that in 1952 would win the West Central League title and the Class AA championship. He also was the winning pitcher in a 13–5 triumph over Cold Spring, a 1950 Class A state tournament team.

Sal Theis, former Cold Springs manager who played on the 1950 Springers and later led them to the 1955 State Class B title, remembered the mid-July Brainerd trip and witnessing both the majestic and mortal sides of the teenager. Theis said Score's speed was amazing to all, but not so amusing to one Springer player who caught one of Score's errant darts in the knee.

"I wound up having to take him out the next inning because he couldn't walk . . . his knee swelled way up," Theis said. "Score was really wild. Sometimes his curveball was hitting the dirt way in front of the plate. But he was as fast as everyone said."

Score struck out 15, but in addition to hitting a batter, he gave up eight hits and walked six. Cold Springs' left-handed slugger Joe Schleper had three hits, including a home run to center, off the left-handed Score, and pushed a Braves outfielder to the fence on a long out. Outfielder John Kasper also hit a home run off Score.

"I was good friends with Bill Arendt, who managed the team and caught Score," Theis said, "and he said that years later occasionally Score would call him, and generally would ask about Schleper."

Howie Schultz, a former major-league first baseman, remembers batting against Score. Schultz had coaxed a 3–0 count against the precocious teen, but Schultz said that Score whizzed three darts past him. What Schultz didn't say is that Score entered the game in a relief role and protected a 6–5 Brainerd lead facing the heart of the Willmar order, striking out Chub Ebnet and Schultz and getting Art Granggaard to pop up.

Cook, a Nisswa native who played outfield for Brainerd, said that he had no idea how fast Score threw, since no radar gun was available, but said the youngster's speed awed even his teammates and probably would have been clocked in the mid- to high 90s. For Russ Jacobsen, a New York Mills player, a hit off Score turned out to be a career highlight.

"I was the leadoff hitter one night, and I hit a double that almost went out of the park," he said. "I was no better than a .250 hitter and only hit a couple home runs in my life. Imagine that. But then, we didn't know that Herb Score was going to be Herb Score at the time."

Brainerd, an independent team that left the Class B Great Central League to play an independent schedule, finished the 1951 season 29–8. The Braves were 31–6 and 34–2 the next two seasons, but without Score, things were never the same. After three independent seasons, the Braves folded in 1954, although Brainerd continued to field teams in the Class B Great Central League.

"They were nice people with good intentions," Little Falls baseball legend Lou Filippi said about Brainerd's baseball brain trust, "but the people just never warmed to the [independent Braves].

I don't think they realized how difficult it would be working with a team that didn't have a built-in league schedule."

Bill "Moose" Skowron: Packer Who Packed Clout

Bill Skowron is perhaps the most famous major-league star to have played in Minnesota in the 1945–60 era. He grew up in Chicago and went to Purdue University on a football scholarship but also played on the Boilermaker baseball team, where he led the Big Ten in hitting in 1950 with a .500 batting average (20 for 40). A Purdue alumnus put Austin manager Emil Scheid in touch with Skowron, who was also considering playing in Iowa that summer. Skowron was offered $400 per month to play baseball and work as an apprentice's helper in Scheid's plumbing and heating shop. Skowron accepted but said it was no token job. "It was tough work," he said. "The other guys gave me all the hard, manual-labor jobs, like cutting holes for pipes in concrete walls."

Skowron was still a raw baseball talent. There were no playground baseball programs in his neighborhood, and the only youth ball he played was in the 16-inch Windy City [soft] Ball Leagues. His father played baseball on weekends, however, and he tagged along with him and eventually got to play some with the adults. He played shortstop at Purdue and was still learning to play the game.

Austin had an offensive juggernaut in 1950 and finished the Southern Minny season with a .323 team batting average. Skowron played third base and hit .343—good for only fifth on the team! However, he hit the ball hard and attracted major-league scouts. Skowron signed a $30,000 bonus contract with the New York Yan-

Nebraska native Norm Wilson tired of the professional
life in 1953 and moved to Springfield, where he caught
for the Class AA Tigers. Courtesy of Norm Wilson.

instead of just one of many faces in the crowd.
The former professionals owed Minnesota a debt
of gratitude for a better standard of life, but at the
same time Minnesota fans owed them thanks for
their contribution to a special era in baseball.

Gread "Lefty" McKinnis: Winding Trail Led to Minnesota

Gread "Lefty" McKinnis was a 32-year-old veteran of the Negro Major Leagues when he
showed up in Rochester, Minnesota, in the summer of 1946 to call on the local promoter Ben
Sternberg. McKinnis had pitched for the Chicago American Giants of the Negro American

League in 1944 and 1945 but had deserted them
for promises of big money in the renegade Mexican League in 1946. When that didn't pan out,
he returned and pitched a few games for the
Pittsburgh Crawfords, but he was having trouble finding regular work. The Chicago promoter
Abe Saperstein, owner of the Chicago American
Giants, suggested that McKinnis contact Sternberg for a possible job in Minnesota.

McKinnis was more than an ordinary pitcher.
He pitched for the Birmingham Black Barons in
the 1943 Negro Leagues World Series, where
he lost two games to the champion Homestead
Grays. McKinnis had also appeared in the East-
West All-Star game—the Negro Leagues' mar-
quee event, held annually at Comiskey Park in
Chicago—in 1943 and 1944.

Sternberg arranged for McKinnis to pitch for
nearby Zumbrota in the Class A Southeastern
Minnesota League. He made his first appearance
on Sunday, July 28. The *Zumbrota News* wrote
that "a black gentleman from parts unknown
was in the box for the locals." He pitched under
the name "Al Saylor," probably fearing the lifetime ban that organized baseball and the Negro
Leagues threatened to place on players who had
signed with the Mexican League. It's not known
exactly why he picked the alias, but he'd been a
teammate with right-handed pitcher Al Saylor in
1941–43 with the Birmingham Black Barons.

With "Saylor" on the mound, Zumbrota won
the league playoffs, but he had joined the team
too late to be eligible for the State Tournament
roster. Without him, the team was trounced 23–
2 by Albert Lea in the first round of the Class
AA tournament. The Southeastern Minnesota
League had been bumped to Class AA during
the playoffs because of excessive use of outside
players by several teams in the league.

Sternberg signed McKinnis to pitch for his

Gread "Lefty" McKinnis was a veteran of the Negro Major Leagues when he came to Minnesota to pitch for Zumbrota in 1946. Courtesy of Phil Dixon.

Bulletin pictured him operating a shoe-shine stand at the Boston Shoe Shine and Hat Shop—he made frequent trips back to Chicago and left the team in early July to pitch for a South Bend, Indiana, team in a Michigan-Indiana semipro league.

He returned to the Queens for an August 30 exhibition game and then beat the Winona Merchants twice to win the Bi-State League playoff championship and a berth in the Class AA State Tournament. McKinnis lost the opening game of the State Tournament, 3–2, to the St. Paul Union Printers. He started against Albert Lea, who were on the way to their fifth consecutive Class AA championship, the following day, but was pulled after giving up single runs in the second, third, and fourth innings in a 4–0 loss.

In 1949 Sternberg took over Rochester's Southern Minnesota League team, renamed the "Royals," but McKinnis went back to pitch for the Chicago American Giants in the Negro American League, where he went 12–7 to lead the team to the Western Division title, and appeared once again in the East-West All-Star game.

McKinnis and Sternberg were reunited at Rochester in 1950, where McKinnis's 11–3 record was the best in the Southern Minny. The Royals finished 19–16 and in a four-way tie for third place, with McKinnis mixing starting and relief roles. Rochester won a double-elimination playoff for third place, beat Waseca in the first round of the playoffs, but lost three straight to Austin in the championship series.

McKinnis wandered across the country the next several years. He pitched for Brandon, Manitoba, of the Man-Dak semipro league from 1951 to 1953 but spent partial seasons in organized baseball in 1952 and 1953 with Tampa, Florida, of the Class C Florida International League. He returned to Rochester in 1954 but pitched ineffectively and was released before midseason. His

Rochester Queens in 1947, where he had a sensational season, going 26–4 overall and averaging 16 strikeouts per game. He started all four of the Queens games in the Class A State Tournament, going 3–1, with 39 strikeouts in 23⅔ innings, while giving up only 9 hits. He shut out Glencoe 1–0 in the semifinals and hit a home run for the game's only score, but lost to Chaska in the championship game when he tried to pitch his third game in four days. He lasted only 2⅔ innings but was selected as the tournament MVP for his iron-man performance.

McKinnis returned to the Queens in 1948. However, unlike in 1947, when he lived in Rochester most of the season—the *Rochester Post-*

record disappears after 1955, when he pitched for St. Petersburg, Florida, in the Class D Florida State League, and 1956, when he appeared for Minot in the Man-Dak League.

McKinnis's baseball fate was shared by many other black players who were in their late twenties or older when organized baseball finally began to be integrated in 1946. They were too old to receive serious trials with major-league teams and were faced with a rapid decline in black baseball when the Negro National League folded after the 1948 season. Consequently, men like McKinnis turned to barnstorming black teams and integrated semipro leagues to find baseball jobs. Some, like Mc-Kinnis, signed minor-league contracts, but they were used primarily to fill out rosters.

Johnny Herr: Lone Star Refugee, Northern Star

Johnny Herr arrived in Litchfield six games into the 1951 West Central League season, and the slender left-hander was playing catch when Jerry Schaber noticed the newest Optimist pitcher. Not particularly impressed by Herr's unique motion or his presence, Schaber approached manager Dick Siebert and asked about the new guy. Siebert, sensing Schaber's skepticism, told the scrappy infielder, "Don't worry, he's going to do just fine."

Siebert's confidence was based on Herr's professional past, which began 13 years earlier as a 16-year-old, when he signed a contract with the St. Louis Cardinals. His bonus offer included either a gun or a radio. He accepted the radio and headed for Daytona Beach to begin a 10-year professional career in which he was 102–84, including a 13–9 record in 1950 with Texarkana, Texas, in the Class B Big State League.

"I've never seen a pitcher like Johnny Herr. He was so smooth and had an excellent curve," former Litchfield outfielder Jim Hannan said. "I'm just glad that I never had to bat against him. He also was a nice person, not cocky or a smart aleck . . . just a very nice guy whose teammates liked him."

If Herr lacked a presence, it was possibly because he was road weary. He was only 28 years old, but he had been a professional since 1939 and also was a war veteran. He reached Columbus in the American Association by 1944, but after the season entered the U.S. Navy and missed all of the 1945 season, as well as contracting an illness that caused severe swelling in his feet. Herr returned to Columbus in 1946, but he was released after the season and began a professional and personal tailspin. Siebert found Herr through Hogo Pearson, a former Baylor player whom he'd called to play at Litchfield. Pearson and Herr played together at Texarkana in 1950.

Schaber needed little time to become a believer in Herr, an instant success who posted several low-hit, high-strikeout victories. He finished the West Central League season 12–2, chalked up 190 strikeouts in 128 innings, and was the Optimists' ace through the playoffs. Litchfield won the Class AA state title, with Herr finishing 1–1, defeating Marshall 11–0 but losing to Austin 4–2. Herr allowed only four hits, but Austin's Carl DeRose—who five seasons earlier had pitched a perfect game at Kansas City in the Class AAA American Association—outdistanced him.

The next season, Willmar dominated the regular West Central League season from beginning to end. Herr beat the Rails twice in the playoffs, but Litchfield lost three games to two. Willmar's Art Grangaard drafted Herr for the state tournament and started him in the opener against Albert Lea. In a return match with DeRose, now a draftee from Austin, Herr went the distance in a 1–0 victory that was arguably the defining decision in the tournament.

"The Herr-Carl DeRose pitcher's battle was one of the best in state tournament history," Will Gullickson, a *West Central Tribune* sports editor and a former town team player, wrote after the tournament.

Herr led Litchfield back to the State Tournament in 1953, but resurfaced in 1954 with the Willmar Rails, now in the Western Minnesota League. Herr and Kelly appeared to be a one-two punch capable of dominating the Class AA league, but not even the dynamic duo was capable of offsetting Willmar's lack of offense. In an effort to cut financial losses, Willmar released Herr and finished the season using Howie Schultz and Lefty Ranweiler as its secondary starters.

Although Herr was 3–10, sports editor Gullickson emphasized that in Herr's 115 innings, only 27 of the 56 runs scored against him were earned, while the Willmar offense scored only 39 runs. Herr lost four games by one run, one game by two, and two by three runs—the offense providing only one earned run in the pair of three-run losses.

"When future bosses discuss contract next year, they'll look at his won and lost record to be sure," Gullickson wrote, "but they'll also be interested in his 2.11 ERA, and there John has nothing to be ashamed of in the least."

For Herr, there was no next season in Willmar. He began the 1955 season at Mankato and was 3–4 in nine starts before being released, and he finished the season in Pipestone, where he lost two games in the playoffs to Marshall ace Rex Wade, 7–0 and 1–0. Marshall scored seven

runs in the first three innings against Herr in the first game, but Herr demonstrated his previous grit in the second loss—his last game in Minnesota.

Slayton's Refugees: Class AA School for Scoundrels

Among the men who wandered into Minnesota to play baseball in the 1945–60 era were a number of scoundrels, rascals, and deadbeats—some of whom were pretty good ballplayers, too. The Slayton Rockets had a burst of glory with the Class AA First Night League in 1950–51 and seemed to capture more than their fair share of the rascals.

Slayton installed lights on its field in the infield of the Murray County Fairgrounds track after the war and joined the First Night League

This Slayton advertisement in the *Sporting News* in 1951 is representative of similar ads placed by Minnesota towns during this era. Courtesy of *Sporting News*.

in 1949. The Rockets joined the signing frenzy in 1950 when the First Night League decided to play in Class AA—the "big leagues" of Minnesota baseball. First they hired Jerry Smith—a Minnesota Gopher star who played in Fergus Falls in 1948 and 1949—to be player/manager. Smith talked his friend Glenn Gostick into joining him. Gostick, who played service ball in the Pacific during an 18-month enlistment in 1946 and 1947, and was the regular Gopher catcher from 1949 to 1951, in turn brought his friend Dick Cassidy. They were friends from North High and had played together at Waverly in 1948. Cassidy tried his hand at pro ball in 1949, pitching for Cedar Rapids in the Class C Central Association.

Clarkfield native George Medchill was also signed. He'd played with Marshall in 1949 and had the well-deserved reputation as an enforcer. Medchill played football at South Dakota State and was also heavyweight on the school's boxing team. At Marshall his manager had once pulled him from a game after he injured two members of the black Broadway Clowns touring team with aggressive play. Art Vande Velde, a top local player, who was on Iona's 1946 State Tournament team, also signed.

Slayton had placed an ad for players in the *Sporting News* and was deluged with responses. Several pitchers—with obviously inflated résumés—were dispatched after only a couple of games. Bill Bolin, the team's batboy, said they really had three teams that summer: "One coming, one going, and one playing."

One of the more unlikely recruits was John Caulfield, a baseball team captain and 1950 graduate of Harvard University. Caulfield was walking home from a coaching clinic in Cambridge when the grocer next to his apartment ran out and told him that he had a call from a guy in Minnesota. Caulfield didn't have a phone but

was able to return the call to Heinie Fitzgerald, a member of Slayton's baseball association, who offered Caulfield $300 per month to play baseball for the Rockets. Fitzgerald had seen a small one-paragraph story in a Minneapolis paper about Caulfield leading the Ivy League in hitting with a .438 average. It's not easy to call someone who doesn't have a phone, but Fitzgerald managed. He kept calling Cambridge numbers until he found someone who knew Caulfield.

Caulfield had never been to Minnesota and figured he was up to the adventure. He boarded a train to Minneapolis almost immediately. The rest of the Slayton Rockets were not very enthused when they heard who was coming. They pictured the stereotypical blueblood "Haaahvahd" prude but were pleasantly surprised when Caulfield showed up. He was a good hitter and first baseman, and a "regular" guy. It turns out he'd grown up in a tough Irish neighborhood called Kerry Corner in Cambridge and entered Harvard on a scholarship created for underprivileged residents from the surrounding neighborhoods.

Shortly after Caulfield arrived in Slayton, the Rockets' new pitcher drove into town in a 1930s-vintage car held together by baling wire and prayer—if, indeed, the driver was capable of prayer. John Burrows, a 36-year-old lefty pitcher with 16 years of professional experience, including 30 games with the Philadelphia Athletics and Chicago Cubs in 1943 and 1944, had responded to one of the *Sporting News* ads. He showed up barely in time to warm up for his first game, but the team found he was so fat that they didn't have a uniform that fit. A local seamstress solved the problem by taking the numbers off their largest jersey, piecing in new material, and then sewing the numbers back on. She also let out the seams on the uniform pants but had to sew in extra material there, too.

Glenn Gostick *(left)*, John Caulfield, and
Dick Cassidy were part of Slayton's diverse
cast of players. Courtesy of Bill Bolin.

Burrows didn't have much zip left in his arm.
He threw a slow curve, a slower curve, and a
straight ball that was more like a changeup. Gostick said he could catch Burrows with a pair of
pliers. He was crafty, though, and knew how to
pitch. He'd seen everything. In his first game,
Cassidy, playing second base, made an error
on the first ball hit to him. Cassidy felt bad and
went out of his way to apologize. Burrows put
his hand on Cassidy's shoulder to console him.
"Don't worry about it, son," he said. "There's been
a million of those behind me." Burrows was a
great storyteller. On Saturday nights, 8 or 10 local farmers would crowd into a booth with him
at the Hub, the local watering hole, and buy him
beers all night while he regaled them with tales
from his baseball travels. The team locked him
up in the local jail one Saturday night to keep
him sober for a Sunday afternoon game.

Several teams had financial difficulties in
1950, but the First Night League decided to stay
in Class AA again in 1951. Slayton decided to
get a jump on recruiting by placing ads in the

Sporting News in January. Howard
Palmer, a journeyman who had not
gotten above Class C in six seasons
in the minor leagues, saw ads from
Slayton and Iona (another First
Night team) while free-reading the
weekly paper at a newsstand in his
hometown, Columbia, Illinois, just
south of St. Louis. Palmer was de-
pressed. He had just quit his job
in an automobile parts assembly plant. A year earlier he'd lost
a teaching job after just one year.
The 1950 baseball season had been a disaster—
he'd sprained an ankle and could hardly run all
year—and now he was broke, unemployed, and
living at home with his mother.

Palmer wrote a letter to Slayton, and Buck
Rauenhorst wired back that the Rockets could
use him. They offered $300 per month. Palmer
accepted immediately—he'd only made $175
per month in 1950 at Paris, Illinois, in the
Class D Mississippi-Ohio Valley League. In addition, Rauenhorst said he could get Palmer a
replacement-teaching job at Currie, Minnesota, if he could make it to Slayton by April 1. In
mid-March Palmer borrowed bus fare from his
mother and left for Minnesota. It took him five
days to get to Slayton—he was snowbound one
day in Sioux City, Iowa, and for two and a half
days in Worthington. Rauenhorst gave Palmer
a $100 advance on his first baseball check, and
the Bolin family rented him a room without payment until he got his first teaching check.

Palmer loved the teaching. On the side, he
ran an eight-week square-dancing class and ref-
ereed a professional wrestling show—where the
female "villain" kicked and tossed him across
the ring. Alas, Palmer was released by Slayton
barely a month into the season. However, Iona

Lefty Caulfield and Vallie Eaves flank one of Slayton's own. The town embraced the players, and the summer visitors spent much of their leisure time on Main Street. Courtesy of Bill Bolin.

picked him up, and he finished the season there. After the season he went back home to Columbia and finally got a real job. It was tough, he said. "Baseball was a devastating profession," he later wrote in a self-published book, *The Baseball Story*. After "playing ball three or four hours a day, drinking beer, dancing till about two, getting up about noon and eating ham and eggs, attending a matinee, and going to the ball park, who wants to go back to carrying a lunch basket and punching a clock!"

At midseason in 1951, 40-year-old righty pitcher Vallie Eaves came to town, the latest to respond to a *Sporting News* ad. He'd pitched in 24 games in the major leagues in his career, spread over five seasons, but drank a lot and had a reputation as a troublemaker. When he was relatively sober he had some good years—he won 21 games and led the Class AA Pacific Coast League in strikeouts in 1945, and he was 26–10 for Leesville in the Class C Gulf Coast League in 1950. Of course, Eaves hadn't put the drinking on his résumé. He also wore a brace to support his right knee, which was withered from a boyhood bout with osteomyelitis. Some opposing

batters bunted on him to take advantage of his lack of mobility but quickly stopped the practice when Eaves threw at their heads during their next at-bat.

Like the veteran Burrows the year before, Eaves knew all the tricks. He showed batboy Bolin how to scuff the seam of a baseball with a bottle cap. The signal for Bolin to bring the scuffed balls to the umpire was when Eaves tossed two consecutive balls back to the ump, requesting new ones. Eaves's performance was up-and-down at Slayton. He returned to pro ball in 1952 and turned in 13–6, 19–11, and 12–11 records the next three years in Class B leagues.

Class AA baseball turned out to be too expensive for the towns in the First Night League. Worthington—the biggest town in the league—dropped out in midseason 1951, and Pipestone's and Slayton's baseball associations nearly voted to do the same. The league dropped down to Class A in 1952. Slayton didn't even field a team. It would be a mistake, though, to think that the towns were soured by the experience. When questioned about it, most said, "It was great while it lasted!"

Joe Kelly: Double Play Combination

Tom Kelly will forever be regarded as one of the Minnesota Twins' all-time managers, a former journeyman player who managed 1,140 victories and two World Series championship teams. The stoic Kelly, however, wasn't the first family member to leave his mark on Minnesota baseball. His father, Joe, came down from the professional Class C Northern League in 1949 and enjoyed two productive Class B town ball seasons at Chokio, a tiny hamlet about 160 miles west of his son's future workplace. In fact, Tom Kelly qualifies as a Minnesota native, having been born on August 14, 1950, shortly before Joe Kelly and his family departed for their home in Elizabeth, New Jersey.

"He was sort of a laid-back fella . . . not a sparkplug type," Chokio fan Ervy Nelson recalls. "He had a slow gait and he really didn't look that formidable. But when he was on the diamond, he definitely was special."

One might wonder what a former professional player from a metropolitan setting near New York City was doing in Chokio, population 541. But like many Minnesota baseball towns, Chokio was willing to invest in the game and its players. Chokio installed lights in 1948, earlier than many towns more than twice its size. The team directors paid players and provided them with jobs, and Kelly was given a salary for baseball and also paid to drive a school bus and to work at the McNally Oil Company.

Chokio, like many towns in 1949 and 1950, tapped into black baseball and brought infielder Louie Wesson up from Hot Springs, Arkansas. In addition to a baseball salary, the black recruit was given a job at McNally Oil, pumping gas. Roger Gerdis remembers being delighted to go with his father to gas up the car because he had never seen a black man up close. Minnesota had liberal views about race overall in the 1940s, but blacks were unique in rural parts of the state.

Kelly, who was 14–14 in a two-year career at St. Cloud, was also unique. He was so good that no catcher in town could handle him. A catcher had to be hired out of the Minneapolis area to complete the team's battery. Kelly was also a good hitter whose power won a few games for Chokio, though not enough games to get the team to the state tournament.

In one of Kelly's first starts, Chokio defeated Clontarf 21–7, with the town phenom striking out 12 batters and collecting three hits, two of them doubles. He pitched two no-hitters, striking out 17 batters and not allowing a ball out of the infield in one of them. Kelly's reputation earned him exhibition opportunities. After his first season, he was hired by Clark, a town in South Dakota, for a tournament. Clark defeated Watertown 7–0 in a game highlighted by Kelly's five-hitter and home run.

"I went out once to Graceville, where I was born," Tom Kelly said referring to the closest town near Chokio with a hospital. "But when my dad came back to Minnesota, he'd occasionally go out [to Chokio] because he made a lot of good friends during the time he was there."

Bert Shepard: So Much Accomplished

Bert Shepard is the only player to pitch in a major-league game wearing an artificial leg. Considering the large number of professional baseball players who wandered in and out of state between 1945 and 1960, one shouldn't be too surprised to learn that Shepard also played for a time in Minnesota, with the Fergus Falls Red Sox in the Class AA West Central League in 1953.

He was shot down on May 21, 1944, on his 34th combat mission, flying a P-38 fighter on a strafing mission over Germany. Shepard, who'd played three years of minor-league ball before enlisting, had been playing service baseball in England and was the 55th Fighter Group's player/manager. He'd volunteered for an early-morning mission so that he could be back in time for a late-afternoon practice.

German doctors amputated his right leg about a foot below his knee. A Canadian POW made a crude artificial leg for Shepard, who immediately started exercising and running and practicing pitching motions. Shepard returned to the United States in February 1945 as part of a prisoner exchange program and was sent to Walter Reed Hospital in Washington, D.C. The War Department saw a chance to improve the morale of wounded soldiers and sent Shepard to the spring training camps of the Senators and Yankees. He pitched for the Senators in an exhibition game against the Norfolk Naval Training Station team before 8,000 fans, mostly servicemen.

His pitching wasn't considered major-league caliber, but the Senators signed him as a coach. On July 10 he pitched against the Brooklyn Dodgers in an exhibition game played to benefit war charities. He gave up only four singles in four innings and got credit for the win. He made his only official major-league appearance on August 4, in a game against the Boston Red Sox. He pitched 5⅓ innings in relief, giving up only one run on three hits. The crowd of 13,000 gave him standing ovations when he returned to the dugout after each inning. General Omar Bradley and secretary of war Robert Patterson presented Shepard with the Distinguished Flying Cross at a home-plate ceremony between games of a doubleheader with the Yankees on August 31.

The War Department called Shepard back into uniform after the season, and he made tours of amputation centers and various children's hospitals and rehabilitation centers. He made some motivational films for the army and became an outstanding speaker. In the next 10 years, Shepard pitched for various minor-league, semipro, and barnstorming teams all over the country. He eventually settled down in California and became a safety engineer.

In the midst of this amazing journey, Shepard showed up in Fergus Falls near the end of June 1953. He'd been hired after responding to an ad in the *Sporting News*. He wasn't hired as a publicity stunt. The *Fergus Falls Daily Journal*, in the last paragraph of a game story on June 26, merely noted that "the new [Fergus Falls] Red Sox pitcher, Bert Shepard, former major leaguer for the Washington Senators, will pitch against Morris Saturday night." It is doubtful whether Shepard mentioned his disability in his response to the ad. Morris beat Fergus Falls 11–0 in that game. The *Daily Journal* said that he did a fair job, but the team committed nine errors behind him. No mention was made of Shepard's artificial limb.

Shepard won his first game on July 1 when the starting pitcher and another reliever spotted Willmar four runs in the first inning. Shepard finished off the first inning and shut out Willmar the rest of the way, winning by a 7–4 margin on a three-run homer in the ninth. The *Daily Journal* now described Shepard as "the new one-legged pitcher."

Unfortunately Shepard's pitching skills weren't competitive in Minnesota's Class AA West Central League, and he was used mostly as a spot reliever. He was a colorful character, though, and his teammates and local fans loved him. Shepard coached third base when he wasn't pitching, and amused fans by using his artificial leg to deflect foul balls into the stands. He had a million stories. One of his teammates said, "we called him B. S.— and not because those were his initials!" Shepard cleaned up in pool against all local competition.

Business manager LeGrand released Shepard on July 17. Fergus Falls was struggling to make financial ends meet and couldn't afford to pay a starter's salary to a spot reliever, no matter how popular he might be.

Frank O'Rourke: Novel Approach to Town Ball

Frank O'Rourke was a nationally acclaimed author, known best for his western short stories and novels. Three of his books were adapted for the silver screen with box office luminaries like

Gregory Peck, Joan Collins, Burt Lancaster, Lee Marvin, Zero Mostel, and Kim Novak playing lead roles. He also wrote about baseball with a passion, but rather than drawing from his imagination as he did in his western sagas, O'Rourke mixed fact with fiction in his baseball tales.

Frank and his wife, Edith Carlson, who was raised in the region, arrived in Minnesota approximately two years after O'Rourke, a native Nebraskan, was severely wounded in Sicily during World War II. They rented a cabin on Lake Hubert and two years later moved over to Gull Lake, both near the small town of Nisswa, just north of Brainerd. They spent summers there through 1952. In addition to his civilian attire, O'Rourke brought his baseball gear and typewriter, items that he used frequently during his summers.

"Frank was a person of enormous charisma," Edith Carlson O'Rourke said. "He simply went to Nisswa, the first or second day after we arrived, introduced himself, and asked if there was any baseball in the region."

O'Rourke quickly discovered the Nisswa team's practice site and attended an evening workout in which he met Dick Cook, Jimmy Thompson, Barney Briggs, Harry Olson, the Wallin brothers, and a few others. He became a regular at practices, and although he played sparingly the first summer, he finished the season managing the team. Briggs said that O'Rourke had played for pay during his Nebraska days in the Depression, and he did everything well. He was a solid infielder who played mostly second and short and could hit for power.

Edith said that Frank maintained a profound respect for his teammates' work ethic, and cited some of the players' occupations: the Wallins were loggers, Harry Olson was a plumber, Jimmy Thompson worked in a hardware store, Dick Cook worked on his father's turkey farm. All the players had jobs, but they were never late, never absent, and hustled throughout the practices as if they were preparing for a championship game. In a letter from her Salt Lake City home, Edith O'Rourke recalled one of her husband's drives to practice early the first summer.

"When he arrived near the field, he noticed a big truckload of logs parked beside the road, and he saw Vic and Carl Wallin on top, each with a peavey hook in hand," she said. "When they saw Frank, Vic waved to Frank with one hand, said 'We'll be there in a minute, Frank!' and with the other hand he jabbed his peavey hook into a log and tossed it overboard as though it were nothing more than a big toothpick. Whenever Frank told the story, he would explode, 'With one hand! Forever in awe of such strength.'"

Nisswa came within a game of qualifying for the 1947 Class A tournament, losing 7–5 to Backus in the regional. Although that was one of the most exciting summers, the most memorable was 1949, when the O'Rourkes returned from Florida, where they rented a winter home in Clearwater, the spring training home of the Philadelphia Phillies.

Frank got to know Bob Carpenter, the Phillies owner, who permitted O'Rourke to take part in the team's spring training. O'Rourke was issued a locker and uniform and participated in practices, sometimes pitching to batters until they were prepared to swing in earnest. That spring was his inspiration for his novel, *The Team*, a saga about a fictional major-league team called the Quakers, a thinly disguised alias for the Phillies. The players were recast under assumed names, as well.

That summer he delighted the Nisswa gang with vivid recollections of his spring training adventure, but he also shared with his players a

Frank O'Rourke *(right)* talks to Phillies pitcher Russ Meyer and team official Babe Alexander during spring training in Clearwater, Florida, in 1949. Photograph given to O'Rourke by Babe Alexander; courtesy of Edith Carlson O'Rourke.

plethora of the equipment and memorabilia that he received before the Phillies headed north to Pennsylvania.

In 1951, O'Rourke was invited to play with the independent Brainerd Braves, a team with two future major leaguers, Herb Score and Gordy Coleman, and a future NBA star, Whitey Skoog. O'Rourke, still playing at Nisswa, wasn't available full-time, but he occasionally suited up and played for the Braves. Cook, one of the Braves top hitters in 1951, said that O'Rourke

was popular with fans, particularly when he patrolled the third-base coaching box.

"He was really fun to watch," Cook said. "He'd use all the gestures and signals the big-time coaches used."

Not all of O'Rourke's time was spent on the diamond. He and Edith blended in with the community, playing host to activities including penny ante poker and calling on team members and their wives. O'Rourke did, however, mix business with pleasure. After all the activities were over and most residents were calling it a night, the author would head for his typewriter and began the clacking, sometimes working until dawn and then sleeping in.

Alas, the pleasant Minnesota summers couldn't last forever. Frank and Edith bought a

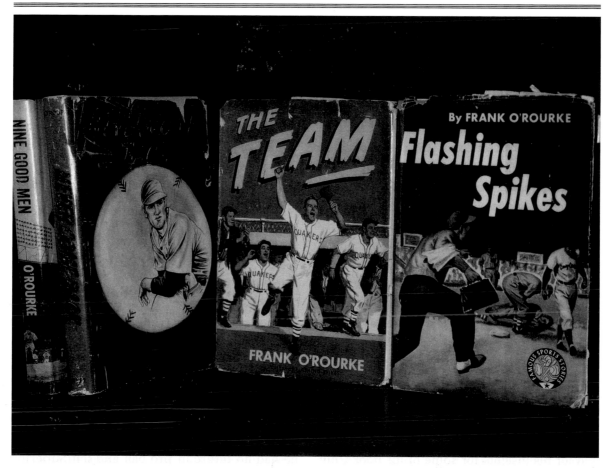

home in Taos, New Mexico, in the fall of 1952, and Frank's writing began to focus on westerns. The Minnesota baseball days were now part of the O'Rourkes' past, but they took many memories with them and left many behind for their friends in Nisswa, Leader, Pine River, and South Long Lake to share.

In 2002, 13 years after O'Rourke's death, Edith Carlson O'Rourke worked with Carroll and Graf to publish *The Heavenly World Series,* a 275-page compilation of 18 baseball short stories written by her husband. His stories included names of players he met and game situations he encountered during his stays in Minnesota.

Dick Cook, who became one of O'Rourke's closest friends from the moment he arrived in the summer in 1946, can be found in "Look for

Frank O'Rourke's baseball stories appeared regularly in national publications like the *Saturday Evening Post* and *Colliers,* and in novels like these. Photograph by the authors; covers courtesy of Edith Carlson O'Rourke.

the Kid with the Guts." The tale is about a kid named Dick Cookson, a former Golden Gloves boxer who plays third base for Waniss, a small town in northern Minnesota near Brainerd. The real-life Dick Cook played third base, boxed in Golden Gloves, and played for Nisswa, a town with the same letters used to spell "Waniss."

In "The Kid," Barney Briggs—the real name of another close friend of O'Rourke's—picked up a baseball scout named Gorham (and Clay Gorham happened to be a Brainerd insurance man) at the Radisson in Minneapolis and drove

were good enough. But Dick just snapped, 'Yes we are.' That was the major difference between the two of us: confidence."

The Stigmans had another brother, Dave, four years younger than Dick, and he developed into a solid pitcher much later than his older brothers. Dick and Al, who grew up together and developed into strapping left-handed pitchers, were obsessed by the game from the moment someone tossed them their first baseball. They constantly played catch and together saved enough money to buy a left-handed catcher's mitt from a Sears and Roebuck catalog, enabling them to take turns pitching to the other.

Their mother cleaned a large hall in Nimrod, the same one in which the movies were shown, and it was big enough for the Stigmans to play catch during the winter and inclement spring and summer days.

They attracted considerable attention for their pitching prowess early and quickly worked their way up the ladder from sandlot to Sebeka High and Legion and finally town team. Al somehow escaped the eye of Cy Slapnicka, a Cleveland scout, who missed Al's no-hitter for Callaway one spring but the next spring in the same town saw Dick pitch a three-hit, 21-strikeout masterpiece and persuaded him to sign a contract with the Cleveland organization.

Dick Stigman was quickly shuffled off to Tifton, Georgia, in the Class D Georgia-Florida League, while Al was working at a Callaway lumberyard and pitching town team ball.

"Al was a very good pitcher. He also was a very good hitter," Dick Stigman said of his brother, a pitcher and position player throughout his town team days. "I don't know why things worked out the way they did. I guess it was a matter of seizing opportunity. Al has always had been a laid-back, calm person."

Not as calm as Dick Stigman suggests. By his own admission, Al Stigman had his bouts with anxiety, particularly before game time. Pitching before tens of thousands, as his brother did through seven major-league seasons, was not Al Stigman's idea of enjoyable. A hundred or so fans in the New York Mills or Perham stands was about all he could comfortably handle.

But his nervousness is not reflected in his record. Although career statistics are rare at the town team level, he won far more games than he lost before and after his military days. He pitched four no-hitters and achieved baseball's holy grail, a perfect game during the 1955 Region 14B Tournament when he was pitching for New York Mills against pretourney favorite Ashby. Stigman struck out 18 batters along the way and didn't allow a ball to escape the infield.

Erv Tolkinen, the New York Mills catcher that night, savored the memory of Stigman's gem long after that magical night. "Al was always a crowd favorite," Tolkinen said, "and that night the people went crazy every time he struck a batter out. He had a lot of good games in his career, but that night his fastball really had a tail and his curveball was like something falling off the table."

Al Stigman, however, said that he owed his good friend Emil Porkkenen a debt of gratitude for his gem. Porkkenen operated a New York Mills gas station, and when Stigman stopped off to see his friend before heading to the park, his friend offered him an antidote for his nervousness: a three-finger shot glass of whiskey. His family probably would have gone for him saying the rosary, as some had suggested many times, but the whiskey obviously served the purpose. By the time he reached the park, he was feeling "loosey goosey" and quickly took charge.

Stigman briefly toyed with the thought of

professional ball and attended a tryout camp in the Fargo-Moorhead area, but he stayed only briefly because jobs were scarce at the time and he felt that he might jeopardize his job working in a New York Mills hatchery.

"I always loved baseball. I still do," said Stigman, who pitched in a 30-and-over league after quitting town team ball. "But I have no regrets. While I loved the game, I just never got over the nervousness." A three-finger jigger of whiskey worked wonders once but probably wouldn't have been a great long-term plan.

COLLEGE RINGERS: SUMMER JOBS BETWEEN SEMESTERS

UNIVERSITY OF MINNESOTA COACH Dick Siebert relied predominantly on home-state talent to win the 1956, 1960, and 1964 NCAA College World Series. Approximately 90 percent of the players on these three rosters were from Minnesota, the majority having developed in the state's town team system. Rod Oistad, who won three games in Benson's 1954 Class A championship run, and Jack Hoppe, a Paynesville draftee who helped pitch Cold Spring to the 1955 Class B title and was voted the State Tournament's MVP, were on the University of Minnesota's 1956 NCAA championship pitching staff. Gophers' 1956 All–Big Ten players Jack McCartan, Jerry Kindall, and Jerry Thomas were seasoned in the state's town team leagues.

Siebert used some of his players on the town teams he managed, and farmed others out to make sure they were able to play regularly against tough competition. Many of his former players continued to compete in the state after graduation. Minnesota Intercollegiate Athletic Association schools like St. Thomas and St. Johns also fed players into the summer town team programs,

and other schools like Moorhead State also made significant contributions. Roger McDonald, a St. Thomas all-around athlete, became the first pitcher to pitch no-hit ball in a State Tournament championship game, shutting down Mayer 4–0 for Excelsior in the 1945 Class A final.

Minnesota's abundance of teams willing to find college players well-paying summer jobs— in return for their baseball skills—attracted athletes from all over the country. The majority of Big Ten schools were represented on Minnesota town team rosters, as were other colleges and universities from the Midwest and from as far away as Pennsylvania, Florida, Texas, Arizona, and California. The Western Minnesota League invested heavily in college talent, with Marshall being the major proponent of recruiting from other states including Ohio, where the town landed two-sport All-American Paul Ebert from Ohio State. Four men who played in Minnesota became members of the American Baseball Coaches Association Hall of Fame: Dick Siebert (1973), Lee Eilbracht (1979), Tom Petroff (1986), and Jerry Kindall (1991).

No town accomplished more with outside college help than did Fergus Falls. The Red Sox established its program using many Gophers in the late 1940s, but when they defeated Austin to win the 1950 Class AA title—one of the biggest upsets in State Tournament history—they relied on six out-of-state college players, including Northwestern's Ed Piacentini, named the State Tournament MVP. When Litchfield won the 1951 title, Dick Donnelly of Stetson College in Florida got the Optimists rolling with an opening-game no-hitter over St. Paul Nickel Joint.

Most of the college ringers got jobs in recreation programs, as coaches or instructors, or on playground and athletic field maintenance, but many also worked on summer construction projects or regular jobs.

Jack Verby: Doc Chose Practice over Baseball

Jack "Doc" Verby was a dominating pitcher in the early years of his career but wound up as one of the most feared hitters in the state. If a vote had been taken in 1950 to select the state's best player, Verby would have been one of the top candidates.

Jerry Schaber, who was a teammate of Verby's in Litchfield, said he'd never seen anyone compete as hard as Verby. "He was dead serious," Schaber said. "I don't think I ever saw him smile during a game."

Pat Ryan, a player on Cannon Falls' Class B team, recalled watching Verby play at Cannon Falls in 1949. "Verby was like a giant," Ryan said. "You could tell when Doc was hitting during batting practice, even if you were just walking up to the park and couldn't see the field. The crack of his bat when he hit the ball was twice as loud as it was for anyone else."

Litchfield didn't have a baseball team when

Verby arrived there in November 1949 to assume the medical practice of a doctor who had died of a heart attack. Verby was instrumental in helping form a team to compete in the Class AA West Central League, and his leadership and skills ignited baseball interest in the town. The town's youngsters worshipped him. The *Litchfield Independent Review* reported a conversation between two young boys. The first suggested they go to the park to play baseball. The second replied, "You can be Joe DiMaggio. I'll be Jack Verby."

Verby starred in basketball and baseball at St. Paul Johnson High School, graduating in 1941. He played basketball and baseball at Carleton College and pitched in state amateur leagues in the summers. Albert Lea drafted him from Owatonna for the 1943 State Tournament, where he lost a heartbreaker in the Class AA championship game. He had a no-hitter for seven innings against Minneapolis Mitby-Sathers. In the top of the 13th he gave up a leadoff double to Casey Dowling. Russ Brovold, the next hitter, hit a home run on a 3–0 count. Albert Lea came back with one run in the bottom of the inning but lost 2–1. Verby had given up only four hits in the game while striking out 17. Years later Dowling remembered that game and thought Verby had grooved the pitch to Brovold only because he thought he wouldn't be swinging on a 3–0 count.

By taking a heavy credit load, Verby graduated from Carleton in three years and enrolled in the University of Minnesota Medical School in the fall of 1944. He was enrolled in the U.S. Navy V-12 program—roughly equivalent to the modern ROTC—which exempted him from the draft until he finished college. He pitched for the Gophers in 1945, using his last year of college eligibility.

Verby pitched for Honeywell in the Minneapolis Park National League in 1945 and led them to the State Tournament. There were only four Class AA teams in the tournament, with games scheduled on consecutive days. Honeywell appeared to be overmatched, and their only chance to win rode on Verby's strong right arm. He tried to pull an unprecedented iron-man feat by pitching both weekend games—and almost pulled it off. On Saturday he shut out West St. Paul 3–0 on three hits, but on Sunday he lost the championship game to Albert Lea, giving up a scratch single in the bottom of the ninth with two outs to lose 1–0.

Following the tournament, he was contacted by nine major-league scouts, as well as by officials from several Minnesota amateur teams. Verby was still enrolled in the V-12 program, however, and could not sign until he was discharged. The New York Yankees put a $7,500 signing bonus offer on the table and offered to establish a baseball schedule that would permit him to finish medical school. Verby was tempted but, in the end, decided to concentrate on getting good grades and pursue baseball merely as a hobby.

He pitched for New Ulm in the Western Minny in 1946, ringing up a 10–0 regular-season record. He faltered in the playoffs, though, losing two games to Gibbon in the semifinals. This was the first hint of the arm problems that would ultimately lead him to quit pitching. Playoff winner Springfield drafted him for the State Tournament, however, and he helped them win the Class A Championship with a two-inning relief job in the 4–1 quarterfinal win over Blackduck and a 6–4 semifinal win over Detroit Lakes as a starter.

Verby completed medical school in 1947 and signed to pitch for the Rochester Aces of the Southern Minny. He made the All-Star team as a pitcher but told team officials he wanted to quit pitching. He said his duties as an intern made it impossible to work out between starts and keep his arm in shape. He did not admit it to the team, but his sore arm had also returned.

Rochester released him when he was no longer available to pitch. Mankato picked him up, and he played outfield there the rest of the season. Verby finished the year with a .352 batting average. He rejoined Mankato in 1948 and set

Jack Verby, shown with Honeywell in 1945, was one of the state's most respected players. He turned down an attractive offer from the New York Yankees to pursue a medical career. Photograph by Earl Evans; courtesy of Don Evans.

a modern Southern Minny hitting record with a .404 batting average. (This record was finally eclipsed in 1957, the last year of the league's operation as a Class AA league, by Rochester's Dick Newberry, who hit .420.) In 1949 Verby moved to Cannon Falls, where he worked in an established medical office. He hit .518 for Cannon Falls in the Class AA St. Paul Suburban League.

Lee Meade, then a 20-year-old sportswriter for the *Litchfield Independent Review*, recalled that Doc Verby made quite an impression when he moved to town in the fall of 1949. "I didn't know who he was at the time," Meade said, "but it seemed like everyone in town was coming up to me and asking, 'did you hear about the new doctor in town?' " Meade introduced himself to

Verby, and they became good friends, and joined with several other local businessmen who were working to establish a team for the 1950 season.

The team finished in fourth place at 21–14, four games behind pennant-winning Willmar. Verby's .370 batting average was second in the league, and he led the league in home runs and RBIs. He even took up pitching again in the last half of the season, when the Optimists were struggling at the mound. He went 4–1 in the regular season and pitched one more game in the playoffs. He beat Willmar ace and former

Doc Verby greeted after another home run for Litchfield in 1950. Note that each player's uniform carries the name of a different sponsor. Courtesy of Gerald W. Schaber.

Gopher teammate Gene Kelly 3–2 before an overflow crowd of 2,700 at Willmar in the crucial third game of the best-of-five playoff finals to give Litchfield a 2–1 lead in the series. He gave up only seven hits but struck out 11 and looked like he was recovering some of his old zip. It was to be the last game Doc pitched in his career, however. Litchfield won the next game 4–0 behind pitcher Pork Chop Kinsel and advanced to the State Tournament, where they finished third in the eight-team Class AA field.

Litchfield signed Dick Siebert as player/manager in 1951. Verby had played first base in 1950, but moved to the outfield to make room for Siebert, and occasionally filled in at third base. Unfortunately, by early July he had also received his draft notice, one of 13 doctors in the state called to medical service in Korea. Verby was scheduled to report in late August and decided to ask Siebert to find a replacement immediately, as he knew he wouldn't be available for the playoffs.

Litchfield went on to win the Class AA State Championship. If any proof was needed to determine how much Verby was respected, the Minnesota Amateur Baseball Association permitted Litchfield to draft Willmar's Howie Schultz—a former Brooklyn Dodgers first baseman and, perhaps, the state's most feared hitter—to replace Verby on their State Tournament roster. The MABA had an "Emergency Serviceman's Rule" at the time that allowed a team to replace a player lost to military service with a player of equal ability.

Verby spent a year at a field medical unit in Korea, and then a year in Okinawa. He returned to Litchfield in the fall of 1953 but soon moved to Rochester to join some old friends from the University of Minnesota Medical School at the Olmsted Medical Clinic. He put on his spikes a

few times in the next two years but decided his medical practice no longer gave him the time to get into the top physical shape he demanded of himself.

Verby joined the staff at the University of Minnesota Medical School in 1969, where he applied himself with the same determination he displayed on the baseball field. He was responsible for developing the Minnesota Rural Physician Associate Program. In 1991 he was given the Thomas W. Johnson Award by the American Association of Family Practitioners for his work on the program. In 2003 he was given a Lifetime Achievement Award by the University of Minnesota Medical Alumni Society.

Dick Durrell: Right Person for the Right Time

Dick Durrell was still a Minneapolis Washburn High School student when Brooklyn Dodgers and Chicago Cubs baseball scouts expressed an interest in the two-sport athlete. At the time the Minneapolis prospect wasn't ready to sign, and before he could even think about playing professionally, along came World War II and his tour with the U.S. Marines.

Once the war ended and he received his discharge, Durrell enrolled at the University of Minnesota, where he played baseball and basketball, including a starting role as a first baseman and outfielder on Dick Siebert's inaugural Gopher team. Durrell enjoyed a modicum of success both at Minnesota and for two summers of town ball at Fergus Falls, but this time when offers were made, he adamantly declared that he had no interest in playing baseball professionally.

Years later, Durrell explained that his decision was based neither on family advice nor on counsel from Siebert, who several years earlier had ended a long and successful major-league career at first base. A future major-league great, Durrell explained, was responsible for his decision.

"I was flattered by the attention, but I knew that I wasn't that good, and I was almost 24 years old," he said. "I had seen Duke Snider play outfield for the old St. Paul Saints, a Dodger franchise, in old Lexington Park, and no way did I consider myself to be at that level. I figured that if I couldn't play baseball at the highest level, why even try to play professionally."

Dick Durrell, shown with the 1947 Gophers, was one of many University of Minnesota players attracted to Fergus Falls. Courtesy of the University of Minnesota Athletic Department.

Durrell's decision not to reach for the sky in baseball led him to reach for the top in the communications business. But there was some occupational indecision and town team baseball before he embarked on his lofty corporate climb. He spent six weeks in the University of Minnesota's law school before deciding he didn't like law. He took a sales job with Wilson's Sporting Goods, but that didn't last long.

Meanwhile he split the 1949 town ball season between Lake Lillian and Atwater and returned to Atwater in 1950 before the 140-mile round-trip commutes prompted him to quit the West Central League team and join Soderville, based just outside the Twin Cities.

"In 1949, Lake Lillian let me go on the Fourth of July," Durrell said. "I had caught a ride out with the umpires that day, but after taking a shower I discovered they had left. The only thing they did for me [at Lake Lillian] was point me to the road back to Minneapolis. I wound up traveling part of the way with truckers who were picking up dead livestock."

In the fall of 1950, Durrell's father spotted an advertisement for a regional newsstand representative for Time, Incorporated. His father thought *Time* was a great magazine and urged his son to apply. Durrell was one of a couple hundred applicants for the job, but he insisted that his business acumen wasn't the only reason he got it. "The guy doing the interviews was a North High grad and a baseball fan," Durrell said. "He heard of me through my association with baseball."

Durrell began the 1951 town team season at Faribault, commuting briefly with John Blanchard before Blanchard signed with the New York Yankees. He had begun to lose his competitive fire and was released by the Class AA team before the season ended. "I would have let me go too," he said. He finished the season with Class A St. Peter, his last in town team ball.

In 1953, he and his wife, Jackie, moved to New York, his first major professional step up the ladder. He was appointed publisher of *People* magazine in October 1973, was selected vice president of Time Incorporated in 1977, and served as director of the television network HBO from 1981 through 1983.

Jack Hannah: Western Minny to Carnegie Hall

Not long after Jack Hannah arrived in Marshall for the 1954 Western Minnesota League season, the Fresno State standout became a celebrity. The man described by his teammate and future Coaches Hall of Fame member Jerry Kindall as "the California Heartthrob" came to play baseball and played it well, but he was also a churchgoing singer who earned civic respect in this conservative southwestern Minnesota community.

Hannah was uncertain how he caught the attention of Marshall baseball organizers, but he suggested that University of Minnesota coach Dick Siebert had something to do with it, because Siebert saw him pitch in an NCAA regional tournament for Fresno State, where Hannah also played football. In addition to college baseball, Hannah had pitched two seasons in a Western Canadian semipro league, one at Saskatoon, where future NHL Hall of Fame member Gordie Howe was a teammate.

In Marshall, Hannah was 6–1 and had a 3.86 earned run average. He and Paul Ebert, an All-American baseball and basketball player at Ohio State, were the one-two punch for a Marshall team that finished 17–11 and tied for second in the Western Minnesota league, a game behind Fairmont.

Playing baseball in a top-notch league and receiving $250 a month to care for Legion Field was a pleasant experience for the personable Californian, but making the stay that much more special was the opportunity to sing a duet in church with operatic soprano Exine Anderson Bailey, a Marshall native.

"Hannah had a beautiful voice. Church attendance would really jump up when word got out that he was going to sing a solo," said Marilyn Mills, a former Marshall resident.

Bailey offered Hannah a music scholarship at the University of Oregon, where she taught, but he declined because he wanted to finish his Fresno State education and then pursue a professional baseball career. After the 1954 season, Hannah could have returned to Marshall, but he was recruited by Spencer in the Iowa State League, where he received $400 a month. Among

Jack Hannah *(right)* and Jack Wilson were among many college stars who played in Marshall. Hannah was from Fresno State, and Wilson from Ohio State. Courtesy of Herb Schaper Historical Baseball Collection/*New Ulm Daily Journal.*

his teammates was Bob Gibson, then a Creighton University student and position player who would attain Hall of Fame status as a St. Louis Cardinals pitcher.

Hannah seemed destined for the good life, and a good life he did enjoy, although it was as an entertainer, not as a baseball star. An arthritic right arm ended his professional career in 1962, and he returned to Fresno and became a counselor and high school baseball coach who had a 314–148 career record. He had always enjoyed singing, and during a family reunion, he and his brother, Joe, and nephew, Lon, sang as a trio and discovered they had a special harmony. They eventually launched a music career as the "Sons of the San Joaquin," singing traditional cowboy music. In 1992 they recorded their first album, *A Cowboy Has to Sing*. The Sons have appeared at venues as disparate as the Grand Ole Opry and Carnegie Hall.

Decades have passed since Hannah's summer in Marshall, but the pitcher-coach-singer did not forget those Minnesota days. "I was only seventeen years old my first summer in Canada . . . before my senior year in high school," Hannah said. "I was young, but it wasn't so bad because a bunch of my friends were also up there. That's what made Marshall so special. I went there not knowing a soul, but people made me feel welcome. They showed interest . . . they couldn't have been nicer."

Paul Ebert: Doctor Was in the House

Paul Ebert was a student-athlete from 1951 to 1954 at Ohio State. He was NCAA All-American in both basketball and baseball in 1954. He made the All–Big Ten basketball team from 1952 to 1954, and the All–Big Ten baseball team in 1952 and 1954.

Right after his college graduation, Ebert headed west with Ohio State teammate Jack Wilson to play summer baseball with the Marshall Tigers of the Class AA Western Minny League. Marshall assembled a strong club that season. Besides Ebert, the pitching staff included Fresno State star Jack Hannah, Northern League veteran Jack Wilcox, and Don Tauscher. Veteran pro Ted Lotz—who spent seven years in the minor leagues, including two in the Class AAA International League—led the league in hitting at .394. Jack Wilson was fifth at .344. University of Minnesota freshman Jerry Kindall played shortstop for the team.

Ebert was the workhorse for the pitching staff. He finished 8–4, throwing 98 innings. Hannah was 6–1 in 63 innings, while Tauscher was 4–1 in 56 innings and Wilcox 1–5 in 63 innings. Marshall finished the regular season tied for second place with Springfield at 17–11, one game behind Fairmont's 18–10 record. The Western Minny held a seven-game round-robin playoff that year, with the top four finishers moving on to play best-of-three series.

Fairmont and Litchfield finished 5–2 in the playoffs, while Marshall and New Ulm tied at 4–3. Ebert's 3–0 shutout at Fairmont was the pitching gem of the playoffs, but he lost 4–3 to Litchfield in the first game of the semifinal round of the playoffs. Following that game, he returned to Columbus to be married and to start his first year in medical school at Ohio State.

Ebert was paid $400 per month—for the three-month season—and worked three mornings a week for the City Recreation Department. He lived with a family in town and paid a small

Paul Ebert, an Ohio State baseball and basketball star, played two seasons with Marshall. He became a nationally acclaimed surgeon. Courtesy of Paul Ebert.

rent. "It was not a lot of money," he said, but more than he could make at a seasonal job back home. "Besides, it was a lot of fun playing baseball." He said the local fans and townspeople were very gracious and helpful. "The players were really looked up to by the town."

Ebert had been considering an athletic career when he graduated from Ohio State. He had offers from professional baseball and basketball. However, he also wanted to go to medical school. The Giants and Pirates made him good offers—a $20,000 bonus plus a guaranteed $20,000 salary over two years. Rules at the time required "bonus players"—those receiving more than $4,000 to sign—to stay with the major-league club for two years. Neither team would permit him to attend medical school, though—they would require him to report to spring training on February 1. Ebert also worried about the salary structure in the minor leagues. He saw that he would not be making much money if he didn't stick with the club after the two-year period. Class AAA salaries at the time were only about $4,000 per year.

The NBA's Milwaukee Bucks were willing to work with him on his schedule. They would permit him to attend medical school at Marquette and would require him to play only home games and weekend road games.

"But the NBA wasn't very well established at the time," Ebert said. He remembered making weekend road trips to Minneapolis when he was playing basketball at Ohio State. "We always seemed to play the Gophers on Monday night," he said. "We'd take an overnight train trip from our Saturday game, and arrive in Minneapolis sometime after noon on Sunday." The team would go to a Minneapolis Lakers game that night, if the team was in town.

"The Lakers played in the Armory or some other small high-school-like auditorium," he re-

called. "They'd draw about 3,000 fans—minor league compared to Monday night in Williams Arena, where the crowds were always around 18,000."

Ebert decided to go to medical school full-time.

He returned to Marshall in the summer of 1955, where the Tigers had dropped down to the Class A First Night League. The league did not compare to the Western Minny, and Marshall's team wasn't as strong as in 1954. Jack Wilson left to try professional baseball, and Ted Lotz and Jerry Kindall also moved on. Ebert and Kansas University's Rex Wade split pitching duties and alternated at shortstop. Wade had pitched for Marshall in 1952, when they were in the Class A Western Central Minnesota League.

Marshall easily won the pennant in the six-team league. They swept Pipestone in the first round of the best-of-three playoffs, on back-to-back shutouts by Wade and Ebert. Milroy upset Worthington two games to one in the other series.

Ebert lost the first game of the finals 4–3 against Milroy, who had been the 1954 Class B State Champions. Coming into the game, Ebert was 10–0 in First Night League play, and 3–0 against Milroy. Upstart Milroy won the league championship two days later in a 14–12 slugfest. Ebert, on only one day's rest, relieved starter Rex Wade in the seventh, and was tagged with the loss.

Milroy would have drafted Ebert for the regional and state playoffs, but he had to return to Columbus for the start of his second year of medical school. Ebert said that 1955 was his last year of organized baseball, as school and family life now demanded his full-time attention.

It's hard to argue with that decision. He graduated from medical school in 1957 and did his internship at Johns Hopkins. He had a distinguished career as a doctor and surgeon, and was a longtime director of the American College of Surgeons. The NCAA recognized his achievements when they made him the 1989 Theodore Roosevelt Award winner. The "Teddy" has been described as the "Nobel Prize of Athletics." Previous winners include notables such as Dwight D. Eisenhower, Ronald Reagan, Jesse Owens, George H. W. Bush, William Cohen, Roger Staubach, Robert Dole, Bill Richardson, Althea Gibson, Gerald Ford, Omar Bradley, Jack Kemp, Rafer Johnson, Byron White, and, in 2004, Minnesota Supreme Court Justice and former Minnesota Viking Alan Page.

Jerry Schaber: Infielder Won Siebert Respect

Jerry Schaber was a Hamline University infielder who played second base for the West Central League Litchfield Optimists in 1950. Dick Siebert was the University of Minnesota head baseball coach who managed the 1951 Optimists after player/manager Pete Kramer moved 25 miles down the road to Willmar and played for Art Grangaard.

In April 1951, Schaber, one of the town's favorite adopted sons, received a telephone call from Siebert asking him if he was available for an infield practice. Schaber told Siebert he had time and reported for what he assumed would be a casual meeting with his new manager, but it turned out to be an unsettling experience. When Siebert began the practice, Schaber felt as if he was a target in a shooting gallery rather than an infielder chasing ground balls.

"The guy was hitting bullets at me. I mean bullets," said Schaber, feigning outrage. "I remember thinking, 'Hey, this sucker is trying to get rid of

me.' I found out later that it was true, but by that time he and I had become good friends."

Life was good the previous season in Litchfield, a small farming community 80 miles west of St. Paul, where Schaber had been a three-sport standout at Harding High and the city's 1946 High School Athlete of the Year. Enrolled at Hamline, where he was a starting infielder and an all-Minnesota Intercollegiate Athletic Conference quarterback, he joined Litchfield after an outstanding 1949 season with the St. Paul AAA League Harding Boosters, where his .429 average

Jerry Schaber was a tough competitor whom Dick Siebert described as "pound for pound, the best player in the state." Courtesy of Brian Larson.

and stellar defensive play helped lead the team to a berth in the Class AA State Tournament.

In his first season at Litchfield, Schaber established a excellent rapport with the community and with Kramer, a manager with immense patience. After Schaber struck out three times and committed three errors in Litchfield's 1950 opener, Kramer just shrugged his shoulders, saying it probably wouldn't be Schaber's last bad game, and expressed his faith in the scrappy infielder. Schaber, comforted by his manager's words, settled into a comfortable routine, hitting .291 in one of the state's toughest town team leagues, and played flawless defense. In Litchfield's first Class AA season, the team qualified for the state tourney, and while the Optimists didn't win the tournament, they upset defending champion Austin, and Schaber did his fair share by reaching base ten times in 18 at-bats while committing only one error in the field.

Schaber wasted no time in signing his 1951 Optimists contract, but suddenly Kramer was gone to neighboring Willmar, and the Hamline athlete was playing for the Gophers' formidable college baseball coach. However, Schaber quickly forged a friendship with Siebert and a lot of new teammates, and life away from the city became even sweeter. He admitted that getting used to Siebert's extremely loose style of leadership was fascinating, sometimes comical.

The Optimists led by Kramer surprised Litchfield baseball fans. The Optimists guided by player/manager Siebert awed them. They won the 1951 West Central title by three games, posting a 27–8 record. Schaber had a great year, hitting .409, with only one error. Litchfield barged through the playoffs to win their second consecutive State Tournament berth and then, thanks to their overwhelming pitching, won the State Class AA Championship.

In the final stages of Litchfield's championship run, Siebert demonstrated his respect for Schaber by naming the second baseman acting manager when Siebert's television commitments forced him to miss a game.

Schaber, much younger and less experienced than many of his teammates, said his role as acting manager was simple. He made no inspirational appeal or set down no rules. "I simply told them, 'The take sign is off.'" Schaber said. "We had so much power with our regular lineup, and we also had drafted [Willmar first baseman] Howie Schultz and [Benson catcher] Red Fischer. Why not let them hit away?"

The Optimists opened with three consecutive shutouts, tying a tournament record, lost a 4–2 heartbreaker to Austin in the fourth game, but bounced back behind Willmar draftee Gene Kelly for a championship-game 10–2 victory over the Packers.

When the team returned to Litchfield for a fan appreciation day, Siebert commended the team and the fans and concluded with a special tribute to Schaber, saying that "pound-for-pound" the second baseman was the greatest athlete in the United States.

Once Schaber graduated from Hamline, he received an offer from the Dodgers, and Cleveland also expressed interest, but the terms were less than enticing. He took a job in the Twin Cities in 1952 and signed with Owatonna in the Southern Minnesota League because the trips to games took less time. Although he made the Southern Minny East All-Star team as a utility player, Schaber felt he had a subpar season, mostly because he could not get to the ballparks in time for batting or infield practice.

Next he spent two years on active duty in the National Guard. When he returned to Minnesota, he found that there were only two Class AA leagues left in the state, and that the pay wasn't as good as it once had been. He turned his full attention to fast-pitch softball and earned state and national recognition, but nothing so special that it obscured his memories of the 1951 Litchfield season.

"I played a lot of sports in my time but that season was fabulous. Siebert just turned me loose. I could do whatever I wanted," Schaber said. "It was definitely one of the best years I've ever had in my life in any sport."

Harold "Tubby" Raymond: The Hustling Catcher from Michigan

On a sunny late-summer afternoon in the glow of Notre Dame's Golden Dome, Harold "Tubby" Raymond was awaiting his induction into the National Football Foundation and College Coaches Hall of Fame.

Before the ceremony, the former University of Delaware football coach was introduced to Bronko Nagurski Jr., son of Minnesota's football legend. They didn't talk about football and Ray-

mond's three hundred victories; they talked a little about Nagurski's legendary father and a lot about baseball in International Falls, where Raymond played two seasons for the Mandos in the late forties, and Nagurski was a regular in the late fifties.

Raymond spent the 1947 and 1948 seasons with the Mandos, named for the team sponsor, the Minnesota and Ontario Paper Company. Raymond had planned to spend the 1947 summer playing ball in Flint, Michigan, but he was recruited by International Falls native Jack McDonald, a University of Michigan baseball teammate, as well as the Wolverines' starting hockey goalie. McDonald told Raymond that the Man-

Tubby Raymond *(back row, third from left)* played for International Falls in 1947 and 1948. The 1948 team qualified for the State Tournament, but by that time Raymond was already in Michigan's preseason football camp. *Front row, from left:* Batboy Billy White, Bob Stish, Ken Knutson, Jack McDonald, Fritz VonderHaar, Ralph Morrison, Willard Baker, Skrien, batboy Ken Carew. *Back row:* Seymour, Smerika, Raymond, Darrell Wegner, Pete Flaa, Pat Morrison, Garry Vold, manager Walt Scheela. Courtesy of Tubby Raymond.

dos had an excellent team, manned mostly by college players, but had no catcher good enough to handle ace pitcher Fritz VonderHaar.

"I talked to my dad and told him that if I ever wanted the chance to play major league ball, I needed to play with guys who cared," Raymond said. "I was really unhappy with my team in Flint because our players constantly were arriving late, and even some were drunk when they got there." Given his father's blessing, Raymond quickly packed his gear, taped his glove to his travel bag, stuck a bat through the carrying straps, and caught a train for Minnesota. He arrived the next day in Virginia, a mining town south of "The Falls."

This was the beginning of Raymond's reputation as "That hustling catcher from the University of Michigan," a memory that stuck with some of the Mando fans for decades. He helped direct the community's youth recreation program the first summer and the following season worked in the paper mill, owned by E. W. Backus, a baseball zealot and the team's primary source of support. Unlike some summer jobs offered to outside players, most Mando players did work, but on game days they received special consideration.

"We had a good team and played a lot of games, winning a lot more than we lost," Raymond said. "Everyone in town treated us well. We ate free at Jimmy the Jap's [Restaurant] and when we made a good play the fans would stick money through the wire fence. When I broke my leg in early August the first summer, they had a day for me and raised money to help pay my medical expenses."

Raymond remained healthy throughout the second season, when the Mandos qualified for the Class A State Tournament, but he left early for Michigan to attend the Wolverines' pre-season football drills and wasn't on the state tourney roster. He captained the 1949 Michigan baseball team and then played two years in the minor leagues before he gave it up and decided to become a full-time football coach.

Tom Petroff: A Spartan Invasion

Tom Petroff was sitting in his Lansing, Michigan, home in the winter of 1950, recovering from a hip injury that he had suffered the previous summer playing professional baseball for Easton, Maryland, in the Class D Eastern Shore League. Petroff answered a knock on the door and was confronted by two gentlemen from Minnesota, asking him if he'd be interested in playing for Morris in the summer. He had been recommended by his good friend Charles Gorman, a Michigan State player who played in Morris the previous summer. The offer sounded good, and after two seasons of playing professional ball, Petroff sensed that a summer of amateur ball might be a nice break from the grind.

Petroff wound up spending two full summers in Morris, one as a player/manager, and part of another before returning for one more professional season in 1952. From there, Petroff became a college coach, his first job at Rider in New Jersey, followed by a lengthy career at Northern Colorado. He saw many things he liked about Minnesota baseball and conceded that his experiences helped prepare him to be a better coach.

"They can say what they want about states like Arizona and California, and I don't mean to take anything away from them," Petroff said, "but at that particular time Minnesota was the bedrock state in [amateur] baseball. The state had so many leagues and players that it was unbelievable. A lot was done for baseball and the many young people interested in the game. I was impressed by the quality of baseball played in

Minnesota, and how the communities gave their teams major support."

Petroff was 155–84–2 in ten seasons at Rider and 367–198–1 in 15 seasons at Northern Colorado. He retired after the 1985 season at Northern Colorado and was named to the American Baseball Coaches Association Hall of fame in 1994.

Bob Montebello: Buckeye Found Wife, Home in Minnesota

Bob Montebello was playing summer baseball in his home town of Steubenville, Ohio, in early July 1951 when he was surprised by a phone call from University of Minnesota coach Dick Siebert. Montebello led the Big Ten in hitting that year with a .467 average, but he didn't figure that the coach and former major-league player even knew who he was.

It turns out that Siebert, who was in his first year as player/manager for the Class AA Litchfield Optimists, was looking for a third baseman who could also do some catching. Siebert asked player Ray Gebhardt if he knew anyone who could fill that spot. Gebhardt, who played for Ohio State from 1947 to 1950 (and who was All–Big Ten in 1949), suggested his old teammate Montebello.

Siebert had only seen Montebello play a couple of times but figured he could trust the recommendation by Gebhardt, who was his leading hitter at the time. So he called Ohio State coach Marty Karow to get Montebello's phone number. Siebert offered $325 per month plus a job, and Montebello left immediately for Minnesota.

"The 1951 season was magic," Montebello said. "I worked on a city street department crew during the day, and people would stop and talk baseball all the time. The whole town was crazy

for baseball." Litchfield won the West Central League pennant and playoffs and then went on to win the State Class AA Championship in Faribault.

Montebello came back to Litchfield in 1952 but stayed home in 1953, where he was working on a graduate degree at Ohio State and needed to be on campus during the summer. He came back to Litchfield in 1954 and 1955. "Crowds were definitely a lot smaller than they were in 1952," he said. The West Central League had folded after the 1953 season and the Optimists moved to the Western Minny. Litchfield finished 14–14 and in fourth place in the standings and then went 5–2 in a round-robin series to qualify for the final playoffs. The Optimists beat Marshall two games to none to win the first round but then lost three straight games to Fairmont in the finals.

Litchfield was back in the Western Minny in 1955 but struggled on the field and at the gate. At the end of July, with an 8–11 record and with no other apparent way to stop the red ink, the Litchfield baseball board dropped out of the league.

Several Optimists joined other teams to finish the season. Montebello decided to stay in Litchfield the rest of the summer. "The team paid me what they owed me for baseball," he said, "and I still had my summer job there." Besides, he now had some ties to Litchfield other than baseball: he'd met his future wife, Judy Danielson, the daughter of a local doctor. They were married in 1956.

In the fall, though, Montebello returned to Ohio State, where he had a teaching position and was the freshman baseball coach. He went to graduate school at Columbia University in 1956 and 1957. One of his job offers after completing his Ph.D. was from Bemidji State, and he and his wife didn't hesitate to move back to Minnesota.

Montebello taught and coached at Bemidji State until his retirement. He played amateur baseball for teams in Cass Lake and Bagley, as well as Bemidji, and made a return trip to the State Tournament in 1977.

Howie Peterson: Batboy Grew Up to Share Title

When it came to amateur baseball, Howie Peterson touched most bases from his childhood days through a long town team career at Willmar and Benson.

His charmed baseball life began as a batboy in Willmar's 1934 Class A state championship season, followed by three starting seasons on the Willmar High baseball team. Then it was on to the University of Minnesota, where he was a starting Gopher infielder, as well as a University of Minnesota basketball player.

His playing days were interrupted by World War II, but once he was discharged from the U.S. Navy, he completed his college education, joined his family business as an undertaker, and became a prominent member of Minnesota's town team baseball community. He played five seasons for Willmar, including a starting role in the 1946 state tourney, a week after starting on Willmar's state fast-pitch softball championship team.

"It was not unusual in those days to double-dip," Peterson said of the softball, which he played alongside several of his Willmar baseball teammates. "The tournaments were far enough apart so that they didn't interfere with one another."

Peterson was a complete player; a sure-handed infielder who hit for power as well as average. In 1946, he hit above .500 most of the season, and in Willmar's first game in the state tournament, hit a two-run home run with one

out in the bottom of the ninth to defeat Delano 5–4. "That was one of the greatest highlights of my career," Peterson said.

One season, Peterson managed a Sauk Rapids mortuary and commuted between work and Willmar's games, but his family eventually started a business in Willmar, an investment that saved him considerable time and energy. When the family added a business in Benson, he moved there and began playing for the Chiefs. He missed Willmar's 1952 Class AA State Championship season, but he continued playing town ball with Benson and shared in the town's 1954 State Class A championship.

An unselfish player, the onetime shortstop moved to second base when John Mauer joined Benson and he remained at second when Chuck Bosacker became the team's player/manager. And he was a grateful individual. When he and Roy Berens, the town's veteran third baseman, decided to retire in tandem after the 1958 season, Peterson submitted a public thanks to the Benson fans on behalf of him and Berens.

Casey Dowling: Touched All Bases

Clarence "Casey" Dowling was a 12-year-old farm kid when he played his first town team game for Jessie Lake, a rural township in Itasca County. Barefoot when instructed to pinch-hit against Sand Lake in his first game, he legged out an infield single, the beginning of a long and prosperous run in amateur baseball.

Dowling, who played college ball with the Gophers, graduated from the University of Minnesota in 1943 and briefly played professionally with Minneapolis and Little Rock in 1944, but the majority of his time was spent in town ball throughout the state. He taught vocational agriculture at various schools and became one of

Minnesota's most traveled amateurs until his final season in 1952.

"The Millers grabbed me because they knew
that I could hit and I had a good throwing arm,"
said Dowling, who had hit .385 and .405 in 1942
and 1943 with the Class AA Minneapolis Park
National League Mitby-Sathers. "I didn't want to
play professional ball, but [friends] said, 'Casey,
you'll never know how good you can be until you play with better players.' So I went with
the Millers in 1944 and that season I was sent to
Little Rock [Southern Association] where their
catcher got hit in the head with a pitched ball
and he swallowed a chew of tobacco. I got sent
down on a Friday night and joined the team in
Birmingham that Saturday. I was the lead-off hitter at Little Rock and faced a 15-year-old kid, Joe
Nuxall, who had been optioned by Cincinnati to
the minors."

Dowling injured his throwing hand and returned to Minnesota, where he quit professional
ball and resumed his teaching. In 1945, Hank
Nicklasson, briefly a teammate with the Millers in 1944, talked Dowling into signing with the
New Ulm Brewers of the Class A Western Minnesota League. From this point, he said it was
"have lesson plans will travel," and he also caught
in Sleepy Eye, Bird Island, Winsted, Dassel, Litchfield, De Graff, and St. Peter.

"I played for Winsted in 1949, where we had
a fabulous young team, and I received thirty to
thirty-five dollars a game," Dowling said. "The
following year, I was teaching in Dassel, but
didn't want to play baseball there because it was
Class B and the pitching was poor. But the president of the school board told me that if I played
in Dassel he'd pay me under the table."

The school board reneged, and after catching
an exhibition game for Litchfield, Jack Verby offered him a contract the same night at a local hotel. Dowling signed for $75 a game and was part
of the town's 1950 Class AA tournament team,
but was lost in the shuffle in 1951, when Dick
Siebert replaced Pete Kramer as manager. One of
Siebert's first moves was to invite his old friend
Hogo Pearson, whom he'd met at Baylor University, up to catch for the Optimists.

Dowling caught for De Graff early in 1951
as a favor to manager Jerry Sullivan, who was
waiting for two outside catchers to arrive. At
the end of the 1951–52 school year, Dowling
moved to St. Peter after two years teaching at
Dassel.

"St. Peter opened a new agricultural department, and I got the job," Dowling said. "I played
for St. Peter in 1952, but that would be my last
season of ball. We had a good club that season,
but Belle Plaine eliminated us in the playoffs."
He had suffered all season with the aftereffects
of a winter bout with pneumonia and decided
it was time to retire from baseball and stick to
teaching agriculture.

MINNESOTA'S OWN: LOCAL HEROES AND METRO MERCENARIES

MUCH HAS BEEN WRITTEN ABOUT the outside influence in Minnesota town team baseball during the post–World War II days, and the visitors definitely made a profound impact on state competition. Some of the most widespread off-season speculation focused on rumors regarding professional prospects expected to enhance a team's State Tournament potential.

Minnesota, however, had more than its share of baseball talent, a fact reflected by the game's prolific nature in the early 1950s, when 799 teams were on the Minnesota State Baseball Association rolls. At its peak there were 106 leagues, with some towns fielding more than one team. Dick Siebert, the baseball coach who used state talent to build a Big Ten power at the University of Minnesota, once said you were certain to see three common landmarks when you approached a Minnesota town: a water tower, a grain elevator, and baseball lights.

The Twin Cities undeniably was the state's baseball epicenter, a place where a groundswell of talent included standouts such as Howie Schultz, Dick Kaess, Ken Staples, Alex Roman-

chuck, Jerry Kindall, Jack McCartan, Ken Yackel, and the Mauer brothers. The abundance of talent should come as no surprise considering that 40 percent of the state's population resided in Minneapolis, St. Paul, and suburban areas. But this is not to detract from the volume and quality of out-state talent.

"I always told people, 'You can't believe the caliber of baseball in Minnesota,'" said Schultz, a Twin Cities product who had big league careers in baseball and basketball. "Any town of any size at a crossroads had a ball team. There were enough farms and farmers around the state that there were bound to be guys who could throw a baseball or hit and run."

Teams also relied on the Main Street professionals and merchants, high school teachers and student-athletes, and construction and manufacturing laborers. Doug Dibb was a farmer. Art Marben and Gary Underhill were teachers. Art Grangaard sold insurance. Milt Goemer sold cars. Tom Mee was a media ace. They were each just one of the guys most of the week, but on Sundays and a couple nights a week they were local celebrities, town heroes.

Dean Scarborough: A Star With a Dark Side

Dean Scarborough was one of the more talented—and enigmatic—players of the era. He led the Western Minny in hitting three consecutive years, from 1950 to 1952, with eye-popping averages of .419, .404, and .438, but he didn't make many friends along the way. His story shows the darker side of post–World War II baseball.

Scarborough was born in Windom and graduated from high school there in 1940. He played football, basketball, and baseball and, if not always the most gifted athlete, was a tough competitor. Classmates recall seeing him spend endless hours on the baseball diamond, fielding ground balls. (He'd pay local kids 25¢ per hour to hit to him if he couldn't find a friend who had the time to do it.)

He enlisted in the U.S. Marines right after Pearl Harbor. He signed with the Yankees after he got out of the service. He had a good season with Little Rock of the Class AA Southern Association in 1947, where his .310 batting average earned him a late-season spot with the Hollywood Stars of the Class AAA Pacific Coast League.

Scarborough floundered in 1948, however, and wound up in Class B in 1949. He split time between Lakeland in the Florida International League, where he hit .271, and with Jackson of the Southeastern League, where he hit .321.

He had been plagued by nagging injuries in all of his four seasons in the minor leagues, at least partially attributed to his aggressive style of play. Dean was a slightly built man and began to think that his body might not be suited for the everyday grind of professional baseball. Dismayed, he checked out possible baseball jobs back in Min-

nesota and signed with the Springfield Tigers of the Western Minny in 1950.

At this point Scarborough was like a lot of former servicemen who were giving up on their major-league dreams. While many of these men leveraged their baseball experiences in Minnesota to continue their educations, learn a trade, or settle down in the community with a regular job, Scarborough remained a baseball nomad. He was employed by Ochs Brick and Tile Co. in 1950 but didn't work much. He never showed up on game days. The next two summers he helped coach in the youth summer baseball program.

He left Springfield after the 1950 season and found a temporary job in a Michigan auto assembly plant. He returned to Springfield in 1951 with his wife and two kids and all his belongings stuffed into and on top of his 1947 Chevy.

Scarborough went back to spring training in Florida in 1952 but was slowed by an old leg injury. Discouraged after a few games back in Lakeland, he returned to Minnesota, where he signed a contract with Rochester of the Southern Minny. However, Springfield refused to give him a release. (Under a new rule adopted by the Minnesota Baseball Association that year, a player who was under contract with a Class AA team in 1951 could not sign with another team in any State Class AA or Class A league without obtaining a release from his 1951 team.) Scarborough threatened that he wouldn't play ball if not permitted to play with Rochester, but Springfield held firm. He eventually backed down and signed with Springfield again just before the season started.

The year 1952 was tough for Springfield. They fell from a 25–10 record in 1951 and a State Tournament berth to 15–20, but Scarborough had his best year, with a .438 average. He had 67 hits in 35 league games! Statistics, though, were never

Dean Scarborough *(far right)*, generally known for his no-nonsense demeanor, has fun with Jim McNulty, Ed Albertson, Mel Cook, and Sid Langston before the 1952 Western Minnesota All-Star Game. Courtesy of Herb Schaper Historical Baseball Collection/*New Ulm Daily Journal.*

him. He signed again with the Rochester Royals and began the season in the Southern Minny. Uncharacteristically, he got off to a slow start, and when Paul Furseth—who had hit .402 at Springfield in 1952—was released by the Royals while hitting .371 (they said they were looking for a power hitter), Scarborough started looking for another team. He contacted Redwood Falls of the Western Minny, but they turned him down after showing some initial interest.

Redwood Falls got some help making their decision. Mike Schwaegerl, in high school at the time and a batboy and scoreboard operator for Springfield, recalled going to a game in Redwood Falls with Bassie Wagner, a longtime Springfield resident. Harold Sloper, the Redwood manager, was from California and in his first year in Minnesota. He was impressed by Scarborough's record and asked Wagner for some feedback. Wagner told Sloper that Scarborough would be poison to team unity, and that he was a selfish player and a great second guesser.

Scarborough did find a job with Minot, North Dakota, in the semipro ManDak (Manitoba/North Dakota) League, and picked up right where he left off in Springfield. He led the league with a .356 batting average. He probably doubled his salary by moving. A Springfield resident who was traveling in Canada told Pat Maloney of the *Springfield Advance Press* that a Winnipeg newspaper reported that Scarborough was making $700 per month in Minot.

Scarborough returned to Minot the next two years, continuing his nomadic existence. He moved to the Basin League in South Dakota in 1956 but was lured back to Minot near the end of the season to replace an injured player. His base-

Dean's problem. On the field he was an electric performer, but in an era where it was common for players to slide with their spikes up and when the bean ball was just another pitch, Scarborough was thought to be "too aggressive." He ran the bases hard, always looking to take the extra base, and his tough sliding terrorized opposing infielders.

Scarborough's reclusive nature did not endear him to his teammates. He kept to himself off the field and was seldom part of the team's social gatherings. His teammates never warmed up to him. When he ran through a hold sign to stretch a single into a double, or to score from second, they thought he was a selfish player. He was a great bunter, but when he bunted for a base hit in the top of the ninth with his team leading 5–0, they thought he was "showing up" the other team and just trying to pad his own statistics.

When Scarborough requested his release in 1953, Springfield by now was happy to give it to

ball trail goes cold at that point, but he eventually settled down in California. He wrote a letter to the Windom Class of 1940 on the occasion of their 45th reunion in 1985. He said he was living with his wife and stepson and was a thoroughbred racing judge.

Charles "Lefty" Johnson: Lefty Was Champion of Champions

Charles "Lefty" Johnson's career record was fashioned primarily during the Depression. He did, however, continue to pitch into the early 1950s, and in 1945 he completed a special achievement.

Charles "Lefty" Johnson, shown in 1938, was an ace pitcher in state leagues for almost 20 years. Photograph by Lefty Evans; courtesy of Don Evans.

When the handsome left-hander won a semifinal game in Albert Lea's 1945 Class AA championship, it marked the fourth consecutive year that he was part of a state championship team's pitching staff. In the three previous seasons, he had won the Class A title games for Fairfax, New Ulm, and Springfield and completed his string in 1945 by defeating St. Paul General Drivers 8–1 in the Class AA semifinals, holding the opponents hitless until Bob Stoltz hit a two-out inside-the-park home run in the ninth.

His achievement might have received greater attention, but Excelsior's Roger McDonald and Albert Lea teammate Earl Steier upstaged him. McDonald pitched a no-hitter to beat Mayer 4–0 in the Class A title game, and Steier capped Albert Lea's Class AA championship by defeating Jack Verby and Minneapolis Honeywell 1–0. McDonald was voted the tournament MVP, and Steier won his own game with a ninth-inning RBI single.

Johnson did gain added attention the following week when he pitched a five-hitter for Albert Lea in a 14–2 romp over Excelsior in the Mythical State Championship. Albert Lea also combined for 14 hits off McDonald and Vern Bruhn.

"He's never had a poorly pitched game either in the state tournament or the playoff between division champions that follows each year, particularly when the chips are down," the *Minneapolis Tribune* baseball writer Ted Peterson wrote before the Albert Lea–Excelsior game. "A magnificent pitching duel is in prospect for Sunday."

Including the four Mythical matchups following the four state tournaments, Johnson had eight consecutive winning decisions, three coming in Class A finals. He allowed 18 runs on 43 hits, with Austin collecting four runs and 12 hits in Fairfax's 1942 Mythical State triumph over the Packers.

Unlike the first three years when Johnson was a draft pick for the three championship teams, the veteran pitched the entire season for Albert Lea in Class AA, compiling an overall 18–3 record. He won three Southern Minny playoff games, beating Austin twice and adding a save against the perennial league power. The left-hander allowed one run or less in seven victories and struck out 173 batters.

Johnson signed with Mankato in 1946 and was involved in a historic marathon against Leo Leininger. In a four-hour game that went 18 innings, Leininger beat Johnson 4–3, though Johnson allowed two fewer hits. "He may be the standout hurler of all-time in Minnesota independent baseball," media legend Halsey Hall wrote in a newspaper column, "yet this could be his toughest defeat."

Johnson continued his nomadic career after leaving Mankato, pitching regularly for St. Peter, Belle Plaine, Wanda, and Hector. But the legend was fading, and after an 11–0 drubbing while pitching for Hector in 1952, he went from being a heralded pitcher to a respected umpire in the state circuit.

Ken Staples: Catcher Caught in the Wrong Draft

Twenty-eight-year-old Ken Staples couldn't believe what he'd just heard. St. Thomas College athletic director and football coach Frank Deig had just called him out of the blue and made a very unusual offer.

Staples had signed a $3,000 bonus contract with the St. Paul Saints—then an independently owned member of the Brooklyn Dodgers organization—when he graduated from St. Paul Humboldt High School in 1946. An all-city standout in football, hockey, and baseball, he was also

St. Thomas head coach Ken Staples *(right)* discusses strategy with assistant Walt Dziedzic. Both were former professional baseball players and Korean War veterans. Courtesy of Ken Staples.

contacted by the NHL's Chicago Blackhawks. He hit .382 for Grand Forks that first year to lead the Class C Northern League in hitting. In 1947 he split time between Greenville of the Class A Southeastern League and Mobile of the Class AA Southern Association. In 1948 he was back in Mobile, and then he spent 1949 and 1950 with Fort Worth of the Class AA Texas League.

In early 1951, Staples got his draft notice and was ordered to report immediately for service in the U.S. Army. Just before he left, he got a call from Col. John Kramer, athletic officer at the Brooke Army Medical Center in San Antonio, Texas. Brooke Center was the U.S. Army's primary hospital for the treatment of veterans with severe burns, and Kramer was given the assignment to assemble a baseball team that would provide entertainment for hospital patients, as well as traveling and playing exhibition games at other military installations.

Staples spent two years in San Antonio, primarily playing baseball. Col. Kramer assembled a powerhouse team, which included current or future major leaguers Don Newcombe, Bob Turley, Gus Triandos, Owen Friend, Dr. Bobby Brown, Danny Ozark, Dick Kokos, and Marv Rotblatt. Staples caught for the team, while Triandos, who later caught for 13 years in the major leagues, played first base. (Tommy Kramer, one of Col. Kramer's eleven children, later became quarterback for the Minnesota Vikings.)

Staples was discharged in May 1953 and assigned to Montreal again, but he was now married to Martha Lanier, whom he'd met in Fort Worth, and he asked to stay in Texas. The Dodgers reluctantly sent him to Fort Worth, where he played for the next two years. In 1954 the Dodgers signed him to a major-league contract—$5,000 per year—to protect him from the free-agent draft, but they were set with Roy Campanella and Rube Walker at catcher, and he didn't make the major-league roster.

In 1955, though, the Dodgers would only offer him a minor-league contract and insisted he play in Montreal. Staples was fed up and held out for more money. When the Dodgers wouldn't budge, he moved back to Minnesota and got a job running the West St. Paul summer recreation program. He also became player/manager for West St. Paul's Class A St. Paul Suburban League team.

St. Thomas athletic director Frank Deig called early that fall and made his proposition. He offered Staples the head coaching job for the St. Thomas hockey and baseball teams. (Deig wasn't coming completely out of nowhere to make this

offer. Staples coached youth hockey teams most winters during his professional baseball career and had played in several senior amateur and semipro hockey leagues.) In return, the college would pay his tuition in addition to the coaching salaries. It was too good an offer to pass up—Staples would have the GI Bill to live on, so money wouldn't be a problem for his growing family. (He and Martha had a five-year-old daughter and a two-year-old son at the time. They eventually had two more sons.)

That's when Deig threw a curveball. "I'll need you to come out for the football team, too," he said.

Staples was almost speechless. "But I haven't

Ken Staples in Fairmont, 1957. His fierce brand of play fit in well with manager McNulty's veteran crew. Courtesy of Ken Staples.

played football for ten years," he pleaded. "I've got a family to think about." Deig didn't listen. He just told him when fall practice started.

Staples accepted the offer. He became the hockey coach immediately and started classes in the winter term. He coached the St. Thomas baseball team in the spring. His assistant coach was Walt Dziedzic, who, like Staples, was a former minor-league player and service veteran.

Staples ran the West St. Paul summer recreation program again in 1956, and his West St. Paul team won the St. Paul Suburban League playoffs and qualified for the Class A State Tournament (where they lost two straight: 6–3 to Pipestone, and 13–0 to Little Falls). Staples tried to keep in shape over the summer, but dreaded the start of fall football practice. "I damn near died during the two-a-day workouts," Staples said. But he stuck it out. St. Thomas, with a few Korean vets like Staples, went 8–0 and won the MIAC championship.

Early in the summer of 1957, Staples received a call from Fairmont manager Jim McNulty, who offered Staples a combined $1,000 per month for playing baseball and working in a grocery store. (Staples said he was just a glorified carryout boy.) The Southern Minny had imposed a salary cap in 1956, limiting players' salaries to $500 per month (except for pitchers, who could be paid $650 per month), so the contract had to be carefully structured.

Staples was receptive to the offer. It was much more money than he would make at the recreation department, and he also liked the idea of playing in a more competitive baseball league. He and his family had a few trepidations, though, as they made their first trip down to Fairmont. Their fears were relieved when most of the team and their families turned up to greet them at a welcome party barbecue at a local park. Mc-

Nulty had even found them a house to rent for the summer at a ridiculously low cost. The Martins were a close-knit team, and full of veterans like Staples.

Staples returned to Fairmont in 1958. The Southern Minny retained its salary cap at $5,800 per month even though the league had dropped to Class A, but the teams were trying to cut back. Staples took a pay cut from the team but supplemented that with a job as groundskeeper at the baseball field. It was a tough year for the league, which now only had four teams—Fairmont, Austin, Albert Lea, and Mason City, Iowa. Fairmont won the pennant but lost in the playoffs to Austin, which went on the win the State Championship.

He graduated from St. Thomas in 1959—he was voted "Mr. Tommie" his senior year—and, when it looked like salaries were going to be cut back even more severely at Fairmont, took a job (paying $3,000 for the summer) as manager of the Watertown, South Dakota, Lake Sox in the college-dominated Basin League.

Staples started his teaching career at Robbinsdale High School that fall and in 1960 played for Mankato, which returned to the Southern Minny after a two-year absence. His pay was down to $300 per month, but Mankato was closer than Fairmont and permitted him to live in the Twin Cities and drive to games.

Staples had a long and successful hockey and baseball coaching career. He moved to Robbinsdale Cooper when that school opened in 1964, managed in the Midwest Collegiate League and with several teams in the Minnesota Twins organization. He also conducted clinics for the Twins and was a spring training coach for many years. In 2004 he managed an amateur team in Osceola, Wisconsin, and worked once again in the 2005 Twins spring training camp.

Tom Mee: Player Became Promoter

When the Minnesota Twins made their American League inaugural in 1961, Tom Mee was banging out press releases and fielding media questions in his Metropolitan Stadium office. The Minneapolis native and graduate of St. Paul's Cretin High School and the University of Minnesota was the Twins' public relations director, a position he filled for 30 years after several seasons with the American Association's St. Paul Saints.

The Twins became the state's newest baseball name, but in Mee they had someone close to Minnesota ball. He played several town team seasons at Redwood Falls, Iona, Marshall, Lamberton, Delano, and Detroit Lakes. He played professionally briefly in 1950 and 1952, but the University of Minnesota communications major wound up leaving the game to become a ra-

Tom Mee was good enough to play Class AA town team and professional baseball, but a radio career led to an administrative spot in the Twins organization. Photograph from the collection of the Minnesota Historical Society.

dio announcer after being certified through the Brown Institute of Radio.

He got his first job at Detroit Lakes. "I did four games on the radio, and all of a sudden they began playing night games," Mee said. "We were a daytime station, and when their shortstop got hurt, they asked me to play. I figured, why not, and had one of the best seasons of my life."

But the experience was not good enough to keep him in Minnesota for the following season. In November 1953 he accepted a sports job with a Montana radio station, and the next year he moved to New Mexico, where he did play-by-play broadcasts of Class C West Texas–New Mexico minor-league games. The league began to struggle, and his radio station did not renew its radio rights, but about that time Mee received an offer from a St. Cloud station. He resigned from the New Mexico station only to learn that the job fell through, but he decided it was time to go home. He and his wife threw their two children in the backseat of their car and headed north without a job.

"I was driving to my parents' place in March, I think it was on St. Patrick's Day, and driving past Midway Stadium I decided to stop in and submit an application," Mee said. "I talked to Mel Jones, who told me to fill out an application, and I did PR for the [St. Paul] Saints from 1957 through 1960."

In the fall of 1960, with the Washington Senators ready to move to Minnesota, owner Cal Griffith and some of his staff came to town. Mee was asked to handle the off-season transition in Minnesota and later declined a radio opportunity in Omaha to become the Twins' public relations director, a job he held until retiring in 1991. He also became the official scorer for Twins home games, a position he still held in 2006.

In 1965, Minnesota won the American

League pennant. Mee needed assistance for the World Series and immediately thought of Jim Rantz, a former town team player who pitched and won the deciding game for the Minnesota Gophers in the 1960 College World Series. Rantz had just completed the season as manager of the Twins' St. Cloud Northern League team. He'd retired as a player in 1964 after five seasons in the Twins' minor-league organization. (He originally signed with the Washington Senators but became Twins property when the franchise moved to Minnesota.)

Rantz was hired on a part-time basis to assist Mee for the World Series. "Jim did an excellent job. They really liked him," Mee said. "So they offered him a full-time job once the Series ended." Rantz eventually became the Twins' director of minor-league operations.

Clint "Timber" Dahlberg: Northern League to South Pacific

Clint "Timber" Dahlberg is another example of a man whose professional baseball career was interrupted in the middle of his prime developmental years. In 1941, at age 21, the Howard Lake native appeared to be maturing physically. His six-foot, three-inch frame had finally filled out and, in his third year in the minor leagues, he hit 17 home runs for Crookston and Wausau in the Class C Northern League. The ball was jumping off his bat, and he was able to hit for distance to all fields. Who knows where he might have gone had it not been for Pearl Harbor?

Like many men of his generation, Dahlberg didn't wait for his draft notice. He enlisted in the Marines Corps on February 25, 1942, and was in basic training in San Diego on February 28, and by early 1943 he was on Guadalcanal. He won a battle star, but contracted malaria while there,

was eventually sent back to the States, and assigned to the Portsmouth, New Hampshire, Naval Prison. He remained there for the rest of the war. Asked years later if he remembered when he was discharged, Timber replied that he did: "November 22, 1945, at 11:17 a.m."

Dahlberg recovered from the malaria well enough to play with the marines' baseball team in the local amateur league in 1944 and 1945 and resumed his professional career in 1946,

Hard-hitting Timber Dahlberg, shown with the Southern Minny Rochester Royals, is one of many Minnesotans who had their baseball careers interrupted by World War II. Courtesy of Ella Dahlberg.

playing for Manchester, New Hampshire, in the Class B New England League. It was slow going, though. He made the All-Star team that year but returned to the same league in 1947. He had his best year in 1948, when he hit .326, with 15 home runs and 106 RBIs for Muskegon, Michigan, in the Class A Central League, but he wound up back in the Central League again in 1949. In midseason—while hitting .330 for Saginaw, but discouraged because he hadn't moved up from Class A—he decided to take a player/manager's job at Clarksdale, Mississippi, in the Class C Cotton States League.

Dahlberg returned to Saginaw in 1950. Although he was the team's most popular player, and was hitting .307 at the time, the organization released him at the end of June. The manager said that Timber's lack of speed and defensive deficiencies were the reason. Furthermore, although they didn't say it publicly, Dahlberg was also 30 years old, and the team wanted to develop its younger players. He finished the season with the London, Ontario, Majors of the Canadian Senior Inter-County semipro league.

Dahlberg returned to Minnesota in 1951, were he was signed to be player/manager for the Rochester Royals of the Southern Minny. He hit .314 that year, but found—as he had at Clarksdale in 1949—that managing wasn't for him. He just didn't like to make difficult personnel decisions. Dahlberg started the 1952 season as manager again but stepped down early in the season. Without the worries of managing, he had his best Southern Minny season, hitting .331 and leading the league with 18 home runs and 45 RBIs.

He had two more good seasons at Rochester in 1953 and 1954, but then he moved back to Howard Lake and purchased a resort on the east side of the lake. He played a few more seasons with the Howard Lake team, mostly as a pitcher,

but didn't have much time to devote to practice and training. Sunday games were even difficult, because that was the big day of the week at the resort's restaurant. Dahlberg usually showed up just before game time and then rushed back to the resort after the game.

It is tempting to engage in "what-might-have-beens" when talking about Dahlberg's war service and its effect on his career. He never saw it that way. Like millions of other men, he just said he was doing his duty. Timber was thankful he was able to play the game he loved as long as he did.

Art Marben: Marines Called Twice

The year was 1946, and life was good for Art Marben. Behind him was World War II and a Pacific campaign that included uncomfortable stops in Okinawa and China. Ahead of him were the prospects of peace, prosperity, and baseball. Free room and board, a lifeguard job, and $15 a game playing a sport he deeply loved were far more appealing than rations, sleeping on the ground, and challenging an enemy on his home turf. Marben loved Springfield and baseball before he left for the war, but the game was even more gratifying when he returned.

"Baseball was the center of activities when we got back," Marben said. "You were really taken care of if you were a ballplayer. I actually could have signed a professional contract after I got out of high school, but why would I have wanted to go to Class D Pocatello, Idaho, for seventy-five dollars a month when I was making much more in Springfield?"

Before the war, Marben—a 1940 graduate of Lamberton High, not far from Springfield in southern Minnesota—was enrolled at Augsburg College and playing in the prestigious Western

Art Marben *(right)*, pictured with Springfield teammate Jack Dolan, twice had his town team career interrupted by war, but he remained one of Minnesota's best homegrown Class AA players. Courtesy of Herb Schaper Historical Baseball Collection/*New Ulm Daily Journal.*

Minnesota League. He earned a reputation as a quality middle infielder and as an explosive offensive force. But with a world war raging on two fronts in October 1942, he enlisted in a Marine Corps program and remained in school until being called into active duty the following July. He entered the war along with several good friends, some of them teammates. He and many others returned. A few others did not.

Once again, Marben was offered a professional baseball contract, but he again declined and reenrolled at Augsburg College. He graduated in 1947 and was hired to teach in his hometown, but played baseball at Springfield. He was called back to the Marines in 1950. He was sent to Quantico and appeared to be headed for Korea, but he remained stationed at the Virginia base, not far from Washington, D.C., and played baseball.

The closest he came to combat was an occasional spat on the diamond. Quantico had a baseball team, and Marben became a major competitor over the next couple seasons, a period in which he played a full schedule against other military bases and college teams. It was good baseball, possibly on par with the Western Minny League. Perhaps better.

"There were a lot of major leaguers in at the same time," Marben said. "I played against Johnny Antonelli [New York Giants] and Whitey Ford [New York Yankees]." One of his teammates was catcher Hal Naragon, a member of the Cleveland Indians' 1954 World Series team and later one of the original Minnesota Twins.

Marben hit .413 in a 70-game schedule and was named the 1951 Virginia Semi-Pro League Championship MVP. Quantico defeated Ford 4–3 in the semifinals but lost to the 43rd Division and Detroit Tiger Art Houtteman, 4–1, in the title game. Houtteman was 19–12 the previous summer with the Tigers.

The infielder, nicknamed "Spider" because of his defensive range, was hitting .375 upon his discharge in June of 1952. He resumed his Western Minny career when he got back to Minnesota. His teaching career led him to Tracy, where he finished his town ball career.

Bill Bolin, a Tracy teammate, described Marben as an outstanding person, "a credit to his community, family, church, and school," as well as an intense competitor. "I remember a game in which he vehemently questioned an umpire's call, and didn't let up," Bolin said. "The umpire finally pulled out a watch and told Art that he had three minutes to calm down and resume play, a threat to which Art responded that the umpire had a minute to decide where he was going to put the watch."

Milt Goemer: Too Little, Too Late for MVP

Milt Goemer appeared poised to make a quantum leap in the New York Yankee chain after a 1948 season in which the Minnesota native went 25–4 for Grand Forks, lifting the previous season's Northern League cellar dweller to the pennant.

Goemer received the Class C Northern League's MVP plaque, and the New York Yankees awarded him a promotion to Beaumont in the Class AA Texas League. But at age 28, having already missed four seasons during the war, he pondered his professional baseball future and decided that it was tentative at best. The burly right-hander from Darwin left pro ball to play town ball with Redwood Falls in the Class AA Western Minnesota League.

His first season lacked the luster of his final professional campaign, but an 8–7 record didn't reflect a lack of drive. "He didn't have spring training when he started the season," said former teammate Tom Mee, a future Minnesota Twins executive. "He began throwing too hard too early and he developed a sore arm. He was a good pitcher, but got off to a poor start."

Goemer, who worked for a Redwood Falls car dealer, pitched for the Redbirds again in 1950 and 1951. He was drafted by 1950 Western Minny champion Fairfax for the State Class AA tournament. Fairfax lost the opener in double-elimination play, but Goemer defeated Minneapolis Mitby-Sathers 7–0 in the next game to temporarily stave off elimination.

Goemer played for Fairfax in 1952 and went 7–3 but moved to Bird Island in the Class A Twin Trails League the next season when Fairfax dropped down to Class B. With him aboard, Bird Island made it to the State Class A Tournament for the third consecutive season.

"He was one of the fastest pitchers I've ever seen," Lake Lillian's Myron Flann said. But though Goemer's arm was back to full strength, his career ended in 1954 when he tore an Achilles tendon. He sat on the Bird Island bench when the 1955 season began, and when the school term ended, and his wife, June, a physical education teacher, completed her Bird Island teaching contract, they moved to the Twin Cities.

Fate works in mysterious ways. While Goemer was crafting his MVP season at Grand Forks, a young Don Larsen went 17–11 at Aberdeen in the same league. Larsen reached the majors in 1953, and in 1956—October 8—Larsen pitched his legendary perfect game against the Brooklyn Dodgers. One can only imagine what went through Goemer's mind when he heard the news.

"Oh, I can remember Milt talking some about having pitched against this or that guy," June Goemer said of her late husband. "I can remember him telling me about playing service ball while he was stationed near Chicago, and how they built a ball field in the South Pacific. But Milt didn't talk a great deal about baseball, especially about his accomplishments. I once told him that he should write some of his baseball memories down. He did, but he didn't write very much."

The memory of Larsen's perfection will forever be preserved by the media and in Cooperstown, New York, home of the Baseball Hall of Fame. Goemer's Northern League MVP ring and several other items from his baseball days can be found in a little Darwin museum, next to "The World's Largest Ball of Twine."

John Garbett: Pitcher Had State Tourney Poise

Sitting in the locker room minutes before Litchfield's 1950 State Class AA tourney game against the highly favored Austin Packers, manager Pete Kramer approached Johnny Garbett and asked him how he felt. Once given a thumbs-up sign, Kramer flipped Garbett a ball and informed the diminutive left-hander that he would start the game.

Kramer's decision was a surprise, especially to Garbett, drafted from Morris after Litchfield won the West Central playoffs and qualified for the state tournament. Willmar's Gene Kelly, arguably the West Central's top pitcher and another draftee, beat Minneapolis Mitby-Sathers 3–1 in the tournament opener, but Litchfield's

Johnny Garbett, shown as a draftee for Litchfield in 1950, led six teams into State Tournament play, but the hard-luck pitcher never won a championship. Courtesy of Brian Larson.

Bob Kinsel or Jack Verby seemed to be the logical choices ahead of Garbett.

He was no stranger to state tourney play, however, having made two previous appearances: with Maple Lake in Class A in 1947, and with Benson in Class AA in 1949. Garbett conceded that, while surprised, he wasn't nervous. He was confident in his ability and the talents of a team that had breezed through the West Central regular season and playoffs. Two hours and three minutes after the game's opening pitch, it was Austin that was surprised after a 3–2 loss. Litchfield gave Garbett a three-run lead in the first inning, and he hung tough to bounce the defending Class AA champs into the losers' bracket.

Garbett escaped bases-loaded situations in each of the first two innings, and he gave up two third-inning runs before settling down. Austin finished with nine hits but no more runs as Garbett—supported by a solid defense—went the distance for the victory. "I think I kept them off balance. That was probably the difference," Garbett said. "I had a fairly good curve, and it was working quite well that game."

Litchfield didn't win the Class AA title—losing back-to-back to Fergus Falls and Austin in double elimination—but the Optimists' victory cost Austin dearly. Rain delays complicated the tournament schedule, and Austin wound up having to play five games on the last two days of the tournament. Austin won the first four but ran out of gas and lost the championship game to Fergus Falls, 3–0.

"It was funny," Garbett said. "Some guy from Fergus came up to me a few years later and said, 'Hey, you were the one who helped us win the State Tournament back in 1950.'"

Garbett, a 1947 graduate of Edison High School and briefly a University of Minnesota pitcher, wasn't so fortunate at State Tournaments during his outstanding career. The majority of his postseason experiences were solid but less gratifying.

In 1947 he was drafted by Maple Lake after spending most of the season with Elk River. (He'd started the year in the Minneapolis Park National League.) After helping to get Maple Lake through the region, he started the team's State Tournament Class A opener against Chaska. Garbett pitched a five-hitter and struck out 14 batters but lost 1–0 to the division's eventual champions, who beat him with a combined no-hitter by Don Anderson and Gene Cooney.

Chaska scored its lone run in the ninth when Bill Wettergren reached first base on a passed ball after striking out. Wettergren stole second minutes later and scored when the Maple Lake shortstop overthrew first base on a grounder deep in the hole, one of three Maple Lake errors in the game.

In 1948, Garbett pitched full-time for Maple Lake in the Class A Wright County League, and in 19 games he compiled a 0.90 earned-run average, allowed an average of 2.48 hits, and struck out 13.3 batters per game. But matched against Shakopee's Gene Cooney in the Region 1A playoffs, Garbett developed a sore back and was pulled in the second inning of a 7–3 loss.

Clara City lured him with a contract for $550 per month in 1949, when the town played in the West Central League's first season in Class AA. Benson drafted him for the State Tournament, where he started and was the losing pitcher in a 6–1 elimination-game loss to runner-up Fergus Falls.

Clara City dropped down to the Class A Western Central League in 1950, and Garbett signed for $100 per game with Morris, a new West Central League franchise whose manager was Paul Scanlon, an old friend dating back to his Minne-apolis playground days. Garbett won 13 games for Morris, highlighted by a 24-strikeout victory over Atwater.

Garbett's next draft call came from Uncle Sam, and with the exception of a couple Minnesota town ball exhibition games while on leave, the only baseball he pitched for the next two years was with military all-star teams. He was discharged in 1952 and signed a minor-league contract with the Chicago Cubs, but he injured an elbow and was released.

He started the 1953 season with Benson-De Graff in the West Central League but caught on with Jordan when the Irish-Chiefs folded in mid-season. Garbett helped lead Jordan to back-to-back State Tournaments in 1953 and 1954, but once again, his good fortune was eclipsed by misfortune.

Matched against Delavan's Rich Weigel in the 1953 State Tournament, Garbett pitched a seven-hitter and struck out 12, but Weigel allowed only four hits in a 1–0 victory. Jordan threatened to tie the game in the bottom of the ninth when Jim Pollard singled and stole second, but Weigel—named the tournament MVP—struck out cleanup hitter Gene Parrish to end the game, and Delavan won its next two games to win the Class A State Title.

Benson foiled another stellar Garbett effort in the opening round of the 1954 State Tournament. The left-hander allowed the Chiefs only six hits and had two hits himself for Jordan, but Benson won 4–2, punctuated by a three-run sixth, and went on to win the Class A State Championship. Jordan won its second game in the tournament, which was double elimination for the first time in Class A, an 11–4 romp over Pipestone, but then was eliminated by Spring Grove, 1–0. Garbett played in the field but didn't pitch in the final two games.

"I just pitched for teams that didn't seem to have much hitting," Garbett said. "But I had a lot of fun. They were terrific days in which a town like Maple Lake with only 800 people would draw two or three times its population. Elk River, Maple Lake, Clara City, Morris, Benson, De Graff, and Jordan were great places to be."

Garbett quit pitching in the mid-1950s but played outfield and comanaged with Minneapolis Cozy's in 1958 and 1959 before retiring for good.

Doug Dibb: Lefty Had the Right Stuff

Doug Dibb was an unlikely pitching standout in his youth, and would certainly have been an unlikely candidate in any other era. The five-foot-eight, 150-pound left-hander was not overwhelming and had an outwardly mild-mannered disposition. He had the use of only his right eye after losing the left in a welding accident at age 16. And while his father was involved in the town's baseball administration, Earl Dibb had nothing to offer in terms of instruction.

"I had two brothers who played, but my father never did. He didn't even know what a baseball was until he saw his sons play," Dibb said. "He became interested in the game, however, and was active in the [Crow River Valley] league and Minnesota state amateur baseball for 14 years." Doug Dibb hadn't made the Minnesota Baseball Hall of Fame in the twentieth century, but his father was inducted in 1965, based on his off-field contributions.

But Doug Dibb compiled an enviable record before leaving the game long after the 1960 season. He was good enough to have pitched exhibitions on Class A or Class AA teams, but he enjoyed his friends and the Lester Prairie baseball atmosphere, so he remained at home. The only

Lester Prairie's Doug Dibb, shown in 1945, pitched in 10 State Tournaments between 1945 and 1960. Courtesy of Doug Dibb.

time he left was for exhibitions and as a draft selection when Lester Prairie failed to qualify for the state tourney. From 1945 through 1960, he was part of 10 state tournament teams, more than any player at any level during the era.

The high-water mark for Dibb was in 1950 when Lester Prairie won the State Class B title. Norwood went undefeated in league play during the regular season, but Lester Prairie upset its neighborhood rival in the playoffs. Dibb combined with drafted pitchers Bert McCarthy of Green Isle and Ed Hoese of Mayer to take Lester Prairie the distance, but Dibb was the winning pitcher in two of the four tournament games.

Dibb won the opener, McCarthy and Hoese each followed with a win, and Dibb completed the job. The left-hander with the uncanny curve defeated Ulen for openers, allowing only three hits and striking out nine, then outlasted Duluth Teve's in the final, matching Sam Koskovich's four-hitter while striking out 11 batters.

That Dibb was drafted so often by Crow Valley teams was a major compliment, considering the league's wealth of pitching talent that included McCarthy, Hoese, Hamburg's Lefty Graupmann, and Norwood's Willy Willemsen. He linked up with each for some competitive epics in the 1940s and 1950s.

"When we and Norwood played, we always drew big crowds because of the rivalry," he said, referring to some close games against Willemsen. "But I liked pitching against all those other guys because they wanted to win just as much as I did."

In 1953, the only year Lester Prairie was eliminated in the first round of the State Tournament, comanager Dibb was playing first while Mayer's Hoese pitched against eventual State B runner-up Holdingford.

Dibb discussed his pitching record as one might discuss a marriage. He said he couldn't have asked for a more supportive wife or a more trustworthy battery mate than Oscar Rolf, who caught almost every game Dibb pitched. "He was a good catcher, a big guy who also could hit the ball a mile when he made contact."

Marty Ledeboer: His Heart Gave Out

Marty Ledeboer came to Sleepy Eye in the summer of 1945, and in a heartbeat the Moorhead State College kid had the townsfolk smiling. He was a welcome addition to the community, a solid baseball player with a matching charac-ter and sunny disposition. On a hot summer afternoon in Redwood Falls in 1947, however, he would become the source of one of Sleepy Eye's darkest days. At age 21, Ledeboer collapsed after crossing home plate and died several hours later in the Redwood Falls hospital with his father and a Sleepy Eye minister at his side.

Ledeboer's death, attributed to a cerebral hemorrhage, came as a shock to all, although a later newspaper account revealed that several years earlier he had been diagnosed with high blood pressure and told that his life span could be severely limited by his condition. He chose to continue playing baseball and played well enough to be recruited by Sleepy Eye, where he was given a job in a local drugstore.

Ledeboer was mired in a battling slump before Sleepy Eye headed for Redwood Falls, and he was hitless until the eighth when he lined a single to right. Casey Dowling, the Sleepy Eye catcher, told the fleet center fielder that the steal sign was on, but Lebeboer shook his head and asked to have the steal sign lifted because he was too fatigued to run.

"But the next batter, Carl Sperl, tripled and Marty had to run," Dowling said. "He started to weave once he got past second base and by the time he was headed for home he was staggering." Ledeboer collapsed shortly after crossing home plate and was rushed to the Redwood Falls hospital, where he briefly regained consciousness, but died four hours later.

Sleepy Eye, with former major-league pitcher Dick Lanahan on the mound, won a meaningless 14–8 decision but several hours later lost a teammate. Three days later Ledeboer was buried at a packed church ceremony in Prinsburg, his birthplace situated between Montevideo and Willmar. Six cousins served as pallbearers. Later that season, the Western Minnesota

League dedicated its All-Star Game to Lede-boer. The game matched league-leading Spring-field against an all-star cast that included five of Ledeboer's teammates. Proceeds were presented to the Ledeboer family, which included his three brothers and seven sisters.

Gary Underhill: A Memorable Summer

Gary Underhill has fond baseball memories go-ing back to his high school days at Austin, where he compiled a 29–6 career record, including a no-hit victory and two other winning decisions in the team's 1954 state championship run. The diminutive left-hander was and will always re-main one of the state's most heralded high school players, and a top-notch town ball pitcher.

In Underhill's memory banks are other golden oldies such as a 6–0 record in his lone college season at Upper Iowa State, a 28–26 four-year professional mark in the St. Louis Cardinal or-ganization, and a 14–3 mark in three seasons with Austin in the tough Southern Minnesota League.

But any trip back in time for the soft-spo-ken Underhill included a special stop in Spring Grove, where the summer before his senior year in high school he pitched town team ball in the Class A Fillmore County League. The five-foot-eight, 140-pound pitcher was 10–4 with a 1.62 earned run average. He struck out 132 batters in 119 innings for a team that qualified for the 1954 State Tournament, where they won one game before losing to eventual champion Benson. Un-derhill pitched through the regional playoffs but missed most of the state tourney because of a sore arm.

"He was some pitcher," former Austin High coach Dick Seltz said of his four-year starter. "If he had been two or three inches taller, he possi-bly could have made it to the majors. He had a curve ball you couldn't believe, and he had a very good fastball."

Underhill was the coach's teammate at Spring Grove, where Seltz started at second base and hit in the cleanup spot. Underhill delighted in play-ing alongside his coach and other older players. One of his favorites was Lyle "Bunny" Johnson, the team's player/manager and local high school principal. "There was a baseball banquet after the season, and Bunny told me that when I got my college degree, I should come back and be a teacher and coach at Spring Grove," Underhill said. "I never did go back, but I can remember at the time thinking how nice that would be. I en-joyed the closeness with the people in town and the baseball atmosphere was wonderful."

In his career, Underhill experienced a vari-ety of baseball environments, beginning with his childhood days in Austin watching South-ern Minny baseball, admiring local heroes Seltz, Red Lindgren, Bill Campau, and Moose Skow-ron, as well as opposing players including pitcher Sad Sam Jones with Rochester. He also played for Austin when the crowds were still large, and af-ter signing a $5,000 bonus with the Cardinals, he pitched in front of thousands while assigned to Sioux City, Daytona Beach, Winnipeg, Stockton, Fresno, and Eugene.

"I can remember my first season [1956] at Sioux City in the Western League, the same sea-son Dick Stuart hit 66 home runs for Lincoln," he said referring to the future Pittsburgh slug-ger. "He'd probably have hit 150 home runs that season if he had been playing in Amarillo where center field was only 350 feet from home. I was so relieved that I got him to pop up the first time I pitched to him."

But Underhill's most vivid memories were of his town team days, particularly the summer of

1954 in Spring Grove when he was a kid playing among men. Much like a first love, this gave him butterflies. At Spring Grove, the farmers would hustle to the park after a long day of work; some would quit early to get to the ballpark, which was often encircled by automobiles. Pandemonium would erupt after a local hit a home run, and boos would cascade throughout the park when a visitor would make a big hit or have an altercation with an umpire or Spring Grove player.

As for the baseball, the game served Underhill in many ways, both personally—he met his wife, the former Thea Miller, the Seltz's babysitter during the 1954 State High School Tournament—and professionally.

"Once I was so upset at an umpire's call that I threw my glove on the ground and stomped on it, and soon after I received a letter from a fan who told me how bush league I'd been," Underhill said. "From that time I always kept my emotions in check. Everything that has happened in my life related to baseball has been good. The game helped turn my life around."

Red Fischer was an outstanding catcher who seemed capable of handling everything except authority. Courtesy of Herb Schaper Historical Baseball Collection/*New Ulm Daily Journal*.

Red Fischer: Big League Swing, but Career Foul by Inches

Many who saw Arnold "Red" Fischer compete described the former Washington High athlete as one of the greatest to come out of St. Paul. His first love was baseball, but not everyone in baseball loved the hard-nosed catcher. He had tremendous ability but limited people skills.

"You heard a lot of different stories, but I heard that he ran into disfavor with somebody [in professional baseball]," said College Hall of Fame coach Tom Petroff, who managed and played against Fischer in the West Central League. "But he was an excellent player, and he should have been in the majors. He was that good."

Fischer could hit for power and had a tremendous arm, a combination that earned him a shot at professional baseball after his high school days. The six-foot, 220-pound catcher signed with Cleveland after graduating from high school in 1947, determined to one day catch Bob Feller. After a modest start in Burlington, Iowa, of the Class C Central Association, Fischer hit .356 with 11 home runs and 70 RBIs in 1948 for Green Bay in the Class D Wisconsin State League, but then came back to Minnesota to play for Benson in 1949. He returned to pro ball in 1950 but was back in Benson again in 1951. Then he went back to the minors in 1952, where he hit .272 with 10 home runs and 58 RBIs for Lancaster, Pennsylvania, in the Class B Interstate League, and he also made a brief appearance with the St. Paul Saints of the American Association.

Lancaster would be his final professional stop. He caught for Benson–De Graff in 1953 and Litchfield in 1954, hitting a season-record 13 home runs with Litchfield in the Western Minny. Paul Giel got most of the attention when Litchfield beat Marshall 11–5 before Giel signed a professional contract in 1954, but it was Fischer's three home runs—and almost a fourth—that powered the victory.

Pitcher Ron Tucker, a former teammate of Fischer, had two favorite stories about playing with the hard-nosed catcher at Benson. Just before their first game together, Fischer walked out to the mound and told Tucker that if anyone reached first and looked prepared to steal that he should hit the ground or he'd catch the ball between his eyes.

The second tale involved Fischer's dispute with an umpire. "I was behind on the count and Red was upset by the calls," Tucker said. "So, all at once, he started piling dirt on the corners of the plate, and the umpire asked him what he was doing. Red looked at [the umpire] and told him that as long as he wasn't going to pay any attention to the corners, why have them. The umpire was ready to kick Red out, but didn't. As for me, Red's escapade calmed me down, and I didn't have much trouble the rest of the way. He didn't smile much, but he had a dry sense of humor, and I found him fun to be around."

Fischer's actions, however, didn't amuse or settle down some of his teammates and managers. One reason cited for his checkered professional career was that he was difficult to manage. Cleveland was set at catcher with defensive wizard Jim Hegan and wanted to convert Fischer to an outfielder, but he refused to make the switch. "Red was his own worst enemy," said Howie Schultz, a former major-league player who became friends with Fischer.

One St. Paul columnist wrote a glowing piece about Fischer, the player and the man, and the article was completed by this observation: "When Red Fischer dies and arrives at the pearly gates, St. Peter had better let him in because if he doesn't, Red will just kick the door down."

APPENDIX: STATE TOURNAMENT HIGHLIGHTS AND BRACKETS

1945–1960

1945 State Tournament at Albert Lea

- Albert Lea successfully defended its Class AA title, the first successful title defense since the tournament began in 1924. Albert Lea scored the winning run in the bottom of the ninth on a single, walk, and run-scoring single by pitcher Earl Steier.

- Honeywell's Jack Verby, pitching for a second straight day, threw a four-hitter but lost 1–0 in the ninth. He had shut out West St. Paul 3–0 a day earlier. Honeywell almost scored in the seventh, but Albert Lea third baseman Shanty Dolan scooped up an error by the shortstop and threw a runner out at home.

- Excelsior first baseman Al Litfin was the tournament MVP, having hit 8 for 19 with three home runs and going errorless in 44 chances.

- Excelsior's Roger McDonald, a native of Tacoma, Washington, pitched a no-hitter in the championship game, striking out 11 against one walk and not allowing a ball to escape the infield. The no-hitter was the fourth in tournament history and the first since 1932.

- Excelsior outscored its opposition 41–2, opening with a 16–2 victory over Clear Lake in the opening round and then recording three consecutive shutouts. The three shutouts tied a tournament record set by Chaska in 1932.

1945 Class AA

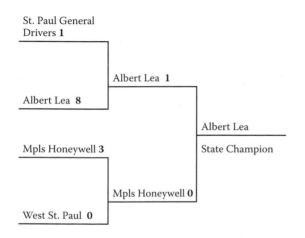

St. Paul General Drivers **1**

Albert Lea **1**

Albert Lea **8**

Albert Lea
State Champion

Mpls Honeywell **3**

Mpls Honeywell **0**

West St. Paul **0**

1945 Class A

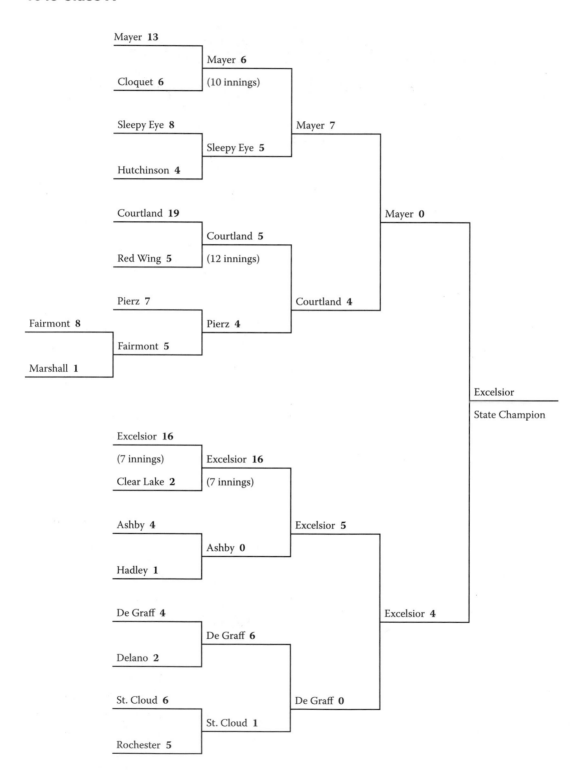

Mayer **13**
Cloquet **6**
Mayer **6**
(10 innings)

Sleepy Eye **8**
Hutchinson **4**
Sleepy Eye **5**

Mayer **7**

Courtland **19**
Red Wing **5**
Courtland **5**
(12 innings)

Pierz **7**
Fairmont **5**
Pierz **4**

Courtland **4**

Fairmont **8**
Marshall **1**

Mayer **0**

Excelsior
State Champion

Excelsior **16**
(7 innings)
Clear Lake **2**
Excelsior **16**
(7 innings)

Ashby **4**
Hadley **1**
Ashby **0**

Excelsior **5**

De Graff **4**
Delano **2**
De Graff **6**

St. Cloud **6**
Rochester **5**
St. Cloud **1**

De Graff **0**

Excelsior **4**

1946 State Tournament at Owatonna

- The rain-plagued tournament attracted a record 23,513 spectators, more than double the previous record of 10,629 set two years earlier in New Ulm, and the fans were not disappointed.

- Albert Lea won a record third consecutive Class AA title, the program's fifth since the tournament's 1924 inaugural, winning three games by margins of five or more runs.

- The champions' Walt Menke was tournament MVP after hitting .563 with three home runs and 14 RBIs in three games. He and his brother, John, combined for seven home runs and 26 RBIs.

- In a 23–2 romp over Zumbrota, tying the tournament record for margin of victory, Walt Menke also set a tournament single-game record of six hits. His brother, John, had five hits in the same game.

- Austin's Whiz Kids rallied from a two-run deficit to defeat Iona 6–2 and claimed a berth in the finals. They didn't have a player in their lineup over 21 years of age.

- Springfield defeated Detroit Lakes 6–4 in the semifinals, and the winning pitcher was Jack Verby, who had been the losing pitcher for Honeywell in the 1945 Class AA championship game.

1946 Class AA

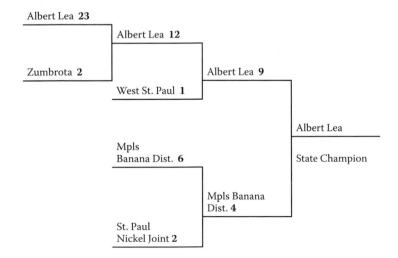

Albert Lea **23**
Albert Lea **12**
Zumbrota **2**
West St. Paul **1**
Albert Lea **9**
Mpls Banana Dist. **6**
Mpls Banana Dist. **4**
St. Paul Nickel Joint **2**
Albert Lea
State Champion

1948 State Tournament at Shakopee

• Albert Lea won a record fifth consecutive Class AA title.

• Albert Lea catcher Spike Gorham, tournament MVP, led the way with a .533 average that included eight hits and errorless fielding in 56 chances. Gorham opened Albert Lea's scoring with a second-inning home run in the Class AA championship game.

• Winsted got solid pitching from Lloyd Lundeen, a former Minneapolis West athlete, and supported him with 14 hits off three Belle Plaine pitchers. Alex Romanchuck paced the winners with three hits in the Class A championship game.

• Jack O'Brien, youngest of three brothers on the Belle Plaine team, was a starting guard on the St. Thomas football team, so he drove to Wausau, Wisconsin, to join his football team for their Saturday game and then returned for the Sunday showdown against Winsted.

• In the tournament's first year of three-divisional competition, 26 teams represented 91 leagues. A record 34,280 spectators attended the nine-day event.

• Springfield entered two teams, the Tigers in Class AA and the Cubs in Class B. The Tigers went 2–2, while the Cubs lost to the St. Cloud Moose in the Class B championship game.

1948 Class A

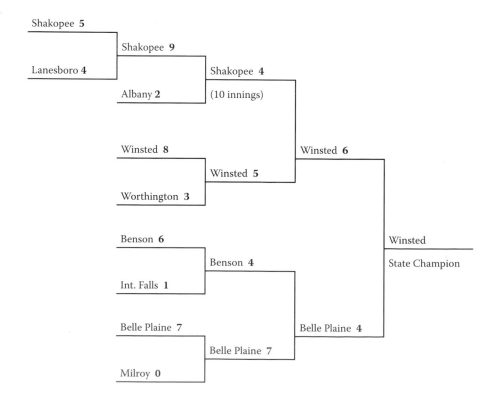

Shakopee 5
Shakopee 9
Lanesboro 4
Shakopee 4
Albany 2
(10 innings)
Winsted 8
Winsted 5
Worthington 3
Winsted 6
Benson 6
Benson 4
Int. Falls 1
Belle Plaine 7
Belle Plaine 7
Milroy 0
Belle Plaine 4
Winsted
State Champion

1948 Class B

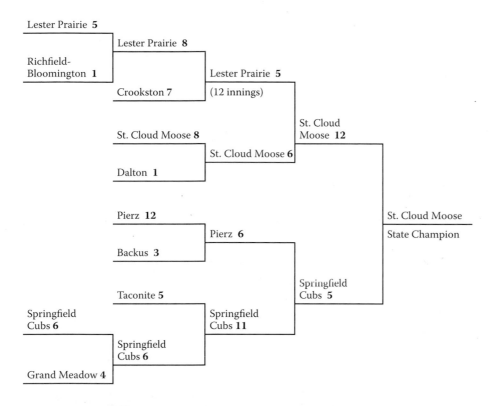

Lester Prairie **5**
Lester Prairie **8**
Richfield-Bloomington **1**
Crookston **7**
Lester Prairie **5**
(12 innings)

St. Cloud Moose **8**
St. Cloud Moose **6**
Dalton **1**
St. Cloud Moose **12**

Pierz **12**
Pierz **6**
Backus **3**

St. Cloud Moose
State Champion

Taconite **5**
Springfield Cubs **11**
Springfield Cubs **6**
Grand Meadow **4**
Springfield Cubs **6**
Springfield Cubs **5**

1949 Class AA
Double Elimination

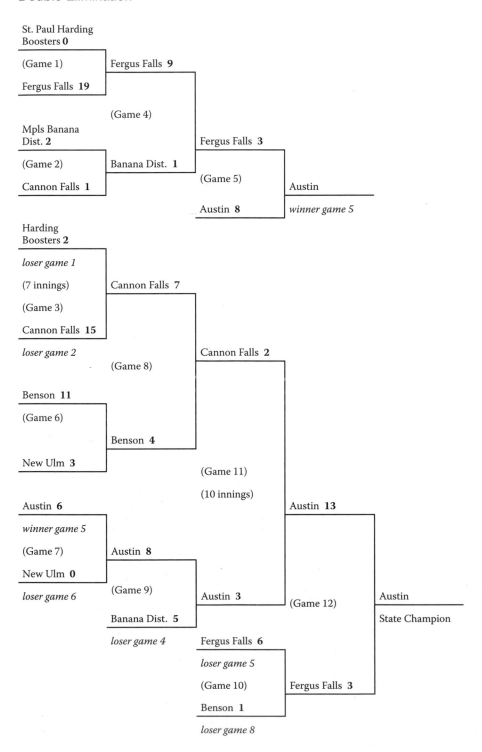

St. Paul Harding
Boosters **0**

(Game 1)

Fergus Falls **19**

Fergus Falls **9**

(Game 4)

Mpls Banana
Dist. **2**

(Game 2)

Cannon Falls **1**

Banana Dist. **1**

Fergus Falls **3**

(Game 5)

Austin **8**

Austin

winner game 5

Harding
Boosters **2**

loser game 1

(7 innings)

(Game 3)

Cannon Falls **15**

Cannon Falls **7**

loser game 2

(Game 8)

Cannon Falls **2**

Benson **11**

(Game 6)

New Ulm **3**

Benson **4**

(Game 11)

(10 innings)

Austin **13**

Austin **6**

winner game 5

(Game 7)

New Ulm **0**

Austin **8**

loser game 6

(Game 9)

Banana Dist. **5**

Austin **3**

loser game 4

(Game 12)

Austin

State Champion

Fergus Falls **6**

loser game 5

(Game 10)

Benson **1**

Fergus Falls **3**

loser game 8

1949 State Tournament at Detroit Lakes

- Austin defeated Albert Lea—winner of the last five Class AA crowns—in a controversial playoff and went on to win the championship. Austin won five games, breezing through all with the exception of a 3–2 semifinal extra-inning victory over Cannon Falls.

- On a day when the wind was blowing at 30 miles per hour, Austin hit seven home runs in the Class AA championship with Fergus Falls, including two by pitcher Bob Kuhlmann and two by Mel Harpuder. Kuhlmann and Harpuder each also had four RBIs.

- Excelsior won the Class A title for the second time in five years, and second baseman Rollie Seltz was voted the tournament MVP. In three games, Seltz hit .643 and was errorless in 27 chances. The winners eliminated defending Class A champion Winsted 17–1 in a semifinal game stopped after seven innings.

- Excelsior pitcher Gene Cooney won two games, including the title contest. Seltz, Hamline basketball star Joey Hutton, and Vance Crosby had two hits each in the final.

- Little Falls didn't enjoy the same winds as Austin, but the Class B champions showed offensive prowess in what would be the era's highest-scoring effort in a championship game, a 23–10 romp over La Crescent. Catcher Bill Arendt had a home run, a double, a single, and six RBIs.

- Whitey Skoog, better known for his basketball prowess at the University of Minnesota and later with the Lakers, won two games for Little Falls, both on the same day. He also was a starter in the 4–3 semifinal victory but was relieved and didn't get the win.

- Some outstanding individual performances included Benson slugger Harry Elliott's three home runs in a game, 20-year-old Mike Schultz's two-hit, 19-strikeout effort in a 2–0 victory over Milroy, and Mr. September Jack Verby's 3-for-3 with three RBIs in Cannon Falls' 7–4 upset over Benson.

- Warroad made its first of tournament-record 10 consecutive appearances in the postseason competition. The northern club won its first two games but lost a shoot-out to La Crescent in the semifinals, 11–10.

1949 Class A

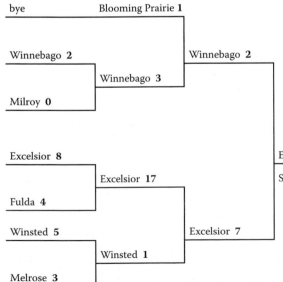

bye	Blooming Prairie **1**	
Winnebago **2**		Winnebago **2**
	Winnebago **3**	
Milroy **0**		
		Excelsior
Excelsior **8**		State Champion
	Excelsior **17**	
Fulda **4**		
Winsted **5**		Excelsior **7**
	Winsted **1**	
Melrose **3**		

1949 Class B

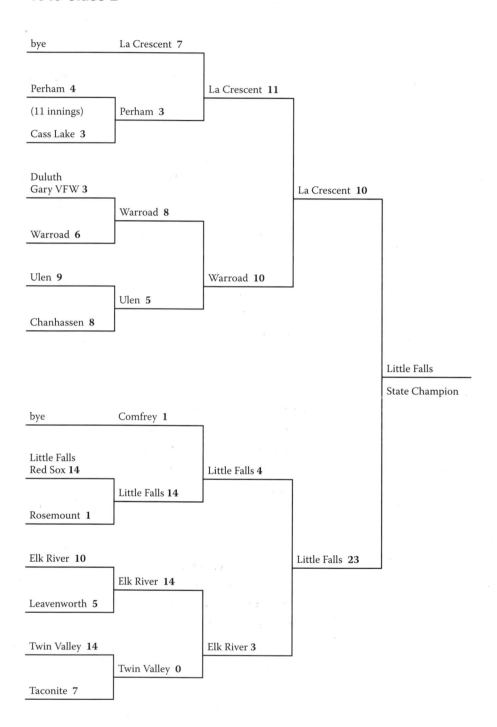

bye

La Crescent **7**

Perham **4**

(11 innings)

Cass Lake **3**

Perham **3**

La Crescent **11**

Duluth
Gary VFW **3**

Warroad **6**

Warroad **8**

Ulen **9**

Chanhassen **8**

Ulen **5**

Warroad **10**

La Crescent **10**

bye

Comfrey **1**

Little Falls
Red Sox **14**

Rosemount **1**

Little Falls **14**

Little Falls **4**

Elk River **10**

Leavenworth **5**

Elk River **14**

Twin Valley **14**

Taconite **7**

Twin Valley **0**

Elk River **3**

Little Falls **23**

Little Falls

State Champion

1950 Class AA
Double Elimination

St. Paul
Nickel Joint **0**

(Game 1) Austin **2**

Austin **16** (Game 4)

Mpls Mitby
Sathers **1** Litchfield **1**

(Game 2) Litchfield **3**

Litchfield **2** (Game 11)

Fergus Falls **6** Fergus Falls **1**

(Game 5) Fergus Falls **7**

Cannon Falls **1** (Game 9) (Game 14)

Marshall **6** Fergus Falls **3** Austin **0**

(Game 6) Marshall **4** (Game 15)

Fairfax **2** Austin **5** Fergus Falls

Nickel Joint **2** *winner game 13* State Champion

loser game 1

(Game 3) Mitby-Sathers **0** Fergus Falls **3**

Mitby-Sathers **7** *loser game 14)*

loser game 2 (Game 8) Litchfield **0**

Cannon Falls **1** *loser game 11*

loser game 5 Fairfax **0**

(Game 7) Fairfax **7** (Game 13) Austin

Fairfax **10** *winner game 13*

loser game 6 (Game 12)

Austin **3**

Marshall **1**

loser game 9

(Game 10) Austin **5**

Austin **3**

loser game 4

1950 State Tournament at St. Cloud

- Defending champion Austin got off to a great start when Roman Bartkowski threw a no-hitter to defeat St. Paul Nickel Joint 16–0, but the Packers were upset in the second round by Litchfield 3–2. Bartkowski later threw a two-hitter and struck out 12 in a 3–0 victory over Litchfield, eliminating the Optimists.

- Bartkowski's no-hitter was the centerpiece in a series of strong pitching efforts. In 36 games played in three divisions, 9 were shutouts, and the losing team scored only one run in 10 others. The 10-run rule was applied only four times.

- Austin scored four runs in the ninth on the final day to force a final game against Fergus Falls. Future Yankee Moose Skowron hit a two-run homer; however, Harley Oyloe harnessed Austin with a three-hitter in the title game to win 3–0.

- Fergus pitchers allowed one or fewer runs in three of five games and never allowed more than four in the other two. Fergus Falls third baseman Ed Piacentini was the MVP, hitting .667 in 15 at-bats and going errorless in 20 chances.

- Le Center won the title in its first state appearance ever, with NHL regular Bob Dill going 3-for-4 and driving in two runs.

- Lester Prairie outscored its opponents 21–3 in four victories. Doug Dibb threw a four-hit shutout against Duluth Teve's, but he needed two unearned runs in the eighth to win 2–0.

- The tournament attendance was a record 35,318, culminating a year in which 799 teams competed in 106 leagues.

1950 Class A

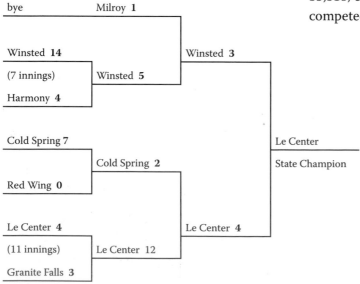

bye — Milroy **1**

Winsted **14**
(7 innings) — Winsted **5**
Harmony **4**

Winsted **3**

Cold Spring 7
— Cold Spring **2**
Red Wing **0**

Le Center **4**
(11 innings) — Le Center **12**
Granite Falls **3**

Le Center **4**

Le Center
State Champion

1950 Class B

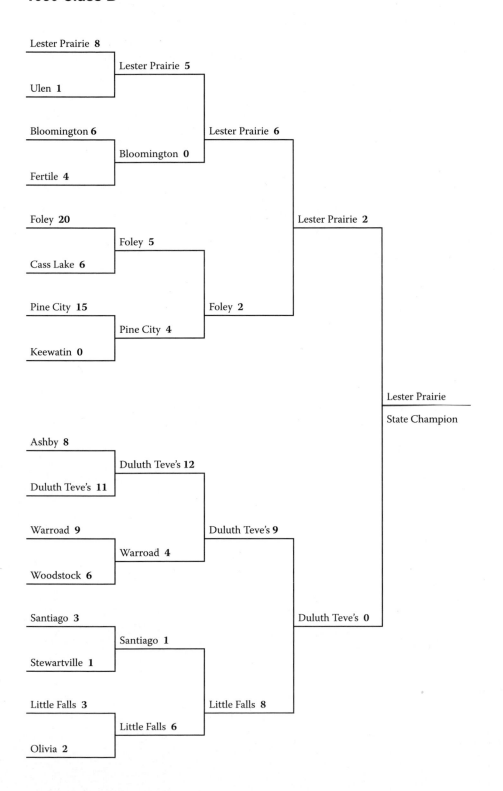

Lester Prairie 8
Ulen 1
Lester Prairie 5

Bloomington 6
Fertile 4
Bloomington 0

Lester Prairie 6

Foley 20
Cass Lake 6
Foley 5

Pine City 15
Keewatin 0
Pine City 4
Foley 2

Lester Prairie 2

Lester Prairie
State Champion

Ashby 8
Duluth Teve's 11
Duluth Teve's 12

Warroad 9
Woodstock 6
Warroad 4
Duluth Teve's 9

Santiago 3
Stewartville 1
Santiago 1

Little Falls 3
Olivia 2
Little Falls 6
Little Falls 8
Duluth Teve's 0

1951 Class AA
Double Elimination

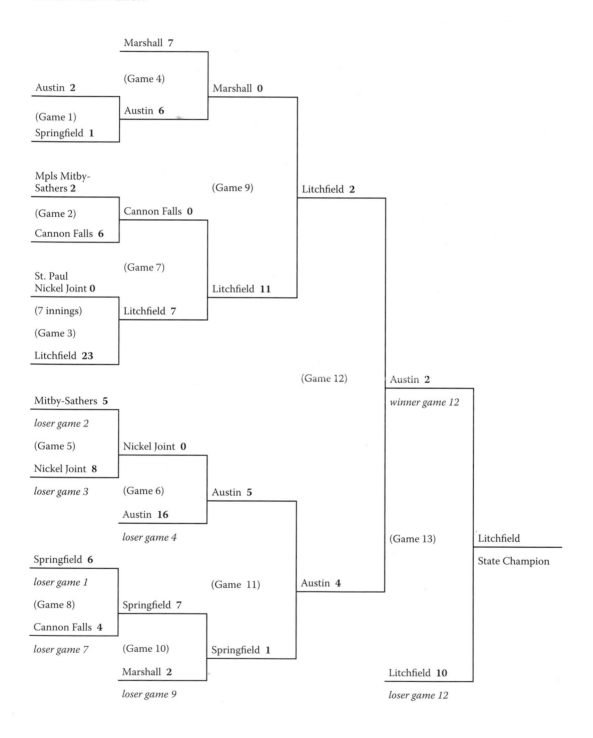

Marshall **7**

(Game 4)

Austin **2**

(Game 1)
Springfield **1**

Austin **6**

Marshall **0**

Mpls Mitby-
Sathers **2**

(Game 2)

Cannon Falls **6**

Cannon Falls **0**

(Game 9)

Litchfield **2**

St. Paul
Nickel Joint **0**

(7 innings)

(Game 3)

Litchfield **23**

Litchfield **7**

(Game 7)

Litchfield **11**

(Game 12)   Austin **2**

winner game 12

Mitby-Sathers **5**

loser game 2

(Game 5)

Nickel Joint **8**

loser game 3

Nickel Joint **0**

(Game 6)

Austin **16**

loser game 4

Austin **5**

Litchfield

State Champion

(Game 13)

Springfield **6**

loser game 1

(Game 8)

Cannon Falls **4**

loser game 7

Springfield **7**

(Game 10)

Marshall **2**

loser game 9

(Game 11)

Springfield **1**

Austin **4**

Litchfield **10**

loser game 12

1951 State Tournament at Faribault

- Soderville's Dave Spencer started his team's championship run with a no-hitter in a rout that went only seven innings. Spencer also tossed a one-hitter to close the Soderville title run; Spencer's second no-hit bid was broken by a seventh-inning single. The game's lone run was scored in the first.

- Litchfield's Dick Donnelly also threw a seven-inning no-hitter, a 23–0 whitewash of St. Paul Nickel Joint.

- Spencer was the tournament MVP, having allowed no earned runs and striking out 20 in 16 innings. Soderville scored its only run in the first inning of the title game, but Spencer made it stick.

- Litchfield got two victories from Gene Kelly, drafted from Willmar. Kelly pitched a three-hitter to beat Cannon Falls and defeated Austin in the championship game, giving up six hits. Litchfield pitchers allowed only 15 hits in 44 innings.

- Mike Dressen's solo homer in the ninth against Fergus Falls gave Watertown a 4–3 win and kept the eventual champions alive. Dressen added two hits in the 9–4 title game win over Le Center, with Winsted draftee Alex Romanchuck earning the victory on 4⅔ innings of relief.

- Defending Class AA champion Austin lost its second game but hung on to reach the title round. Despite southpaw John Herr's four-hitter for Litchfield, the Packers beat the Optimists on the final day and forced a second game before losing the title.

1951 Class A

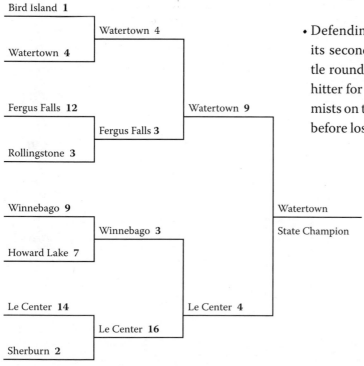

```
Bird Island  1
                    Watertown  4
Watertown  4
                                    Watertown  9
Fergus Falls  12
                    Fergus Falls  3
Rollingstone  3
                                                    Watertown
                                                    State Champion
Winnebago  9
                    Winnebago  3
Howard Lake  7
                                    Le Center  4
Le Center  14
                    Le Center  16
Sherburn  2
```

1951 Class B

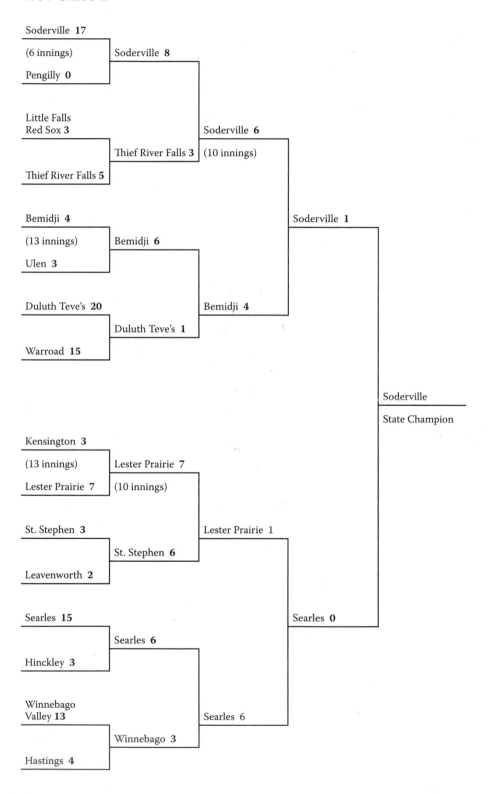

Soderville **17**

(6 innings)

Pengilly **0**

Soderville **8**

Little Falls
Red Sox **3**

Thief River Falls **5**

Thief River Falls **3**

Soderville **6**

(10 innings)

Bemidji **4**

(13 innings)

Ulen **3**

Bemidji **6**

Duluth Teve's **20**

Warroad **15**

Duluth Teve's **1**

Bemidji **4**

Soderville **1**

Soderville
State Champion

Kensington **3**

(13 innings)

Lester Prairie **7**

Lester Prairie **7**

(10 innings)

St. Stephen **3**

Leavenworth **2**

St. Stephen **6**

Lester Prairie **1**

Searles **15**

Hinckley **3**

Searles **6**

Winnebago
Valley **13**

Hastings **4**

Winnebago **3**

Searles **6**

Searles **0**

1952 State Tournament at Austin

• Willmar's Art Grangaard announced before the tournament that this would be his final season, and the Rails' player/manager and seven-year veteran third baseman went out in style. He was named the tournament MVP after hitting .417 in 12 at-bats and was errorless in 12 chances.

• Warroad entered its fourth consecutive Class B tournament with only one loss but was eliminated by Kensington 4–3 in the first round. Warroad ace Jim Fish, who struck out 19 in the Region 12 title, lost in the ninth when Kensington had a leadoff triple and game-winning single.

• Soderville successfully repeated in Class B. Soderville won the 1951 title in its first State Tournament appearance, and its two-year record was 8–0 with an 82–20 scoring advantage.

• Albert Lea, making its first tournament appearance since winning its fifth consecutive title in 1948, had its 15-game tournament winning streak snapped by Willmar 1–0 in the opening round. The former titans won their next two but lost to Willmar in the championship game.

1952 Class AA
Double Elimination

Willmar **1**

(Game 1)   Willmar **12**

Albert Lea **0**

                (Game 3)

Mpls Mitby-
Sathers **0**
                            Willmar **12**
(Game 2)   Fairmont **4**

Fairmont **9**

                                        (Game 6)   Willmar

Albert Lea **12**
                                                    State Champion
loser game 1

(Game 4)   Albert Lea **8**

(7 innings)

Mitby-Sathers **0**   (Game 5)   Albert Lea **8**

loser game 2

                Fairmont **0**

        loser game 3

1952 Class A

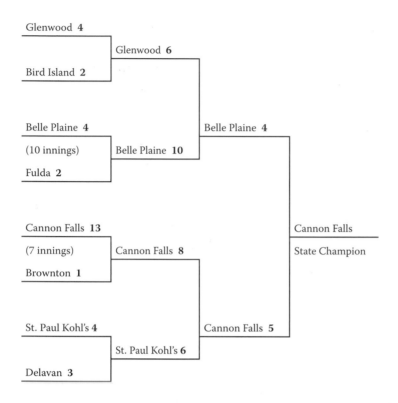

Glenwood **4**

Bird Island **2**

Glenwood **6**

Belle Plaine **4**
(10 innings)
Fulda **2**

Belle Plaine **10**

Belle Plaine **4**

Cannon Falls **13**
(7 innings)
Brownton **1**

Cannon Falls **8**

St. Paul Kohl's **4**

Delavan **3**

St. Paul Kohl's **6**

Cannon Falls **5**

Cannon Falls
State Champion

1952 Class B

Kensington 4
Warroad 3
Kensington 10

Chaska 12
Red Lake Falls 10
Chaska 8

Kensington 3

Soderville 14
Verndale 3
Soderville 9

Bemidji 9
Hibbing 7
Bemidji 2

Soderville 12

Soderville 15

Soderville
State Champion

Rollingstone 2
Pierz 10
Pierz 8

Searles 5
Foley 4
Searles 7

Pierz 6

Pine City 4
Madison 0
Pine City 7

Marystown 13
Lawrence Lake 6
Marystown 4

Pine City 14

Pine City 5

1953 State Tournament at New Ulm

- Austin lost its opener 3–2 against Litchfield but became the first team to win a tournament coming out of the losers' bracket since double elimination was introduced in 1947.

- In 27 games, Delavan was the only team to win by shutout, defeating Jordan 1–0 in Class A first round.

- This would be the last year of three-division tournament play, and the final year that the event would attract more than 30,000 fans.

- Delavan's Rich Weigel was the tourney MVP. He won two games, got the save in the championship game, and in 20 innings gave up two earned runs, 10 hits, and struck out 14.

- Rollingstone won the Class B title in its third attempt. The champions scored 51 runs in four games, including a tournament-high 21 against Park Rapids.

- The Class B final was a small-town dream game, matching Rollingstone (population 315) against Holdingford (458).

1953 Class AA
Double Elimination

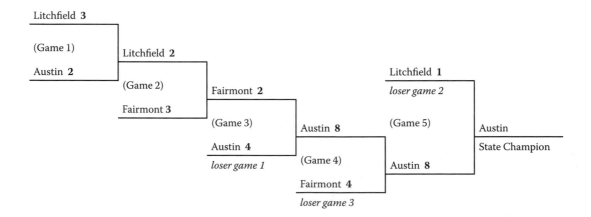

Litchfield **3**

(Game 1)

Austin **2**

Litchfield **2**

(Game 2)

Fairmont **3**

Fairmont **2**

(Game 3)

Austin **4**

loser game 1

Austin **8**

(Game 4)

Fairmont **4**

loser game 3

Litchfield **1**

loser game 2

(Game 5)

Austin **8**

Austin

State Champion

1953 Class A

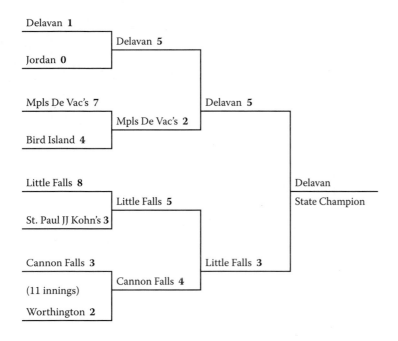

Delavan **1**
Jordan **0**
Delavan **5**

Mpls De Vac's **7**
Bird Island **4**
Mpls De Vac's **2**

Delavan **5**

Little Falls **8**
St. Paul JJ Kohn's **3**
Little Falls **5**

Cannon Falls **3**
(11 innings)
Worthington **2**
Cannon Falls **4**
Little Falls **3**

Delavan
State Champion

1953 Class B

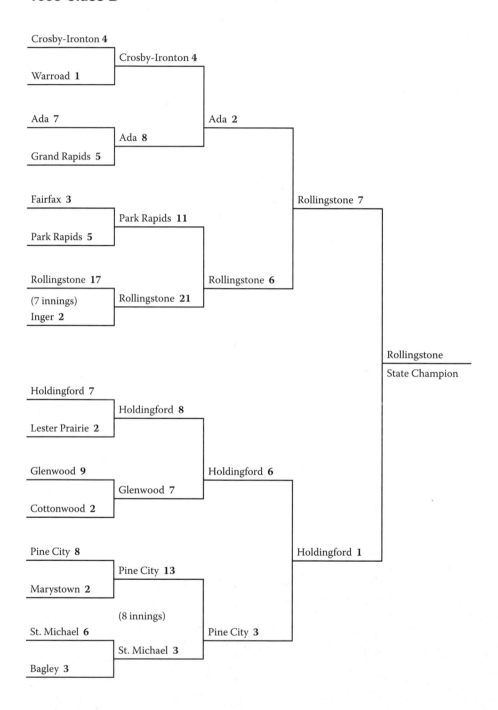

Crosby-Ironton **4**

Crosby-Ironton **4**

Warroad **1**

Ada **7**

Ada **8**

Grand Rapids **5**

Ada **2**

Fairfax **3**

Park Rapids **11**

Park Rapids **5**

Rollingstone **7**

Rollingstone **17**

(7 innings)

Rollingstone **21**

Inger **2**

Rollingstone **6**

Rollingstone
State Champion

Holdingford **7**

Holdingford **8**

Lester Prairie **2**

Glenwood **9**

Glenwood **7**

Cottonwood **2**

Holdingford **6**

Pine City **8**

Pine City **13**

Marystown **2**

Holdingford **1**

(8 innings)

St. Michael **6**

Pine City **3**

St. Michael **3**

Bagley **3**

1954 State Tournament at St. Cloud

- The tournament went back to two divisions: Class A and B. Class A was double elimination, and Class B single elimination.

- Rain stopped the Buffalo–Battle Lake game after 4½ innings, with Buffalo leading 1–0, a contest that prompted the state to declare seven innings the least number of innings for an official tournament game.

- Buffalo got off easy in its opener, but not in the quarterfinals, where it lost a then-tournament-record 15-inning decision to Norwood.

- Milroy, one of the tournament's smallest towns with a population of less than 300, was the sweetheart of the competition, but Benson shortstop Chuck Bosacker was the MVP. Bosacker hit .545 in 22 at-bats and handled 24 chances without an error.

- Benson was undefeated in the double-elimination Class A event, winning two games by shutout. Jordan was the hard-luck team in Class A, losing its two games by a total of three runs.

1954 Class A
Double Elimination

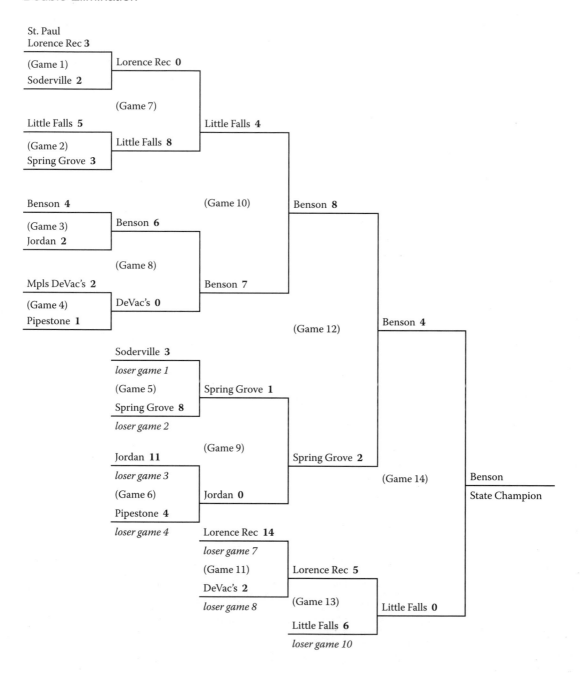

St. Paul
Lorence Rec **3**

(Game 1)
Soderville **2**

Lorence Rec **0**

Little Falls **5**

(Game 2)
Spring Grove **3**

(Game 7)
Little Falls **8**

Little Falls **4**

Benson **4**

(Game 3)
Jordan **2**

Benson **6**

(Game 10)
Benson **8**

Mpls DeVac's **2**

(Game 4)
Pipestone **1**

(Game 8)
DeVac's **0**

Benson **7**

Benson **4**

Soderville **3**
loser game 1
(Game 5)
Spring Grove **8**
loser game 2

Spring Grove **1**

(Game 12)

Jordan **11**
loser game 3
(Game 6)
Pipestone **4**
loser game 4

(Game 9)
Jordan **0**

Spring Grove **2**

(Game 14)

Benson
State Champion

Lorence Rec **14**
loser game 7
(Game 11)
DeVac's **2**
loser game 8

Lorence Rec **5**

(Game 13)
Little Falls **6**
loser game 10

Little Falls **0**

1954 Class B

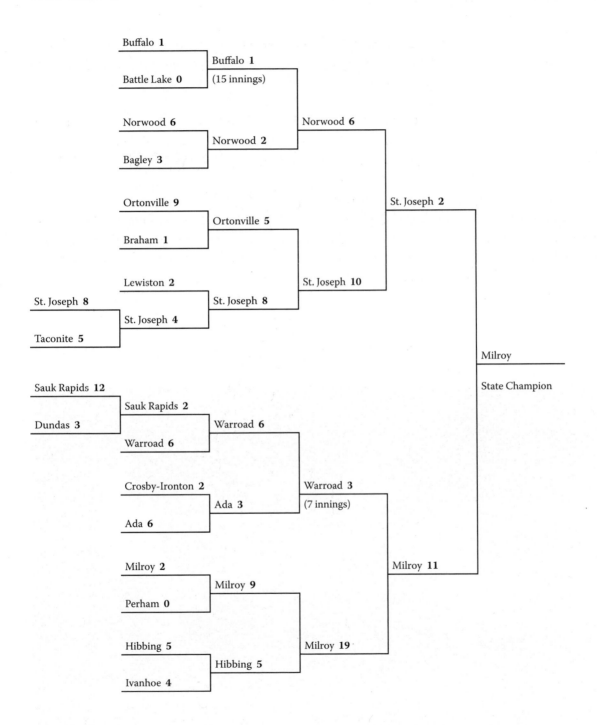

Buffalo **1**
Buffalo **1**
Battle Lake **0**
(15 innings)

Norwood **6**
Norwood **2**
Bagley **3**

Norwood **6**

Ortonville **9**
Ortonville **5**
Braham **1**

St. Joseph **2**

Lewiston **2**
St. Joseph **8**
St. Joseph **8**
St. Joseph **4**
Taconite **5**

St. Joseph **10**

Milroy
State Champion

Sauk Rapids **12**
Sauk Rapids **2**
Dundas **3**
Warroad **6**
Warroad **6**

Crosby-Ironton **2**
Ada **3**
Ada **6**

Warroad **3**
(7 innings)

Milroy **2**
Milroy **9**
Perham **0**

Milroy **11**

Hibbing **5**
Hibbing **5**
Ivanhoe **4**

Milroy **19**

1955 State Tournament at Chaska

• St. Peter catcher Marty Lee, a draftee from Le Sueur, doubled in the 15th inning to drive in the winning run in a 5–4 semifinal decision over Little Falls, which reached the semis by scoring three runs in the bottom of the ninth to defeat St. Paul Briteway Cleaners 6–5 in the quarterfinals. St. Peter was undefeated in Class A.

• In arguably the tournament's top individual performance, Class B Bagley's Dick Lawrence hit for the cycle in an 18–8 victory over Detroit Lakes. Lawrence, recording a tournament first, had two singles, a double, a triple, and a home run and rolled up five RBIs.

• Hutchinson pitcher Jiggs Westergard—facing a two-out, 3–2 pitch—hit a three-run home run in the bottom of the ninth to defeat Milroy.

• Bagley's Ken Severud pitched a two-hitter but lost a 1–0 decision against Rollingstone in Class B. The lone run, coming in the third inning, was unearned.

• Cold Spring outscored four opponents 28–2, with Dave Perl pitching a pair of shutouts. Perl won the final game, giving up seven hits and striking out eight, but his teammate Jack Hoppe, a draftee from Paynesville, also won two games and was voted the MVP.

1955 Class A
Double Elimination

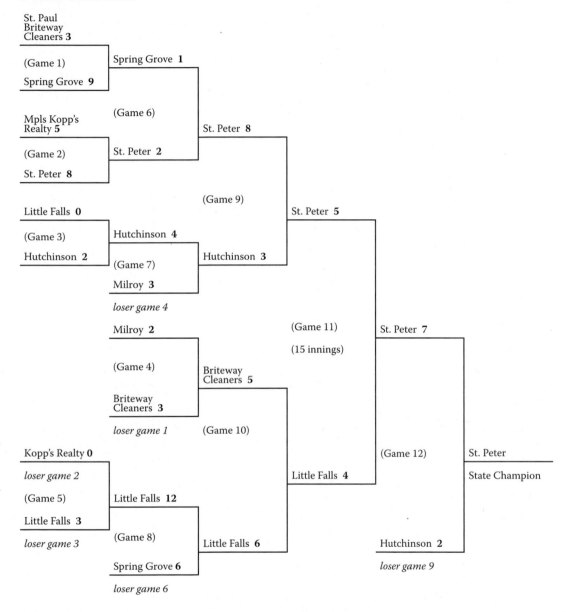

St. Paul Briteway Cleaners **3**

(Game 1)

Spring Grove **9**

Spring Grove **1**

(Game 6)

Mpls Kopp's Realty **5**

(Game 2)

St. Peter **8**

St. Peter **2**

St. Peter **8**

(Game 9)

St. Peter **5**

Little Falls **0**

(Game 3)

Hutchinson **2**

Hutchinson **4**

(Game 7)

Milroy **3**

Hutchinson **3**

loser game 4

Milroy **2**

(Game 4)

Briteway Cleaners **3**

Briteway Cleaners **5**

loser game 1

(Game 11)

(15 innings)

St. Peter **7**

(Game 10)

Little Falls **4**

Kopp's Realty **0**

loser game 2

(Game 5)

Little Falls **3**

Little Falls **12**

loser game 3

(Game 8)

Spring Grove **6**

Little Falls **6**

loser game 6

(Game 12)

Hutchinson **2**

loser game 9

St. Peter

State Champion

1955 Class B

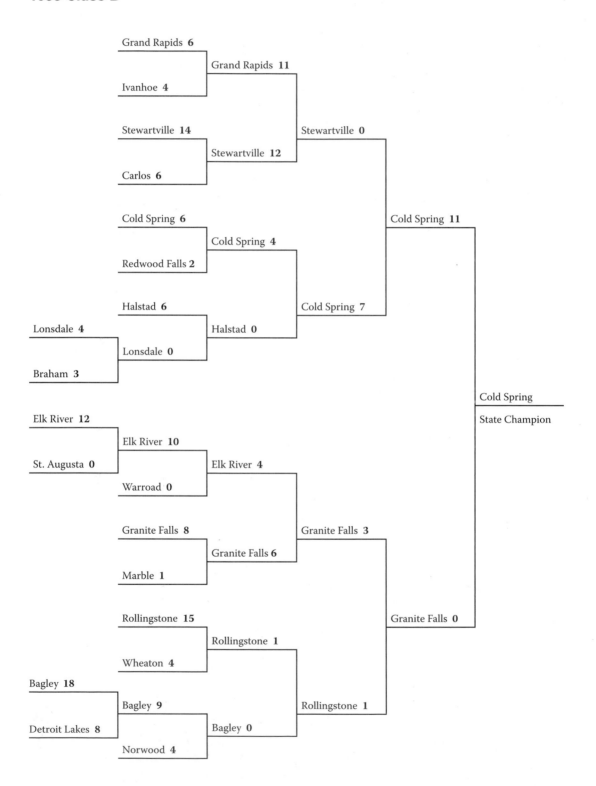

Grand Rapids **6**
Ivanhoe **4**
Grand Rapids **11**

Stewartville **14**
Carlos **6**
Stewartville **12**

Stewartville **0**

Cold Spring **6**
Redwood Falls **2**
Cold Spring **4**

Halstad **6**
Lonsdale **4**
Braham **3**
Lonsdale **0**
Halstad **0**

Cold Spring **7**

Cold Spring **11**

Elk River **12**
St. Augusta **0**
Elk River **10**
Warroad **0**
Elk River **4**

Granite Falls **8**
Marble **1**
Granite Falls **6**

Granite Falls **3**

Rollingstone **15**
Wheaton **4**
Rollingstone **1**

Bagley **18**
Detroit Lakes **8**
Bagley **9**
Norwood **4**
Bagley **0**
Rollingstone **1**

Granite Falls **0**

Cold Spring
State Champion

1956 State Tournament at Little Falls

• Minneapolis Teamsters lost its opener but came all the way through the losers' bracket, winning two one-run games and another pair of two-run decisions.

• Len Feriancek had three hits, including a game-winning home run in the ninth inning of the Teamsters' 9–8 victory over Bloomington. Dick Cassidy had a two-run home run in the 4–2 semifinal victory over Pipestone and a three-run homer in the fifth to cap the Teamsters' 7–5 victory in the title game.

• Despite Cassidy's timely hitting, Little Falls' Dutch Woerner was the MVP after winning two games, saving another, and pitching 17 innings without allowing an earned run. He also had three hits in one victory and two in another, including a home run.

• Bemidji's Dick Lawrence, who hit for the cycle in the 1955 State Tournament, went 4 for 4 in the championship game. The champions also got an eighth-inning home run from Corky Johnson in a 3–2 quarterfinal victory over Perham.

• Defending Class B champion Cold Spring won its opener but lost in the second round to eventual runner-up St. Charles 9–4. St. Charles scored seven runs in the fourth against Cold Spring, whose pitchers had allowed only two runs in the 1955 tournament.

• In St. Charles's 6–1 victory over Appleton, pitcher Jerry Grebin struck out 18. The two teams left a combined 30 runners on base.

• Tournament pitchers were particularly lackluster in both divisions. According to MBA records, they gave up a combined 30 home runs and hit 36 batters in the 29 games played.

1956 Class A
Double Elimination

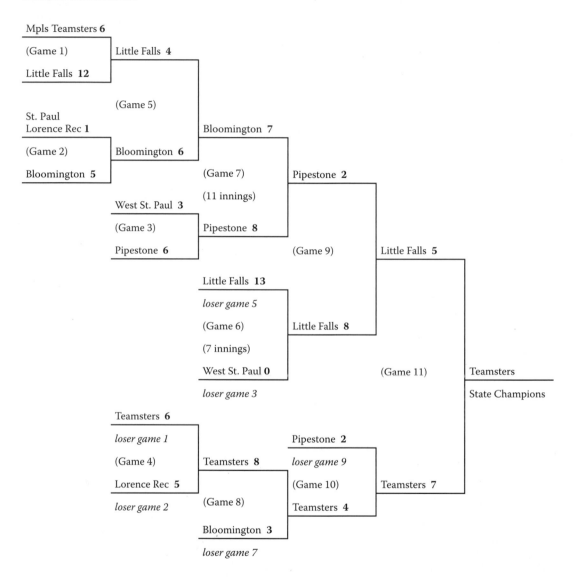

1956 Class B

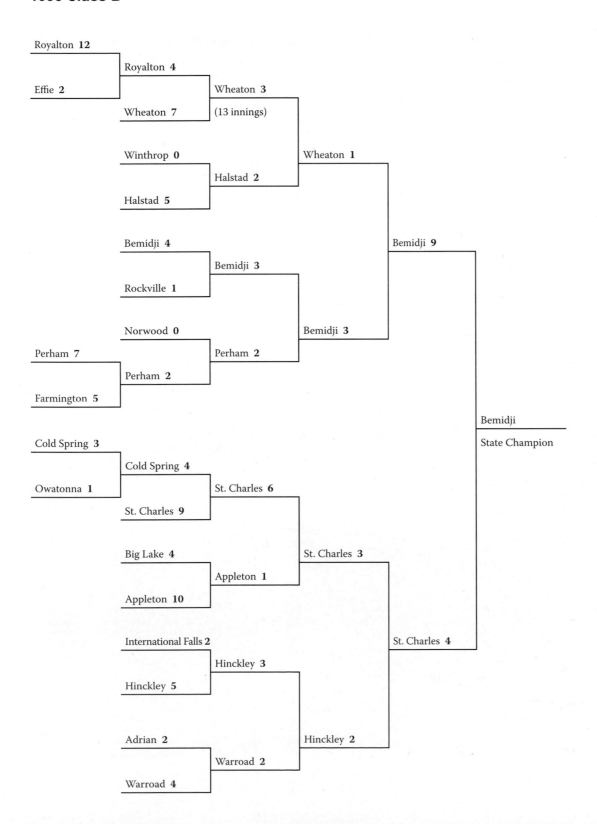

Royalton **12**
Royalton **4**
Effie **2**
Wheaton **3**
Wheaton **7**
(13 innings)

Winthrop **0**
Halstad **2**
Halstad **5**

Wheaton **1**

Bemidji **4**
Bemidji **3**
Rockville **1**

Bemidji **9**

Norwood **0**
Bemidji **3**
Perham **2**
Perham **7**
Perham **2**
Farmington **5**

Bemidji
State Champion

Cold Spring **3**
Cold Spring **4**
Owatonna **1**
St. Charles **6**
St. Charles **9**

Big Lake **4**
St. Charles **3**
Appleton **1**
Appleton **10**

International Falls **2**
Hinckley **3**
Hinckley **5**

St. Charles **4**

Adrian **2**
Hinckley **2**
Warroad **2**
Warroad **4**

1957 State Tournament at Cold Spring

• Waseca's Vern Edmunds was the MVP, winning three games. In 27 innings, he gave up five earned runs, 13 hits, and struck out 40 batters. Edmunds, who held Kiester to one hit in a 2–0 win and had a perfect game entering the seventh, came back two days later to win the championship game 6–4 over St. Paul Briteway Cleaners, striking out 10.

• Pitching was impressive in the six-team Class A field. Overall the losers in 8 of 11 games scored two or fewer runs.

• Class B champion Braham struggled to beat Morris 6–4 in the quarterfinals when Braham was outhit eight to five, but Morris committed six errors and gave up six bases on balls. In the championship game, Braham's Bob Westerlund gave up only three hits and struck out eight, and George Eng's two-run double in the third was the difference in a 3–1 victory over Norwood.

• Braham got two victories out of Fred Brandt, a draftee from Hinckley, including a two-hit, 16-strikeout 5–0 shutout over Pipestone in the semifinals. Pipestone's Ken Kielty spoiled Brandt's no-hit bid with an eighth-inning single.

• Shakopee spoiled Bemidji's title defense in the quarterfinals. Pat Devitt was the winning pitcher and had three hits, while the Shakopee defense had four double plays in the 7–3 decision.

• The Class B final attracted 3,020 spectators, compared to 425 for the Class A final.

1957 Class A
Double Elimination

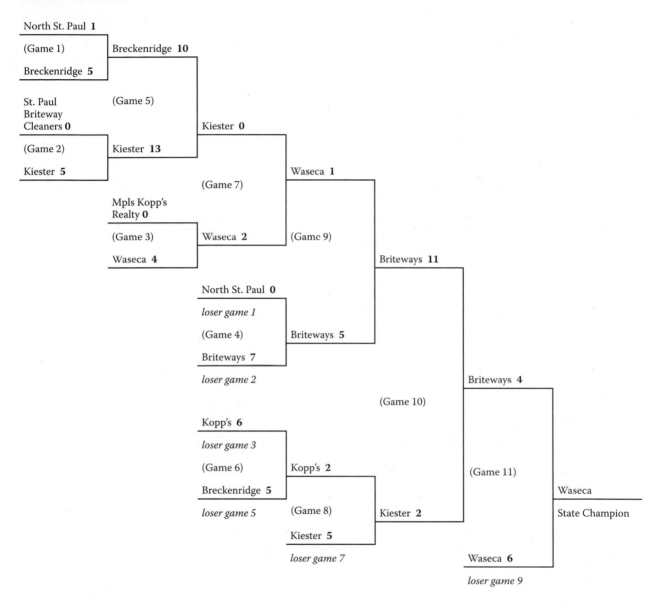

North St. Paul **1**

(Game 1)   Breckenridge **10**

Breckenridge **5**

St. Paul   (Game 5)
Briteway
Cleaners **0**   Kiester **0**

(Game 2)   Kiester **13**

Kiester **5**
                                                 Waseca **1**

                        (Game 7)

Mpls Kopp's
Realty **0**
                                                       Briteways **11**
(Game 3)   Waseca **2**   (Game 9)

Waseca **4**

North St. Paul **0**

loser game 1

(Game 4)   Briteways **5**

Briteways **7**
                                                       Briteways **4**
loser game 2

                        (Game 10)

Kopp's **6**

loser game 3

(Game 6)   Kopp's **2**   (Game 11)
                                                                   Waseca
Breckenridge **5**
                                                                   State Champion
loser game 5   (Game 8)   Kiester **2**

Kiester **5**

loser game 7   Waseca **6**

                                          loser game 9

1957 Class B

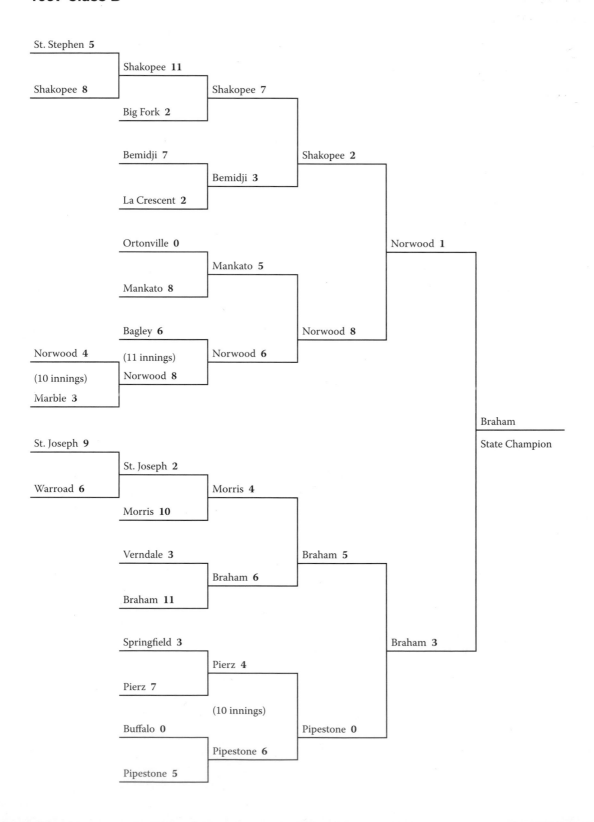

St. Stephen **5**

Shakopee **11**

Shakopee **8**

Shakopee **7**

Big Fork **2**

Bemidji **7**

Bemidji **3**

La Crescent **2**

Shakopee **2**

Ortonville **0**

Mankato **5**

Mankato **8**

Norwood **1**

Bagley **6**

(11 innings)

Norwood **4**

Norwood **8**

Norwood **6**

(10 innings)

Marble **3**

Norwood **8**

St. Joseph **9**

St. Joseph **2**

Warroad **6**

Morris **10**

Morris **4**

Braham

State Champion

Verndale **3**

Braham **6**

Braham **11**

Braham **5**

Springfield **3**

Pierz **4**

Pierz **7**

Braham **3**

(10 innings)

Buffalo **0**

Pipestone **6**

Pipestone **5**

Pipestone **0**

1958 State Tournament at New Ulm

• The Austin Packers were defeated in their opener by Minneapolis Cozy's but won five in a row to claim the Class A title. Austin clinched the title with a pair of 7–6 victories over Little Falls, the first in 11 innings and the second in 10.

• Austin's 10-inning 7–6 victory over Little Falls was the first State Championship decided in extra innings since the 1943 Class AA tournament in which Minneapolis Mitby-Sathers defeated Albert Lea 2–1 in 13 innings. Packer Dick Noterman's two-out single produced the winning run.

• The Packers also needed two extra innings to defeat Little Falls 7–6 in the Class A semifinals. Ray Rosenbaum had three hits, including one in the 11th inning that drove in the winning run.

• Austin pitcher Jim Lawler was the MVP, winning three games and giving up only eight earned runs and striking out 29 in 36 innings.

• Little Falls' Vern Deering dismissed St. Paul Park with a tournament-record 79 pitches in a 9–0 third-round victory. Deering pitched a one-hitter; his no-hit game was spoiled by Roger Pribow's leadoff double in the seventh.

• Pipestone's Jack Kelly had four hits, three of them doubles, in a 16–5 victory over Marble in the Class B semifinals. Norwood scored four runs in the seventh and two in the eighth to overtake Willmar 7–5 in the other semifinal.

• Kelly also had two hits and four RBIs in the 5–3 victory over Norwood in front of a crowd of 3,448 in the Class B championship.

1958 Class A
Double Elimination

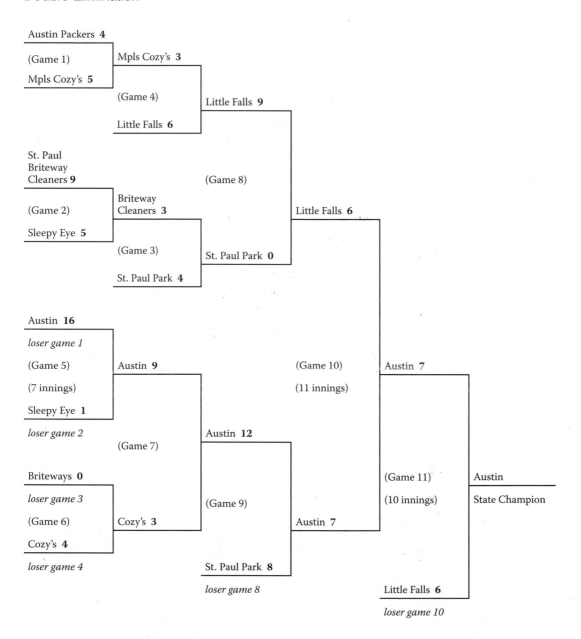

Austin Packers **4**

(Game 1)   Mpls Cozy's **3**

Mpls Cozy's **5**
                                          (Game 4)   Little Falls **9**

                        Little Falls **6**

St. Paul
Briteway
Cleaners **9**   (Game 8)

(Game 2)   Briteway
                        Cleaners **3**   Little Falls **6**

Sleepy Eye **5**

                        (Game 3)   St. Paul Park **0**

                        St. Paul Park **4**

Austin **16**

loser game 1

(Game 5)   Austin **9**   (Game 10)   Austin **7**

(7 innings)   (11 innings)

Sleepy Eye **1**

loser game 2
                        (Game 7)

                                        Austin **12**
Briteways **0**

loser game 3
                                        (Game 9)   Austin
(Game 6)   Cozy's **3**   State Champion
                                                        Austin **7**   (Game 11)
Cozy's **4**
                                                                              (10 innings)
loser game 4

                        St. Paul Park **8**

                        loser game 8   Little Falls **6**

                                                                              loser game 10

1958 Class B

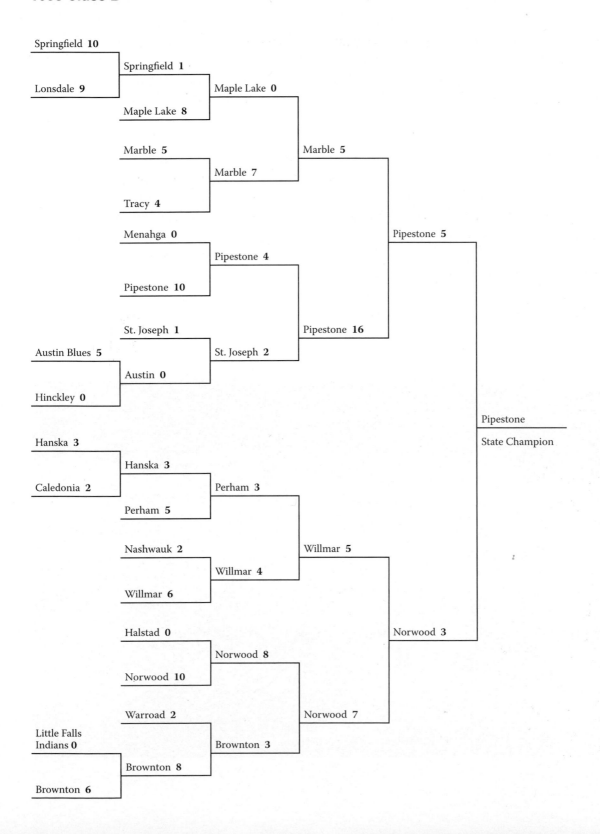

Springfield **10**

Springfield **1**

Lonsdale **9**

Maple Lake **0**

Maple Lake **8**

Marble **5**

Marble **7**

Marble **5**

Tracy **4**

Pipestone **5**

Menahga **0**

Pipestone **4**

Pipestone **10**

Pipestone **16**

St. Joseph **1**

St. Joseph **2**

Austin Blues **5**

Austin **0**

Hinckley **0**

Pipestone
State Champion

Hanska **3**

Hanska **3**

Caledonia **2**

Perham **3**

Perham **5**

Willmar **5**

Nashwauk **2**

Willmar **4**

Willmar **6**

Norwood **3**

Halstad **0**

Norwood **8**

Norwood **10**

Norwood **7**

Warroad **2**

Brownton **3**

Little Falls
Indians **0**

Brownton **8**

Brownton **6**

1959 State Tournament at St. Cloud

• In one of the most decisive State Tournament title games, Fairmont rolled up 20 hits against Bloomington. Milt Nielsen had a home run, three doubles, and three RBIs to lead the 14–2 romp. Fairmont never trailed in four tournament games.

• Jerry Zellner pitched a no-hit game against Minneapolis in Bloomington's second game, striking out 15 batters. The no-hitter was the tournament's first since 1951 and the 10th overall in the event's 36-year history.

• St. Paul 3M left 18 runners on base in its 9–5 loss to St. Peter. Future hockey legend—do you believe in miracles?—Herb Brooks had three hits for 3M.

• Shakopee's pitchers gave up only eight runs in five games. Trailing 2–0 in the bottom of the ninth, the champions scored three runs, including Fred Kerber's two-run homer on a 1–2 count, to win the Class B championship.

• Shakopee's Fulton Weckman was the tournament MVP, winning three games, allowing only four earned runs, and striking out 34 in 23 innings. Hard-luck honors went to Hanska's Denny Bloomquist, who lost a one-hitter in a 1–0 game against Hinckley—Bloomquist's no-hitter was ruined in the eighth.

1959 Class A
Double Elimination

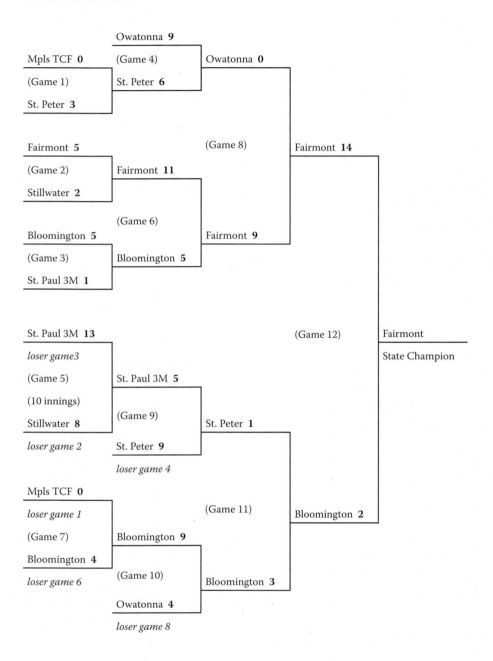

Owatonna **9**

Mpls TCF **0**

(Game 1)

St. Peter **3**

(Game 4)

St. Peter **6**

Owatonna **0**

(Game 8)

Fairmont **14**

Fairmont **5**

(Game 2)

Stillwater **2**

Fairmont **11**

(Game 6)

Fairmont **9**

Bloomington **5**

(Game 3)

St. Paul 3M **1**

Bloomington **5**

Fairmont
State Champion

(Game 12)

St. Paul 3M **13**

loser game3

(Game 5)

(10 innings)

Stillwater **8**

loser game 2

St. Paul 3M **5**

(Game 9)

St. Peter **9**

loser game 4

St. Peter **1**

Mpls TCF **0**

loser game 1

(Game 7)

Bloomington **4**

loser game 6

Bloomington **9**

(Game 10)

Owatonna **4**

loser game 8

(Game 11)

Bloomington **3**

Bloomington **2**

1959 Class B

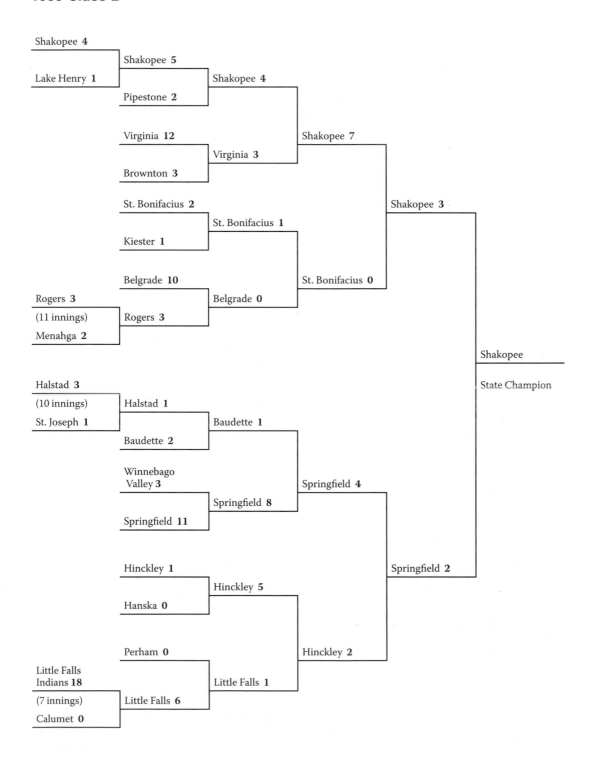

Shakopee **4**

Shakopee **5**

Lake Henry **1**

Pipestone **2**

Shakopee **4**

Virginia **12**

Virginia **3**

Brownton **3**

Shakopee **7**

St. Bonifacius **2**

St. Bonifacius **1**

Kiester **1**

St. Bonifacius **0**

Belgrade **10**

Belgrade **0**

Rogers **3**

(11 innings)

Rogers **3**

Menahga **2**

Shakopee **3**

Shakopee

State Champion

Halstad **3**

(10 innings)

Halstad **1**

St. Joseph **1**

Baudette **2**

Baudette **1**

Winnebago
 Valley **3**

Springfield **8**

Springfield **11**

Springfield **4**

Hinckley **1**

Hinckley **5**

Hanska **0**

Springfield **2**

Perham **0**

Little Falls **1**

Little Falls
Indians **18**

(7 innings)

Little Falls **6**

Calumet **0**

Hinckley **2**

1960 State Tournament at Springfield

• Bloomington opened the Class A Tournament with a loss but came back to win five in a row, the final two victories over St. Paul Como Recreation, who had not lost a game all season.

• Bloomington's Wayne Tjaden was MVP after winning three games, allowing four earned runs and striking out 20 in 23 innings. Mike Larson helped Bloomington reach the championship round, pitching a two-hitter and striking out 12 Stillwater batters in a 5-0 shutout.

• Bloomington brought victory to the growing metropolis, which in the next season would be home to the Minnesota Twins.

• Pipestone won its second Class B title in three seasons, winning five times, including three times in double elimination. Bruce Johnson had four hits in Pipestone's opener against Twin Valley and three hits against Fergus Falls in the semifinals.

• Shakopee lost its opener 2–1 in 14 innings against Grand Rapids, but the decision was overturned because Grand Rapids used two ineligible players. Later, Shakopee beat Warroad 4–2 on three unearned runs to qualify for double elimination, but then lost two straight.

• Fergus Falls scored eight runs in the sixth inning of a 10–4 opening victory over St. Joseph but lost two games to Pipestone, 5–0 and 2–1.

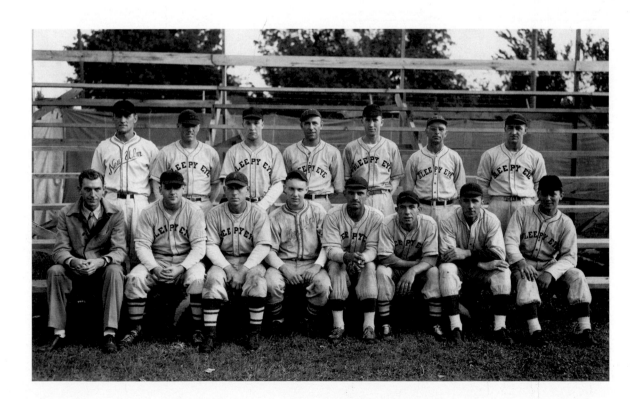

1960 Class A
Double Elimination

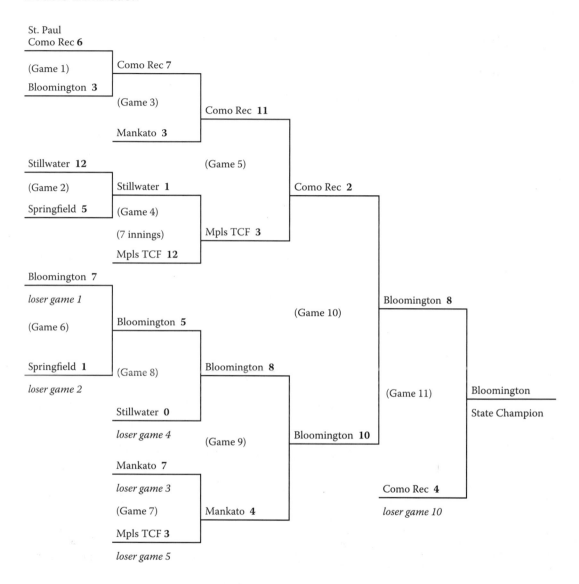

St. Paul
Como Rec **6**

(Game 1)

Bloomington **3**

Como Rec **7**

(Game 3)

Mankato **3**

Como Rec **11**

(Game 5)

Stillwater **12**

(Game 2)

Springfield **5**

Stillwater **1**

(Game 4)

(7 innings)

Mpls TCF **12**

Mpls TCF **3**

Como Rec **2**

Bloomington **7**

loser game 1

(Game 6)

Springfield **1**

loser game 2

Bloomington **5**

(Game 8)

Stillwater **0**

loser game 4

Bloomington **8**

(Game 9)

Mankato **7**

loser game 3

(Game 7)

Mpls TCF **3**

loser game 5

Mankato **4**

Bloomington **10**

(Game 10)

Bloomington **8**

(Game 11)

Como Rec **4**

loser game 10

Bloomington
State Champion

1960 Class B
Double Elimination Quarterfinal Round

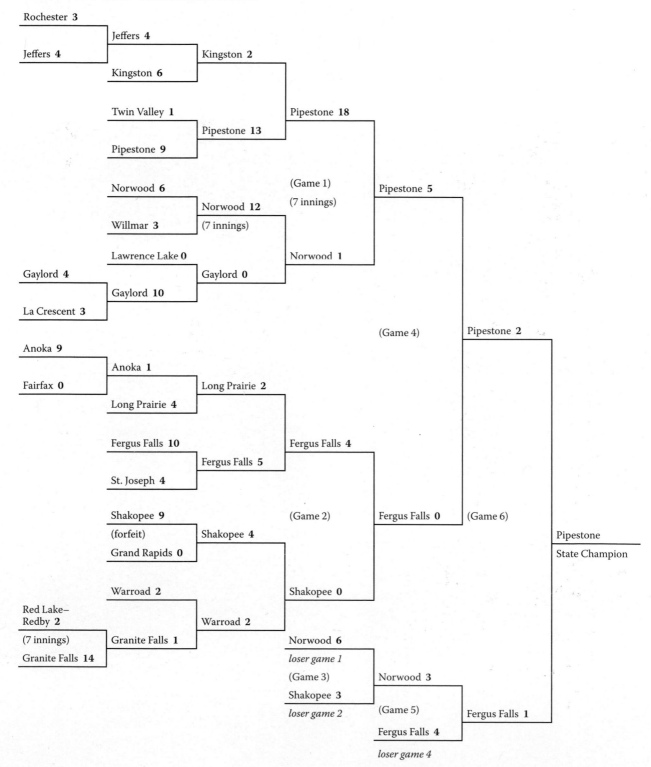

Rochester **3**

Jeffers **4**

Jeffers **4**

Kingston **6**

Kingston **2**

Twin Valley **1**

Pipestone **13**

Pipestone **9**

Pipestone **18**

Norwood **6**

Norwood **12**

Willmar **3**

(7 innings)

(Game 1)
(7 innings)

Lawrence Lake **0**

Gaylord **0**

Gaylord **4**

Gaylord **10**

Norwood **1**

La Crescent **3**

Pipestone **5**

Anoka **9**

Anoka **1**

Fairfax **0**

Long Prairie **4**

Long Prairie **2**

Pipestone **2**

Fergus Falls **10**

Fergus Falls **5**

St. Joseph **4**

Fergus Falls **4**

(Game 4)

Shakopee **9**
(forfeit)
Grand Rapids **0**

Shakopee **4**

(Game 2)

Fergus Falls **0**

(Game 6)

Shakopee **0**

Pipestone
State Champion

Warroad **2**

Red Lake–
Redby **2**
(7 innings)
Granite Falls **14**

Granite Falls **1**

Warroad **2**

Norwood **6**
loser game 1
(Game 3)
Shakopee **3**
loser game 2

Norwood **3**

(Game 5)

Fergus Falls **4**

Fergus Falls **1**

loser game 4

A NOTE
ON SOURCES

*T*OWN BALL: THE GLORY DAYS OF MIN-
nesota Amateur Baseball is based on
interviews with men and women who
played during the years from 1945 to 1960 or
were involved in the game as spectators, officials, or reporters. Our historical database was
established by poring over microfilm copies of
newspapers in the Minnesota Historical Society.
Exhibits and files at county historical societies
around the state were also invaluable sources of
information. We owe a debt of gratitude to those
who permitted us to read their old family scrapbooks and helped us find others who might also
have valuable information and memories.

We obtained photographs from a wide vari-
ety of sources. Our biggest disappointment was
in how few we actually found. We discovered, to
our dismay, that most newspapers had thrown
away or lost their old photograph and negative
archives. Furthermore, the snapshot cameras
common in the 1940s and 1950s were not very
useful for distance shots (the ones you'd take at
game) or for evening shots, and consequently we
found very few photos taken by spectators during games in the era.

Three sources of negatives were particularly
helpful: the *Dispatch–Pioneer Press* and *Star-Tribune* Newspaper Negative Collection at the Minnesota Historical Society, the Myron Hall Collection at the Stearns County History Museum, and
the Herb Schaper/*New Ulm Daily Journal* Historical Collection. We can all thank Herb for inter-
cepting the New Ulm negatives from a garbage
collector and preserving them in his home office.
Our thanks also to Don Evans, who preserved
the collection of photographs taken by his father,
Lefty Evans, during the 1930s and 1940s.

We used a number of books to provide historical and social context for the events taking
place in Minnesota from 1945 to 1960. William
B. Mead's *Even the Browns* (Chicago: Contemporary Books, 1978) and Frederick Turner's *When
the Boys Came Back: Baseball and 1946* (New
York: Henry Holt, 1996) provided insight on
the struggles of major-league and professional
baseball during the war and the turbulent year
of 1946. Both books contain some useful economic data as well as social commentary. J. Ronald Oakley's *Baseball's Last Golden Age, 1946–
1960* (Jefferson, N.C.: McFarland, 1994) offers a

history of the major leagues—which, like Minnesota's town teams, saw rapid growth in the late 1940s and a slow decline in the 1950s. For serious researchers or for fanatical baseball fans, Oakley published an extensive bibliography.

For more specific baseball research, the CD *Professional Baseball Player Database, version 5.0* (Old-Time Data, Inc., Shawnee Mission, Kansas), was essential for finding the records of the hundreds of minor-league vagabonds who wandered into Minnesota during these years. Similarly, James A. Riley's *Biographical Encyclopedia of the Negro Baseball Leagues* (New York: Carroll & Graf, 1994) proved indispensable in finding information on the African Americans who played for Minnesota towns in the late 1940s and early 1950s. Jay Wiener's *Stadium Games: Fifty Years of Big League Greed and Bush League Boondoggles* (Minneapolis: University of Minnesota Press, 2000) gives an excellent description and analysis of the politics involved in the construction of Metropolitan Stadium and bringing the Washington Senators to Minnesota in 1961.

Our readings on the social history of small towns and rural America began with Richard O. Davies's *Main Street Blues; The Decline of Small-Town America* (Columbus: Ohio State University Press, 1998). Davies examined the post–World War II fate of his hometown, Camden, Ohio, and found that it had was losing to forces over which it had no control; he argued that the story was the same for small towns all over the country. More specifically, Joseph Amato and John W. Meyer's *The Decline of Rural Minnesota* (Marshall, Minn.: Crossings Press, 1993) examined small towns in southwestern Minnesota and concluded that they had been declining since 1920 and were fated to continue to decline owing to economic changes that moved jobs to the Twin Cities or other larger regional centers. Amato and Meyer believed that some of the fierce baseball ri-

valries in the 1940s and 1950s mirrored the competition for businesses and jobs. A town that had been outdone economically by a nearby rival, for example, could still prove it "was the greatest town of all" by beating the rival in baseball.

David Halberstam's *The Fifties* (New York: Fawcett Columbine, 1993) and William Manchester's *The Glory and the Dream: A Narrative History of America, 1932–1972* (Boston: Little, Brown, 1974) provided valuable background history. Erik Barnouw's *Tube of Plenty: The Evolution of American Television* (New York: Oxford University Press, 1990) presented a very detailed and fascinating history of the development and rise of television.

Two anthologies provided further readings on Midwestern towns: *A Place Called Home: Writings on the Midwestern Small Town*, edited by Richard O. Davies, Joseph A. Amato, and David R. Pichaske (St. Paul: Minnesota Historical Society Press, 2003), and *Main Street on the Middle Border*, edited by Lewis Atherton (Bloomington: Indiana University Press, 1954).

Art Gallaher Jr.'s *Plainville Fifteen Years Later* (New York: Columbia University Press, 1961) is fascinating follow-up in 1954–55 to a study originally conducted in 1939–40 in a small, unnamed Missouri farming community. Gallaher found, among other things, that the brief period of prosperity experienced from 1945 to 1949 was not sustainable, an experience shared with small towns in Minnesota and the rest of the Midwest. Another anthology, *Recasting America: Culture and Politics in the Age of the Cold War,* edited by Lary May (Chicago: University of Chicago Press, 1989), is a compilation of papers evolving from a national conference and speaker series held at the University of Minnesota in 1987–88. The papers outline and discuss the economic growth in the postwar society and the development of a more homogeneous mass culture.

INDEX

Armand Peterson is a retired engineer and manager from Honeywell and Alliant Techsystems. He lives in Maple Grove, Minnesota.

❖   ❖   ❖

Tom Tomashek worked for more than thirty years as a sports reporter at the *Chicago Tribune* and the *Wilmington News Journal*. He continues to write for several national publications.